U

RMEDIATE BUSINESS ENGLISH TEACHER'S BOOK

NEW EDITION

MARKET LEADER

Bill Mascull
with David Heitler

www.longman.com

Introduction

1 Course aims

Market Leader is an extensive new Business English course designed to bring the real world of international business into the language teaching classroom. It has been developed in association with the *Financial Times*, one of the world's leading sources of professional information, to ensure the maximum range and authenticity of business content.

The course is intended for use either by students preparing for a career in business or by those already working who want to improve their English communication skills.

Market Leader combines some of the most stimulating recent ideas from the world of business with a strong task-based approach. Role plays and case studies are regular features of each unit. Throughout the course students are encouraged to use their own experience and opinions in order to maximise involvement and learning.

An essential requirement of Business English materials is that they cater for the wide range of needs which students have, including different areas of interest and specialisation, different skills needs and varying amounts of time available to study. Market Leader offers teachers and course planners a unique range of flexible materials to help meet these needs. There are suggestions in this book on how to use the unit material extensively or intensively, and how the material in the Practice File integrates with the Course Book. There are optional extra components including a Business Grammar, Videos and a series of special subject books to develop vocabulary and reading skills. This book contains extensive extra photocopiable material in the Text bank and the Resource bank.

2 The main course components

Course Book

This provides the main part of the teaching material. It is divided into 14 topic-based units, plus two revision units. The topics have been chosen following research among teachers to establish the areas of widest possible interest to the majority of their students. The Course Book provides input in reading, speaking and listening, with guidance for writing tasks too. Every unit contains vocabulary development activities and a rapid review of essential grammar. There is a regular focus on key business functions, and each unit ends with a motivating case study to allow students to practise language they have worked on during the unit. For more details on the Course Book units, see *Overview of a typical unit* below.

Practice File

This gives extra practice in the areas of grammar and vocabulary, together with a complete syllabus in business writing. In each unit students work with text models and useful language, then do a writing task to consolidate the learning. Additionally the Practice File provides regular self-study pronunciation work (with an audio CD and exercises), and a valuable survival language section for students when travelling.

Audio materials

All the listening activities from the Course Book (interviews with business practitioners and input for other activities such as role plays and case studies) and the Practice File (pronunciation exercises) are available on cassettes and audio CDs, depending on users' preference.

Teacher's Resource Book

This book provides teachers with an overview of the whole course together with detailed teaching notes, background briefings on business content, the Text bank (28 optional extra reading texts) and the Resource bank (photocopiable worksheets practising communication skills).

Test File

Five copiable tests are available to teachers and course planners to monitor students' progress through the course. There is an entry test, three progress tests and an exit test which reviews the work done throughout the course.

3 Overview of a Course Book unit

A typical unit consists of the following sections.

Starting up

Students have the opportunity to think about the unit topic and to exchange ideas and opinions with each other and with the teacher. There is a variety of stimulating activities such as answering quiz questions, reflecting on difficult decisions, prioritising options and completing charts. Throughout, students are encouraged to draw upon their life and business experience.

Vocabulary

Essential business vocabulary is presented and practised through a wide variety of creative and engaging exercises. Students learn new words, phrases and collocations, and are given tasks which help to activate the vocabulary they already know or have just learnt.

There is further vocabulary practice in the Practice File.

Discussion

There are a number of discussion activities in the book. Their main purpose is to build up students' confidence in expressing their views in English and to improve their fluency.

Reading

Students read interesting and relevant authentic texts from the *Financial Times* and other business sources. They develop their reading skills and acquire essential business vocabulary. The texts provide a context for language work and discussion later in the unit.

Listening

The authentic listening texts are based on interviews with business people and experts in their field. Students develop their listening skills such as prediction, listening for specific information and note-taking.

Language review

These sections develop students' awareness of the common problem areas at intermediate level. They focus on accuracy and knowledge of key areas of grammar. If students already know the grammar point, this section works as a quick check for them and the teacher. If they need more explanation they are referred to the Grammar reference at the back of the Course Book.

There is further grammar practice in the Practice File and in the *Business Grammar and Usage* book (see *Extending the course* below).

Skills

This section helps learners to develop their communication skills in the key business areas of presentations, meetings, negotiations, telephoning and social English. Each section contains a useful language box which provides students with the support and phrases they need to carry out the business tasks in the role play activities.

Case studies

Each unit ends with a case study linked to the unit's business topic. The case studies are based on realistic business problems or situations and are designed to motivate and actively engage students. They use the language and communication skills which they have acquired while working through the unit. Typically students will be involved in discussing business problems and recommending solutions through active group work.

All of the case studies have been developed and tested with students in class and are designed to be easy to present and use. No special knowledge or extra materials are required. For teaching tips on making the best use of the case studies, see *Case studies that work* below.

Each case study ends with a realistic writing task. These tasks reflect the real world of business correspondence and will also help those students preparing for Business English exams. Models of writing text types are given in the Writing file at the end of the Course Book.

4 Using the course

Accessibility for teachers

Less experienced teachers can sometimes find teaching Business English daunting. They may be anxious about their lack of knowledge of the business world and of the topics covered in the course. *Market Leader* sets out to provide the maximum support for teachers. The *Business brief* section at the beginning of each unit in the Teacher's Resource Book gives an overview of the business topic, covering key terms and suggesting a list of titles for further reading and information.

Authenticity of content

One of the principles of the course is that students should deal with as much authentic content as their language level allows. Authentic reading and listening texts are motivating for students and bring the real world of business into the classroom, increasing students' knowledge of business practice and concepts. Due to its international coverage the *Financial Times* has been a rich source of text and business information for the course.

The case studies present realistic business situations and problems and the communication activities based on them – group discussions, simulations and role plays – serve to enhance the authenticity of the course.

Flexibility of use

Demands of Business English courses vary greatly, and materials accordingly need to be adaptable. *Market Leader* has been designed to give teachers and course planners maximum flexibility. The course can be used either extensively or intensively. At the beginning of each unit in the Teacher's Resource Book are suggestions for a fast route through the unit if time is short. This intensive route focusses mainly on speaking and listening skills. If the teacher wants to extend this concentration on particular skills, optional components are available in the course (see *Extending the course* below).

5 Case studies that work

The following teaching tips will help when using case studies.

1 Involve all the students at every stage of the class. Encourage everyone to participate.
2 Draw on the students' knowledge of business and the world.
3 Be very careful how you present the case study at the beginning. Make sure your instructions are clear and that the task is understood. (See individual units in the Teacher's Resource Book for detailed suggestions on introducing the case study.)
4 Ensure that all students have understood the case and the key vocabulary.
5 Encourage the students to use the language and communication skills they have acquired in the rest of the unit. A short review of the key language will help.
6 Focus on communication and fluency during the case study activities. Language errors can be dealt with at the end.

Make a record of important errors and give students feedback at the end in a sympathetic and constructive way. Note good language use, too, and comment on it favourably.

7 If the activity is developing slowly or you have a group of students who are a little reticent, you could intervene by asking questions or making helpful suggestions.

8 Allow students to reach their own conclusions. Many students expect there to be a correct answer. The teacher can give their own opinion but should stress that there usually is no single 'right' answer.

9 Encourage creative and imaginative solutions to the problems expressed.

10 Encourage students to use people management skills such as working in teams, leading teams, delegating and interacting effectively with each other.

11 Allocate sufficient time for the major tasks such as negotiating. At the same time do not allow activities to drag on too long. You want the students to have enough time to perform the task and yet the lesson needs to have pace.

12 Students should identify the key issues of the case and discuss all the options before reaching a decision.

13 Encourage students to actively listen to each other. This is essential for both language practice and effective teamwork!

6 Extending the course

Some students will require more input or practice in certain areas, either in terms of subject matter or skills, than is provided in the Course Book. In order to meet these needs, *Market Leader* provides a wide range of optional extra materials and components to choose from.

Teacher's Resource Book

The Text bank provides two extra reading texts per unit, together with comprehension and vocabulary exercises.

The Resource bank provides copiable worksheet-based communication activities, linked to the skills introduced in the Course Book units.

Business grammar

For students needing more work on their grammar, this book provides reference and practice in all the most important areas of Business English usage. It is organised into structural and functional sections.

Video

Four *Market Leader* videos are now available at intermediate and post-intermediate levels to provide students with authentic and engaging examples of Business English in use.

Each video is accompanied by a set of photocopiable worksheets and a transcript.

Special subject series

Many students will need to learn the language of more specialised areas of Business English. To provide them with authentic and engaging material, *Market Leader* includes a range of special subject books which focus on reading skills and vocabulary development.

The first books in the series are *Banking and Finance*, *Business Law* and *International Management*. Each book includes two tests and a glossary of specialised language.

Longman Business English Dictionary

This is the most up-to-date source of reference in Business English today. Compiled from a wide range of text sources, it allows students and teachers rapid access to clear, straightforward definitions of the latest international business terminology.

Market Leader website: www.market-leader.net

This website offers teachers a wide range of extra resources to support and extend their use of the *Market Leader* series. Extra texts of topical interest will be added regularly, together with worksheets to exploit them. Links to other relevant websites are posted here, and the website provides a forum for teachers to give feedback on the course to the authors and publishers.

The Test Master CD-ROM

The Teacher's Resource Book includes a Test Master CD-ROM which provides an invaluable testing resource to accompany the course.

- The tests are based strictly on the content of the corresponding level of Market Leader Advanced and New Editions, providing a fair measure of students' progress.
- An interactive menu makes it easy to find the tests you are looking for.
- Keys and audio scripts are provided to make marking the tests as straightforward as possible.
- Most tests come in A and B versions. This makes it easier for you to invigilate the test by making it harder for students to copy from each other.
- The audio files for the listening tests are conveniently located on the same CD.

Types of test

The Test Master CD contains five types of test.

- **Placement Test/s**
- **Module Tests**
- **Progress Tests**
- **Mid Course Test**
- **End of Course Test**

Flexible

You can print the tests out and use them as they are - or you can adapt them. You can use Microsoft® Word to edit them as you wish to suit your teaching situation, your students or your syllabus.

Levels

Test Master CDs are available for Market Leader Advanced and all levels of Market Leader New Edition.

Contents

Resource Bank

UNIT 1

Communication

At a glance

At a glance

	Classwork – Course Book	Further work
Lesson 1 *Each lesson (excluding case studies) is about 45–60 minutes. This does not include administration and time spent going through homework.*	**Starting up** What makes a good communicator? Written and spoken forms of communication. **Vocabulary: Good communicators** Ss look at vocabulary related to good and bad communicators. **Listening: Improving communications** Ss listen to an expert on communications talking about communication between companies and their customers and the consequences of breakdowns in communication.	**Practice File** Vocabulary (page 4)
Lesson 2	**Reading: Internal communication** Ss read an article, complete a chart and answer questions about communication in organisations. **Language review: Idioms** Ss do language awareness and practice activities on some common idioms.	**Text bank** (pages 132–135) **Practice File** Language review (page 5) **ML Grammar and Usage**
Lesson 3	**Skills: Dealing with communication breakdown** Ss listen to two phone conversations between a customer and a supplier, and practise skills involved in dealing with breakdowns in communication.	**Resource bank** (page 196) **Practice File** Survival Business English (page 63)
Lesson 4 *Each case study is about 1½ to 2 hours.*	**Case study: HCPS** A private health care organisation has serious internal communication problems following a takeover by another health care organisation.	**Practice File** Writing (page 6)

For a fast route through the unit focussing mainly on speaking skills, just use the underlined sections.

For 1 to 1 situations, most parts of the unit lend themselves, with minimal adaptation, to use with individual students. Where this is not the case, alternative procedures are given.

Business brief

Within companies, communication falls into two main areas. There is the communication of information and technical knowledge needed to do the job at hand. Here, paper-based communication is being replaced by the company **intranet**, with internal websites only accessible by employees. Some very large companies are appointing **knowledge officers** to exploit the information in a company to the full and communicate it effectively to those who need it. (But in this age of increasingly accessible information, there will no doubt always be the **information hoarders**, employees and managers who find power and pleasure in keeping information for themselves, even if it would be useful to their colleagues.)

There is also what might be called 'celebration-exhortation'. The internal **company magazine** is the classic **communication channel** here. It may be produced **in-house** by a 'communications department' or **out-of-house** by journalists who specialise in this area. It may try to demonstrate how the company is putting its **mission statement** into action: the management may try to change employee behaviour by exhortation and by praising the performance of particular departments and individuals.

Externally, **advertising** has been the most visible form of communication with customers. Usually this is designed to increase product sales, but there is also **institutional advertising**, designed to improve **perceptions** of the company as a whole. Companies naturally like to be seen as human and environmentally aware. But the communication between companies and their customers is increasingly becoming two-way, with **customer service centres** designed to gather information, not just complaints, from customers about all aspects of use of a company's products. Ideally, this information feeds back into product modification and new product design. (See Unit 10 for more on **customer relationship management**.)

Equally, a company must communicate with its investors, and **investor relations** are becoming an important specialised area of **public relations**. Investors want to know how their money is being used and what their prospects are.

And then there is the wider public audience to attend to. **Press conferences** may be called to announce important events, such as product launches. **Press releases** may be issued to communicate more routine information. There is also the specialised area of **crisis management** and **damage control**: see Unit 11.

Whatever a company does, it has an **image**. It might as well try to influence (some would say 'manipulate') the moulding of this image. This is one reason why the **communications industry**, in all its forms, is a multibillion-dollar business.

Read on

Paul Argenti: *Corporate Communication*, McGraw-Hill, 1998

Scott Cutlip: *Effective Public Relations*, Prentice Hall, 1999

Steven L. Guengerich (ed.) et al.: *Building the Corporate Intranet*, Wiley, 1996

Richard B. Higgins: *Best Practices in Global Investor Relations*, Quorum, 2000

Cees van Riel, Wally Olins: *Principles of Corporate Communication*, Prentice Hall, 1995

Lesson notes

Warmer

- Divide the board into areas and write one or two words in each area, like this:

drums pigeon post	painting ... ...
newspapers radio	language sign language ... ...

- Get the Ss, in pairs, to list all the forms of communication they can think of by adding to each group. Elicit their responses and complete the table on the board, perhaps to produce something like this:

drums pigeon post smoke signals semaphore Morse code telephone	painting sculpture music
newspapers radio television Internet interactive television	language sign language body language dance

- Invite comments and encourage discussion. (The Ss may come up with other responses, or organise them in other ways, but it doesn't matter.)

Overview

- Tell the Ss that they will be looking at communication, especially in the context of organisations.
- Ask the Ss to look at the Overview section on page 6. Tell them a little about the things on the list, using the table on page 8 of this book as a guide. Tell them which points you will be covering in the current lesson and in later lessons.

Quotation

- Write the quotation on the board.
- Tell the Ss that it is a quotation from a philosopher.
- Ask the Ss to discuss, in pairs, whether they agree with the quotation. (Some might mention music or painting as communicating emotions that cannot be expressed in words.)
- In whole-group discussion afterwards, ask pairs for their opinions, and then ask the group why some areas, like philosophy and law, can be very difficult to understand.

Starting up

These questions introduce the theme of communication, and provide an opportunity for some speaking practice.

- Divide the class into groups of three or four.
- Ask the Ss to choose the three most important criteria in the context of
  a) native speakers **b)** non-native speakers of a language
  (The emphasis on grammatical accuracy will probably be different for **a)** and **b)**.)
- Discuss answers.

- Discuss in small groups or with the whole class. Rather than doing this in the abstract, take some well-known figures from television, politics, etc. and ask Ss what makes them good communicators (or not). Be tactful when discussing political figures. Ss might mention body language, speaking style, ease that people have in identifying with them, etc. You could discuss what makes for charisma, the way that some people have a powerful attractive quality as communicators and leaders that makes people admire them and want to follow them.

(C)

- Discuss question 1 with the whole class and write their ideas on the board under the headings 'Written' and 'Spoken'.
- Ask Ss to discuss, in pairs, which forms of communication they like using, and why.
- Elicit feedback.
- Ask the whole class to brainstorm problems that can occur with the different forms of communication. You may need to prompt them to think about such things as jargon, formality/informality, standard ways of doing things, technology, tone of voice and visual gestures. Again, list their ideas on the board.
- Ask Ss to discuss, in pairs, how these problems can be solved.
- Elicit feedback.
- If you are doing this lesson at the beginning of a course and you have not done a needs analysis, this exercise forms a good basis for one. Agree with the Ss which communication forms are most important for them/or need most practice. Note down what they say and refer to these notes regularly while you are planning and doing the rest of the course, so as to modify activities, emphasis of the course, etc.

1 to 1

This forms a good basis for a needs analysis, if you haven't already done one. It may give you ideas for role play of specific activities to complement those in the Course Book, based on your student's particular work situation.

Vocabulary: Good communicators

Ss look at vocabulary typically used to describe good and bad communicators.

- Work on pronunciation of the words, without going into meanings at this stage. Get individual Ss to repeat the difficult ones after you, paying particular attention to stress: arTICulate, etc.
- Put the Ss in threes and get them to put words into groups: the good and the bad, and then into the more specific groups in Exercise B. If available, get each three to consult a good general dictionary, such as the *Longman Dictionary of Contemporary English*.

A
Good communicators: articulate, coherent, eloquent, fluent, focussed, extrovert, persuasive, responsive, sensitive, succinct
Bad communicators: hesitant, inhibited, rambling, reserved

B
1 focussed, succinct
2 hesitant, inhibited, reserved
3 rambling
4 fluent, eloquent, sensitive
5 articulate, coherent
6 persuasive
7 extrovert
8 responsive

C–D 1.1

- Get the Ss, in pairs, to read the talk and fill in the blanks. Play the recording for them to check their answers.

1 interrupt
2 clarify
3 confuse
4 explain
5 digress
6 ramble
7 engage

E

- In pairs or class discussion, get examples of good communicators. Prompt the Ss by mentioning different occupations: politicians, actors, news presenters, advertisers, etc.

Listening: Improving communications

Anuj Khanna is Marketing Manager of Netsize, a marketing agency for mobile media. He talks about

- **communication between companies and their customers**
- **the consequences of breakdowns in communication**
- **how business communication will develop in the future**

A 1.2

- Get the Ss to listen once or twice to the first part of the interview, depending on their level. Stop at points where Ss can answer questions 1–2.

1 **a)** New technology has provided new communication channels such as the Internet, mobile phones, instant messaging, etc.
b) They can improve in terms of giving more control to customers so that they don't receive unwanted communications, and ensuring that the timing of any communication is right.
2 He gives the example of a bank informing a customer by e-mail or SMS that his salary has been credited or he has gone over the overdraft limit.

- Encourage discussion of any points arising, for example, the importance of communications training and the frustrations of unwanted phone calls and e-mails.

B 1.3

- Play the second part of the interview two or three times, stopping at points where Ss can answer questions 1–2.

1 **a)** Closure of all airports in the country and delays in flights globally.
b) Large hourly fines for the suppliers.
c) The engineering company has to pay a fine for every hour's delay in fixing the machine. The bank loses money.
2 He mentions a), c) and d).

C

- Ask the Ss how *they* think business communication will change in the future.

Reading: Internal communication

This article is about the importance and difficulty of achieving good internal communication in business organisations. The problems can be purely practical; they can result from information overload, or they can be caused by employees developing loyalties within departments or subgroups which, particularly in a climate of fear and uncertainty, prevent sharing of information.

Ⓐ

- Get the Ss to discuss the question in pairs. Discuss the findings with the whole group and ask the Ss about their personal experiences of using e-mail, particularly for communication within their company.

Ⓑ

- Get the students, in pairs, to discuss the items and choose the three best. Then ask them to join another pair and compare their choices.
- Elicit feedback and find out what the most popular items were. Ask Ss who chose these to justify their choices.
- Rather than treating the whole article in the same way, vary the treatment of each section, perhaps in the way outlined here. Read the first two paragraphs with the whole group, explaining and / or practising pronunciation of difficult words and expressions where necessary, e.g. *hard nut to crack* (line 5), *repercussions* (line 8).
- Get the Ss to read the third, fourth and fifth paragraphs silently and individually, or to read and discuss in pairs. Circulate and monitor for difficulties, e.g. *logistical nightmare* (line 21), *customs documents* (line 24), *automated system* (line 27), *duplicating* (line 38).
- Get the Ss to read and discuss the sixth, seventh, eight and ninth paragraphs in pains. Again, circulate and monitor for difficulties, e.g. *screen calls* (line 47), *bombarding* (line 67), *unstructured data* (lines 68–69), *work flow* (line 75).
- Read the final paragraphs with the whole group, explaining and / or practising pronunciation of difficult words and expressions where necessary, e.g. *group dynamics* (line 86), *common loyalties* (line 91), *threatened* (line 102), *identified* (line 103). If there is not enough time, get the Ss to read it as homework.

Ⓒ

- Get the Ss, in pairs, to complete the chart. Check and discuss the answers with the whole group.

1 Senior managers hide behind their computers.
2 Staff use voice mail to screen calls.
3 Employees sitting next to each other send e-mails rather than speak to each other.

Ⓓ

- Get the Ss to read the article again and work in pairs to answer the questions.

1 They had language and geographical difficulties, huge amounts of paperwork and great difficulty tracking and monitoring jobs.
2 They installed an automated system so that data was only entered once but could be accessed by everyone in the company.
3 Theobold recommends checking e-mail only three times a day and allocating a set time to deal with it.
4 People use the 'reply all' button so an e-mail goes to people who don't need it as well as those who do.
5 Both departments felt their job security was threatened so they didn't communicate with their 'rivals'.
6 It is a waste of time unless you also sort out the group dynamics of a company.

Ⓔ

- Ask the Ss to find and underline the words in bold in the article. This will give them one of the collocations. Then ask them to decide which of the other two words does not form a word partnership.

1 information
2 trouble
3 time
4 factories
5 experience
6 truth
7 support
8 ideas
9 e-mails

Ⓕ

- Get the Ss to discuss in pairs or threes for a few minutes, and then to report back to the class. Deal with question 2 tactfully, for example where you are dealing with people from different workplaces.

Language review: Idioms

In this section, the Ss look at different idioms. (Ss usually love them.)

Ⓐ

- With books closed, explain what an idiom is (an expression with a meaning that can be difficult to guess from the meanings of its separate words) and ask the Ss if they have any favourite idioms in English.
- Get the Ss to complete the exercise in pairs and then discuss the answers with the whole class.

a) nutshell **b)** point **c)** grapevine **d)** picture **e)** stick
f) wavelength **g)** tail **h)** purpose **i)** brush **j)** wines

Ⓑ

- Go through the exercise with the whole class. You might like to point out that there are three answers for number 4.

1 g **2** f **3** a **4** jhe **5** i **6** d **7** b **8** c

Ⓒ

- Get the Ss to complete the exercise in pairs and then discuss the answers with the whole class.

1 b **2** f **3** d **4** h **5** i **6** c **7** a **8** e **9** g **10** j

Ⓓ

- Ask the Ss, in pairs, to take turns asking and answering the questions.

Skills: Dealing with communication breakdown

In this section, the Ss discuss the kind of communication problems that can occur on the phone, and listen to two different versions of the same conversation.

- Get the Ss, in pairs, to brainstorm possible expressions for each situation, then to report to and discuss with the whole group. Draw their attention to the 'Useful language' box at the bottom of the page, which has expressions for all 7 situations.

(B) 1.4

- Play the recording 1.4 once and get the Ss to identify the problems the speakers have.

> The speakers have problems 1, 2, 3, 5 and 6.

(C) 1.5

- Play the recording once or twice and get the Ss, in pairs, to make notes on why this second conversation is better.
- Elicit feedback from the whole class.

> Koichi interrupts Bernard and tells him to wait while he gets a pen so he can write down what he needs. He controls the speed of the conversation better.
> Koichi tells Bernard when he hasn't heard what he said and gets him to repeat it.
> Koichi asks Bernard for more details about the materials he needs and then checks that he has got the information correct.
> Koichi asks Bernard to spell the name of the new customer he mentions.
> Koichi asks Bernard to repeat the number of lasers ordered. Bernard clarifies it and so this time Koichi has the correct number – 18 not 80.
> When Koichi doesn't understand the word 'roll-out', he gets Bernard to explain it.
> When Koich can't hear Bernard because the connection is bad, he tells him and asks him to speak up.
> Koichi asks Bernard to e-mail him the details he needs to contact the new customer.
> Bernard offers to call Koichi back to get a better line.

(D) 1.5

- Play recording 1.5 again. Stop at points where Ss can complete the gaps.

> **1** Hold on a second
> **2** didn't catch that; slow down
> **3** check; got
> **4** spell that for
> **5** did you say
> **6** does; mean
> **7** a bad line; speak up please
> **8** call you back

- Read out each of the extracts in turn and ask the Ss to match them with the points in Exercise A.

Extract 1	2	**Extract 2**	2
Extract 3	7	**Extract 4**	4
Extract 5	1	**Extract 6**	3
Extract 7	1, 6	**Extract 8**	1, 6

In this exercise, the Ss look at useful language for dealing with breakdowns in communication, and apply this language in a role play.

- Go through the expressions and practise intonation, getting individual Ss to read the expressions. Get them to complete the three unfinished expressions with possible endings, e.g. *'What do you mean by 'roll-out'?*
- Get the Ss to role play the situation in simultaneous pairs sitting back-to-back, using expressions from the Useful language box. Circulate and monitor. When the students have finished, praise strong points and mention one or two things that Ss should pay particular attention to. Then get 'public' performances from one or two individual pairs in front of the whole group.
- There are more situations like this to role play in the Resource bank, on page 204 of this book.

Case study

HCPS

In this case study, the Ss look at the communication problems in a Swiss private health care organisation, which has just been taken over by Sanicorp, another health care organisation, and suggest solutions.

Stage 1

- Get the Ss to read silently the Background section, the e-mail from Gloria Richter to Gunther Schmidt, and the e-mail from Ursula Krieger to Chris Wright.
- Circulate and answer any queries. Discuss common queries with the whole group.
- Quickly put the headings in the left-hand column of the table below on the board and elicit information from the group so as to complete the column on the right.
- Make sure the Ss understand the situation by getting individual Ss to expand orally on different parts of the table, using complete sentences.

Company	HCPS
Activity	Private health care
Based in	Geneva, Switzerland
Changes in structure since the takeover	More centralised. More decisions made by top management at head office
Gloria Richter's e-mail to Gunther Schmidt	◎ Staff receiving too many e-mails, many of which they don't need to be sent. Checking and sorting these is preventing them from getting on with their real work ◎ Staff lounge has been taken away and her staff don't have the opportunity to meet people from other departments any more
Key points of Ursula Krieger's e-mail to Chris Wright	◎ Middle managers confused about who to report to ◎ Planned reorganisation hasn't happened yet so no one knows what's going on ◎ No one will take responsibility for authorising financial payments – department heads unhappy that they can't get a quick answer when they need to spend money

- Ask the Ss to say what they think is the most important problem mentioned in the e-mails. There is no fixed answer to this and as opinions will differ, this question should generate some discussion.

Stage 2: Listening 1.6

- Get the Ss to read the text about Desiree Roland Consultants. Elicit that they are a firm of management consultants and that the President of HCPS has brought them in to analyse the company's communication problems and to produce a report.
- Establish that the Ss are going to hear some typical comments from the interviews that Desiree Roland Consultants conducted with HCPS staff. Focus their attention on the chart and ask them to make notes under the various headings as they listen.
- Play recording 1.6, pausing for the Ss to make notes after each speaker.
- Check answers with the whole class.

Type of problem	Description of problem
Organisation	Staff concern about forming new teams
Documents	Are too many reports required? Are the contracts with customers too complicated?
Location of premises	The distance between buildings is creating communication problems
Customer relations	Communication problems caused a loss of an important customer. Staff dealing with customer relations want more money for more responsibility/duties.
Other problems	Lack of trust in management. Flexitime unpopular with one member of staff.

Stage 3: Brainstorming and decision-making

In the task the Ss are members of Desiree Roland Consultants. They will discuss the company's problems and come up with a plan.

- First, in small groups, the Ss make a list of all the communication problems that HCPS is experiencing and rank these in order of importance. They discuss these problems and make suggestions for ways of solving them.
- Bring the Ss together as one group and get them to pool their ideas. Write these on the board and try to come to a consensus on which ideas to use in an action plan.
- Again, there are no fixed answers to this question but the Ss may come up with suggestions similar to these:

1 Staff should check e-mails at fixed times throughout the day, e.g. early morning and late afternoon only.
2 'Get together' meetings and social events should be held so that staff from the two sides of the organisation (HCP and Sanicorp) can get to know each other better.
3 The management should consider giving more authority and decision-making power to middle managers, i.e. decentralise the management route.
4 HCPS could produce a new, revised organigram/organisation chart so that reporting procedures are clear.
5 The management could consider setting up a staff lounge for informal communication between staff or consider other ways of developing informal communication, e.g. staff outings, encouraging managers to meet staff after work, etc.
6 The management could review their policy concerning flexitime, following a survey of staff attitudes.

- Finally, the Ss should discuss the timing of the actions that they propose and the amount of investment each will require. Encourage the students to give reasons for their decisions regarding timing and financial investment.

Stage 4: Listening 1.7

- Establish that the conversation is between Susan Westbrook, the President of HCPS, and Chris Wright, the Managing Director.
- Play recording 1.7 and ask the Ss to take notes on what the two people say.
- Get feedback from the whole class on what they heard before asking them to say who they agree with and why.

Stage 5: Writing

- The Ss write an e-mail from the management consultants detailing their recommendations. This should:
  - inform the management of HCPS that the research and analysis has been completed
  - briefly describe the communication problems uncovered
  - outline the recommended plan of action

Writing file page 141

1 to 1

This may give you ideas for role play of specific activities to complement those in the Course Book, based on your student's particular work situation.

UNIT 2

International marketing

At a glance

	Classwork – Course Book	Further work
Lesson 1 *Each lesson (excluding case studies) is about 45–60 minutes. This does not include administration and time spent going through homework.*	**Starting up** The advantages and problems of marketing globally. **Vocabulary: Collocations** Economic vocabulary in an international context and the vocabulary of international marketing.	**Practice File** Vocabulary (page 8)
Lesson 2	**Reading: Coffee culture** Ss read an article about coffee drinking habits in Latin America and Starbucks' expansion into this market, match countries with statements about coffee drinking, do comprehension tasks and work on some of the vocabulary. **Listening: Adapting to markets** Ss listen to a marketing specialist talking about the growth of global markets and how companies set about marketing their products internationally. **Language review: Noun compounds and noun phrases** Ss work on the structure of noun compounds and noun phrases.	**Text bank** (pages 136–139) **Practice File** Language review (page 9) **ML Grammar and Usage**
Lesson 3	**Skills: Brainstorming** Ss look at the principles of brainstorming, listen to a brainstorming session, and work on expressions used in sessions like this. They then put these ideas into action in their own brainstorming sessions.	**Resource bank** (page 197) **Practice File** Survival Business English (page 65)
Lesson 4 *Each case study is about 1½ to 2 hours.*	**Case study: Zumo – creating a global brand** A multinational based in Spain looks at ways of developing one of its products into a global brand.	**Practice File** Writing (page 10)

For a fast route through the unit focussing mainly on speaking skills, just use the underlined sections.

For 1 to 1 situations, most parts of the unit lend themselves, with minimal adaptation, to use with individual students. Where this is not the case, alternative procedures are given.

Business brief

'The world's youth prefer Coke to tea, trainers to sandals,' wrote one marketing specialist recently. This implies that tastes everywhere are becoming similar and **homogeneous**. But the watchword should still be **Think global, act local**. Acting local means having local market knowledge: there are still wide **variations** in taste, customs, behaviour and expectations between consumers in different markets, even markets that from the outside look very similar, such as those in Europe or Latin America. It means, for example, recognising attachments to local brands, how business is done in each place and so on.

Of course, these are issues that a company with a **global presence** has to address. But even companies that seem as if they have been global for ever had to start from a home base. For example, it took Marlboro 30 years and McDonald's 20 years to become truly global organisations.

How to enter overseas markets in the first place? Philip Kotler enumerates the various methods.

- **Indirect export**. Exporters use an **intermediary**, such as an **export agent**, to deal with buyers in the overseas market.
- **Direct export**. Companies handle their own exports, for example by setting up **overseas sales offices**.
- **Licensing**. Companies sell the rights to use a **manufacturing process**, **trademark** or **patent** for a **fee** or **royalty**. In services such as hotels, the company may negotiate a **management contract** with a local business to run the hotels on its behalf.
- **Joint ventures**. Two companies, for example an overseas firm and a local one, may work together to develop a particular market.
- **Direct investment**. The company buys a local firm, or sets up its own **manufacturing subsidiaries**.

Of course, these different arrangements require different levels of commitment, investment and risk. Kotler talks about the **internationalisation process**, where firms move (hopefully) through these stages:

- no regular export activities;
- export via independent representatives / agents;
- establishment of overseas sales subsidiaries;
- establishment of production facilities abroad.

This process will help them to progress towards global thinking and local action as they expand internationally. At different stages, companies will have different levels of understanding of the markets where they are trying to develop. Each step in the process requires different levels and types of support.

Read on

Philip Cateora, John Graham: *International Marketing*, McGraw-Hill, 1998

Harold Chee, Rod Harris: *Global Marketing Strategy*, Financial Times Prentice Hall, 1998

Financial Times: *Mastering Marketing*, Pearson Education, 1999, ch. 10: 'International Marketing'

Philip Kotler: *Marketing Management*, Prentice Hall, 1999 edition, ch. 12: 'Designing Global Market Offerings'

Lesson notes

Warmer

- Ask Ss to consider the place of the international products on the left in the table below in relation to the products on the right in their country / countries. (Write them quickly on the board.) For example:
  - Who drinks Coke or Pepsi? Is it all generations? What do people drink with meals?
  - Who goes to fast-food hamburger restaurants? Do families go there for snacks and family meals?
  - Who wears trainers? Is it only younger people? Do business people wear them to work and then change into shoes when they get there? etc.

Coca-Cola and Pepsi Cola	Tea, coffee and local soft drinks
Fast-food hamburgers	Traditional food of the country
Trainers	Shoes or sandals
Jeans	Trousers
Western rock music	Popular music of the country

- Whole class discussion about the place and use of these products.

Overview

- Tell the Ss that they will be looking at international marketing.
- Ask the Ss to look at the Overview section on page 14. Tell them a little about the things on the list, using the table on page 16 of this book as a guide. Tell them which points you will be covering in the current lesson and which in later lessons.

Quotation

- Ask the Ss what they understand by the quotation on page 14. (It goes against the usual principle of marketing, which is that marketers should understand customers' needs and provide products and services that satisfy them.)

Starting up

This section introduces the theme of international marketing and provides an opportunity for some speaking practice. Get the Ss to discuss in pairs or small groups with one member of each group taking notes. Then ask the notetaker in each group to report their findings to the whole class.

Examples include:
- Food: Nestlé, Danone
- Drink: Coca-Cola, Starbucks
- Electrical equipment: Sony, Zanussi
- Clothing: Gap, Benetton, Zara
- Construction: Bechtel, Halliburton, ABB

1. Advantages include being able to buy raw materials in large quantities at lower prices, and being able to spread administrative and other costs over a larger number of products sold.
2. Problems include not understanding local tastes and habits, and not understanding the structure of local distribution networks.
3. For methods of entering overseas markets see Business brief on page 17.

Vocabulary: Collocations

These exercises develop some of the vocabulary needed to talk about a country's economy.

- Get Ss to work individually or in pairs. Then go round the whole class and elicit answers.

1. monetary regulations (Point out that *currency regulations* would also be possible here.)
2. government bureaucracy
3. political stability
4. buying habits
5. economic situation
6. Income distribution

- Talk about a particular country, using these and related expressions. Don't ask the Ss to 'make up sentences' with the expressions, but have a natural discussion. *In [name of country], the economic situation is good, with low inflation and low unemployment. The country is politically stable ...,* etc. Get the Ss to use correct related forms, e.g. *politically stable* and *political stability.*

- Get the Ss to discuss the questions in pairs or small groups, and then report to the whole class.

1. For business, benefits include stable environment for planning, investment, etc.
2. Talk about inflation, growth, general prosperity, etc.
3. Treat this one with caution. Some Ss might argue that unequal distribution allows some people to accumulate wealth that can then be used for new investment. Others may say that on principles of fairness, wealth should be more equally distributed.

- Get the Ss to do the exercise in pairs or small groups.
- Then check answers with the whole group. Here, it's particularly important to discuss with the Ss *why* the odd one out is the odd one out. For example in question 1 a), b) and c) all are used to talk about markets that are increasing in size, but d) is not.

1 d	**2** c	**3** b	**4** c	**5** b	**6** a
7 d					

2 Examples might include top-of-the range cars, life-coaching, etc.
3 domestic
4 withdraw
5 slogan
6 A retailer sells to the general public. A wholesaler sells to a retailer, usually in large quantities.

Reading: Coffee culture

This article, from the Financial Times, looks at how the Starbucks coffee house chain has expanded into the market of South America.

- Get the Ss to discuss in pairs or small groups and then bring findings together in the whole class.

Ⓑ

- Get the Ss to read the article quickly and then scan it for the information needed to match the countries with the statements.

1 Chile **2** Chile **3** Brazil **4** the US **5** Argentina, Peru

Ⓒ

- Get the Ss to read the first eight paragraphs of the article again. Circulate and monitor. Ask for the Ss for words that are causing difficulty and explain them.
- Ask one student to summarise the article so far in a couple of sentences.
- Get the Ss to read the rest of the article. Circulate and monitor. Ask the Ss for words that are causing difficulty and explain them.
- Get the Ss to answer the questions in Exercise C. If you haven't already explained the meaning of *franchise* (line 90), you may need to in order to help Ss with question 3.

1 Pike Place Market, Seattle in 1971.
2 **a)** 3,907 **b)** 437
3 **a)** 1,378 **b)** 1,180
4 Japan
5 airline offices, sports stadiums, hotels, bookshops
6 home market saturation, bad experience in Japan, security problems in Israel, opposition from the anti-globalisation movement

Ⓓ

- Get the Ss to do this in pairs and then check with whole class.

a) 2, 6, 8, 10, 11, 12
b) 1, 3, 4, 5, 7, 9

Ⓔ

a) 2, 4, 5, 6, 9, 10, 11
b) 1, 3, 5, 7, 8, 12

Listening: Adapting to markets

Paul Smith is a marketing specialist. He talks about the reasons why global markets are growing, how companies prepare for international marketing of their goods and services, and the problems and challenges inherent in global marketing.

Ⓐ 2.1

- Get the Ss to listen once or twice to the first part of the interview. Encourage them to take notes to help them answer the question.

Is the marketplace really attractive or not?
Is there a real need for your product?
Who would the customers be?
Can they pay for it?
Can you beat the present or future competition?
Do you need a local partner?
How easy is it to trade there (taxes, barriers, borders, customs complications)?
Are there any unusual cultural characteristics to take into account?

- Encourage discussion of any points that arise, particularly if any of the Ss have experience of attempting to market a product globally.

Ⓑ 2.2

- Play the second part of the interview, stopping at points where the Ss can note down the problems and challenges.

Differences in language, literacy, the associations of colour, the meanings of gestures, culture, media availability, legal restrictions.

Ⓒ

- Ask the Ss to discuss the question in pairs or small groups and to report back to the class on their ideas.

Language review: Noun compounds and noun phrases

This section looks at a feature which can cause difficulty, particularly to those from certain language backgrounds, such as Latin-based ones.

- Go through points 1 and 2 with whole class, commenting where necessary.

Ⓐ

- Get the Ss to work on these expressions in pairs.

1 consumer profile
2 mass-market café culture
3 speciality shops
4 per capita consumption
5 anti-globalisation movement

Lesson notes

(B)

- Get the Ss to work in pairs.

> **1** leader **2** check **3** market **4** exchange **5** contract **6** conditions **7** product

- Check with the whole class.

(C)

- Get the Ss to work in pairs. Then go round the whole group quickly to get answers.

> **1** really impressive sales figures
> **2** new public relations department
> **3** highly ambitious market research programme
> **4** expanding overseas operations
> **5** rapidly improving balance sheet
> **6** extremely volatile exchange rate
> **7** highly confidential marketing report

- Ask individual Ss to use appropriate intonation, pretending that they are company managers talking to an audience and putting the expressions into short contexts, e.g. *Ladies and gentlemen, last year we had some really impressive sales figures. As you can see from the chart, ...*

Skills: Brainstorming

The idea here is to introduce the Ss to the idea of brainstorming, if they are not already familiar with it.

(A)

- Get the Ss to go through the points in pairs or small groups. Circulate and monitor.
- Round up the findings with the whole class. There are no right or wrong answers, but some of the issues below may emerge.

> **1** Yes, but sometimes it is good to be vague about the purpose of the meeting, so that participants don't look immediately at the specific situation. This will keep the discussion more open-ended and throw up ideas that otherwise might not have occurred.
> **2** Theoretically, no. The idea is to get everyone involved as equals. But people in some cultures would always expect the most senior person to speak first, whatever the type of meeting.
> **3** Probably a good idea.
> **4** This should be one of the main features of brainstorming, but sessions where this actually happens must be rare.
> **5** In theory, yes, but extremely bizarre suggestions would probably be seen as such.
> **6** Easier said than done, but it's probably more acceptable to interrupt in brainstorming than other types of session.
> **7** Theoretically, the speculation should be as wide-ranging as possible, but most participants would probably set limits as to what is relevant.
> **8** Probably a good idea. Details can come later in developing particular ideas.

(B) 2.3

- Play recording 2.3 once and get the Ss to say what the purpose of the meeting is – to develop promotional ideas for the Business Solutions website.
- Play recording 2.3 once or twice more and get the Ss, in pairs, to note the different types of promotional activities mentioned. Then check with the whole class.

> advertising on television and radio; online promotion; direct mailing; press advertising in traditional newspapers, business magazines and journals

(C) 2.4

- Play recording 2.4 once or twice and get the Ss, in their pairs, to note the answers to the questions. Then check with the whole class.

> **1** send a mailing to the names of the contact base, containing a brochure and / or a CD Rom; an event, for example on a river boat; billboard advertising
> **2** next meeting in three weeks; information on the budget and the cost of the different promotional activities

(D)

- Get the Ss, in pairs, to categorise the expressions. At the same time you could ask them to say whether they are tentative / neutral (T/N in table below) or strong (S). Then check with the whole class.

Stating objectives	
The purpose of the meeting this morning is ...	T/N
What we need to achieve today is ...	S
Our objective here is to ...	T/N
Encouraging contributions	
Don't hold back ...	S
'Fire away'.	S
Say whatever comes to mind.	T/N
Any other ideas?	T/N
Would it be worth sponsoring some kind of event?	T/N
What about that?	T/N
Expressing enthusiasm	
That's great!	S
That's the best idea I've heard for a long time.	S
That's an excellent suggestion.	S
Excellent!	S
We should definitely do some of that.	S
Absolutely!	S
Making suggestions	
I think we could ...	T/N
I suggest we ...	T/N
One thing we could do is ...	T/N
I think we'd reach a wide audience ...	T/N
What about press advertising?	T/N
Would it be worth sponsoring some kind of event?	T/N
It would be great to do a presentation. ...	S

Agreeing	
Yes, that's a good idea because ...	S
Exactly because ...	S
You're (absolutely) right because ...	S
Excellent!	S
We should definitely do some of that.	S
Absolutely!	S
That might be one way ...	T/N

(E)

- The idea here is to put into action some of the principles of brainstorming.
- Organise the class into groups of three or four for maximum participation.
- If there is more than one group, get different groups to do different situations in parallel. Appoint someone in each group who will note down the ideas produced, ready to report them to the whole class at the end of the activity.
- Make sure Ss are clear about the background to their situation.
- Start the activity. Circulate and monitor.
- When Ss have finished, get the notetaker in each group to say what ideas they came up with.
- Praise strong points from your monitoring of the brainstorming sessions and mention language points that the Ss should pay particular attention to. Get individual Ss to go back to the context where the mistake occurred and say the new, improved version.

1 to 1

- Encourage the student to come up with ideas for each situation as quickly as possible. Do not interrupt. Afterwards praise and correct language as in the final bullet point above.

Case study

Zumo – creating a global brand

A multinational company based in Spain wants to develop one of its existing products, currently sold only in Europe, for the global market.

Stage 1

- Get the Ss to read the first two sections.
- Circulate and answer any queries. Discuss common queries with whole group.
- Quickly put the points in the left-hand column of the table below on the board and elicit information from the group so as to complete the column on the right.
- Make sure the Ss understand the situation by getting individual Ss to expand orally on a part of the table, using complete sentences.

Background: Zumospa

Company	Zumospa
Activity	food and drinks
Based in	Valencia, Spain
History	developed nationally, then globally, with acquisitions worldwide
Methods	innovative advertising and marketing; careful selection of products; marketing round the world through regional offices
Products	many food and drink products, household names

Background: Zumo

Sales	€30 million, 20% of Zumospa's total sales
Profit	€4.5 million
Position in Zumospa's product portfolio	cash cow
Ambitions	to make Zumo a global brand

Stage 2 2.5

- Write the points in the left-hand columns of the following two tables on the board.
- Play recording 2.5 and ask the Ss to make notes on the company results, future plans and competitive advantage. Also ask them to note down the ingredients of Zumo and its properties.
- Get the Ss to read the next two sections and to use this information and the notes to complete the tables on the board.

Lesson notes

Lesson notes

Zumo's key features

Ingredients	caffeine, vitamins, glucose, plus secret ingredient 'herbora' (rare African plant root)
Properties	body absorbs Zumo faster than water or other soft drinks; unique formula – tasty and thirst-quenching

Zumo as a global brand: initial strategy

Positioning	global; play down Spanish associations
Markets for initial launch	South America, Mexico, southern US, Japan, where Zumospa already has regional offices
Advertising campaign	standard throughout all markets, with local language and content adaptation
Advertising media	TV and radio; some adaptation of media (different media in different places)

Stage 3: Task

- Divide the class into small groups of three or four. Explain the purpose of the brainstorming session and remind them that they shouldn't spend too long on each point.
- Circulate and monitor, noting strong and less strong language areas.
- Praise the strong points and talk about areas for improvement, getting relevant students to reformulate what they said with the corrections you suggested.
- Make sure that Ss understand the situation by getting individual Ss to expand orally on different parts of the table, using complete sentences.

Stage 4: Writing

- Get the Ss to write an e-mail concentrating on two or three key points from the brainstorming session, saying what their particular group came up with in those areas, and whether they, as Marketing Manager for Zumospa, agree with the ideas produced.

Writing file page 139

1 to 1
Get your student to glean the information to complete the tables and then have a 1 to 1 brainstorming session, where you both come up with ideas. Move on quickly from point to point.

Building relationships

At a glance

	Classwork – Course Book	Further work
Lesson 1 *Each lesson (excluding case studies) is about 45–60 minutes. This does not include administration and time spent going through homework.*	**Starting up** Ss discuss important business and social relationships, listen to an interview and do a quiz about their ability to build relationships. **Vocabulary: Describing relations** The vocabulary of relationships, including typical word combinations with *relations*. **Listening: Relationships in a global market** Things to be aware of when doing business in South America and China.	**Practice File** Vocabulary (page 12)
Lesson 2	**Reading: AIG knows everyone** The importance of building good business relationships.	**Text bank** (pages 140–143)
Lesson 3	**Language review: Multi-word verbs** Ss look at multi-word (phrasal) verbs and practise them in context. **Skills: Networking** Ss study networking language in a series of networking situations, and practise the language in role plays.	**ML Grammar and Usage** **Practice File** Language review (page 13) **Resource bank** (page 197)
Lesson 4 *Each case study is about 1½ to 2 hours.*	**Case study: Getting to know you** Ss analyse an Asian car manufacturer, and suggest ways of strengthening customer loyalty to deal with increasing competition.	**Practice File** Writing (page 14)

For a fast route through the unit focussing mainly on speaking skills, just use the underlined sections.

For 1 to 1 situations, most parts of the unit lend themselves, with minimal adaptation, to use with individual students. Where this is not the case, alternative procedures are given.

Business brief

Both employers and employees have expectations about what is reasonable behaviour in a work context. There is a certain level of **trust** between people, and even if the newspapers are full of stories of breakdowns in this trust, we think of them as exceptions to **established norms** in **social relationships**.

Business-to-business relationships

Some say that first impressions count. Others think that someone's character can only be judged after a lot of contact in business contexts and socially. This is why deciding on a **supplier** or **distributor** takes varying lengths of time in different cultures. To emphasise the importance of relationships like these, companies may refer to each other as **partners**.

A new trend is for companies to set up **e-marketplaces** on the Internet where they work together on **procurement** (purchasing) of materials and parts. Suppliers can make bids in competition with each other.

When firms work together on a particular project, they may enter into a **strategic alliance**. This may take the form of a **joint venture** between two or three companies, or a **consortium** between several organisations. An alliance may be the prelude to a **merger** between companies. Journalists often use the language of betrothal and marriage in situations like this.

Companies may overcome legal and other barriers in order to merge, but, as in marriage, there is no guarantee that the relationship will work. The cultures of the two companies may be so incompatible that the promised increase in profitability and **shareholder value** does not materialise.

Relationship networks

Stakeholder theory holds that society is made up of a web of relationships, and that each member of this arrangement has its **stake** of interest and of responsibilities. In a company, the interested parties are its owners (shareholders), managers, employees, suppliers, distributors and customers who may or may not be end-users of its products or services. A large company's activities have an effect on the places where it operates (think especially of **company towns** dominated by one company) and on society as a whole. Some companies publish an independent **social audit** that goes beyond the traditional **annual report** and attempts to give a bigger picture of the company's place in society, the benefits it brings, the effects of its activities on people and the environment (see Unit 1, Communication). Some say that social audits give a false sense of **social responsibility**. Optimists reply that pressure from stakeholders such as shareholders and customers can bring positive changes in the way companies work, and benefits to society as a whole. Companies are increasingly sensitive to accusations of causing pollution, tolerating **racism** or using **sweatshop labour**.

Read on

E. Robert Dwyer, John Tanner: *Building Business-to-Business Relationships*, Irwin, 1998

Francis Fukuyama: *Trust: The Social Virtues and the Creation of Prosperity*, Free Press, 1996

Robert Hargrove: *Mastering the Art of Creative Collaboration*, McGraw-Hill, 1998

Gary Heil: *One Size Fits One: Building Relationships One Customer and One Employee at a Time*, Van Nostrand Reinhold, 1996

James E. Post et al.: *Business and Society: Corporate Strategy, Public Policy, Ethics*, McGraw-Hill, 1995

Lesson notes

Warmer

- With the whole class, build up on the board a 'mind-map' of a typical individual and their relationships. Draw a circle in the centre of the board showing the individual, with 'spokes' going out to other circles representing family, colleagues, boss, friends, clubs the individual belongs to, etc.
- Invite comments and encourage discussion of the map.

Overview

- Tell the Ss that they will be looking at building relationships, especially in organisations.
- Ask the Ss to look at the Overview section at the beginning of the unit. Tell them a little about the things on the list, using the table on page 24 of this book as a guide. Tell them which points you will be covering in the current lesson and which in later lessons.

Quotation

Ask the Ss to look at the quotation and say if they agree with it. (Explain *shark* and who Woody Allen is if they don't know.)

Starting up

This section develops some of the ideas from the Warmer activity, and focusses the Ss on the subject of the unit. There is also a brief listening extract.

- Get the Ss to discuss the questions in pairs. Each individual student should draw two mind-maps like the one in the Warmer activity, one concentrating on company and professional relationships, the other on social relationships.
- Get one or two individual Ss to draw their maps on the board and explain them to the whole class, not forgetting to talk about the benefits of each relationship.

(B)

- In the listening activity in Exercise C, the Ss will listen to Ward Lincoln, the Business Relations Manager of an international training organisation talking about how companies can build good business relationships.
- Before listening to the recording, tell the Ss specifically that Ward Lincoln is going to talk about the key factors companies must consider when communicating with their clients. With the whole group, get the Ss to say what they think the key features of this communication might be and write them on the board. Some examples are:
  - they should get to know each other well
  - they should talk to each other regularly.

(C) 3.1

- Play recording 3.1 once or twice and get the Ss to say:
  - which of the points they came up with were mentioned, and in what order, marking this on the list prepared on the board in Exercise B
  - the points they didn't anticipate, adding them to the list.
- Play the recording again, confirm the key points about communication, and work on remaining unfamiliar vocabulary, e.g. *restless*.

(D)

- Get the Ss to do the quiz individually, then check their answers on page 153.
- Get two or three Ss to say what their 'profile' is and whether they agree with it.

Vocabulary: Describing relations

This section deals with the vocabulary of relationships, looking at some typical word combinations, and prepares the Ss to talk about relationships in the later activities in the unit.

- Ask the Ss to work in pairs, getting them to say whether the words they know are positive or negative. With the whole class, put these verbs into a table on the board.
- Then, with the whole class, explain the verbs they don't know, using full sentences, like this:
  - If something *jeopardises* a relationship, it puts it in danger.
  - If people *resume* a relationship, they start it again after a period when it had stopped.
- After each of your definitions, ask the Ss if the expression is positive or negative and put it on the table on the board.

Positive meaning	Negative meaning
build up relations	*break off* relations
cement	cut off
foster	disrupt
develop	endanger
encourage	jeopardise
establish	damage
improve	sour
maintain	undermine
strengthen	
promote	
restore	
resume	

Ⓑ

- Get the Ss in pairs to discuss the sentences and choose the correct verb in each one.

1 damage	**2** establish	**3** strengthened	**4** undermined
5 improving	**6** disrupted	**7** broke off	**8** jeopardised
9 building up	**10** fostered		

Ⓒ

- Explain any unfamiliar words, e.g. *imposition*, to the whole class.
- If the Ss are unfamiliar with this type of matching exercise, point out that they can look for clues like full stops at the end of the numbered elements, indicating that the following element will be a new sentence. Here, there are no full stops, but in 4, for example, the plural *excellent relations* shows that the continuation must have a plural verb, so a) or b) must be the continuation, but only a) makes sense.
- Get the Ss in pairs to match the two parts of the expressions quickly.
- Round up the results with the whole class.

1 e	**2 d**	**3 b**	**4 a**	**5 c**

- In getting the Ss to make up sentences, it's good to give them specific contexts. You could prompt them to talk about relations between:
  - their country and another country
  - their company and its customers
  - their department and the rest of the company they work for
  - two well-known celebrities or politicians.
- Give the Ss time to think about their sentences and write them down. Don't 'put them on the spot' in front of the whole class.
- Once the Ss have had time to think about their sentences, do a whole-class round-up, writing the best sentences on the board.

Listening: Relationships in a global market

Ss listen to Agnes Chen, who talks about doing business and building relationships in South America and China, and compare the two business cultures.

Ⓐ 3.2

- Go through the three points with the whole class, then play recording 3.2 and ask the Ss to make notes on each point.
- Get the Ss in pairs to compare notes on each point. Play the recording again if the Ss need you to.
- Have a whole-class round-up, checking answers to each point.

1 Doing business in South America
Be aware that people are warm and friendly.
Personal contacts are very important.
They like to get to know you well before doing business with you.
Long business lunches or dinners may be necessary.
They like to take their time before doing business.

2 Doing business in China
The Chinese like to work with friends and relatives.
You often need an intermediary with local knowledge to help you establish business relationships.
They will trust you if you are loyal and respectful.
You have to win trust and respect.
Expensive gifts are part of business culture.

3 The best way to build a business relationship
Have clear objectives at the beginning.
Know what you're trying to achieve and deliver.
Review the relationship from time to time.
Have as much face-to-face contact as possible.
Be open and sharing.
Remember that trust is the foundation of an effective business relationship.
Keep your word.
Deliver what you say you will.
Don't promise more than you can do.

Ⓑ 3.3

- Play recording 3.3 and get the Ss to summarise what Agnes Chen says about building business relationships in China. Encourage them to use the words and phrases given.
- Ask the Ss if what she says is true of their own culture.

Reading: AIG knows everyone

Ss read about the importance of building good business relationships, something that can involve the investment of a lot of time and energy.

- Get the Ss to start skimming the article quickly to find the answer to the question. The answer is near the beginning, so they will not need to look at the whole article. If they don't know the expression *underwriting agency* in lines 3 and 4, then they can find the answer from the word *insurer* in line 5.

b) insurance

- Go through the numbers with the Ss so that they know what they are looking for as they skim the article again. Ask them to make a note of what each of the numbers refers to. Check answers with the whole class.

Lesson notes

Lesson notes

166: AIG's capitalisation in billion dollars
1992: the year that AIG became the first foreign insurer to be allowed into China
1919: the year that AIG was founded
80,000: the number of people employed by AIG
130: the number of countries in which AIG has affiliated agents

(C)

- Go through the names with the Ss and then ask them to find them in the article and note down who they are. Check answers with the whole class.

Maurice Greenberg: the Chairman of AIG
Cornelius Vander Starr: an American entrepreneur, the founder of AIG
Edmund Tse: the man who runs AIG's Asian operations and life assurance worldwide

(D)

- Give the Ss time to read the whole article more thoroughly. Put them in pairs to decide what are the main factors responsible for AIG's success in Asia. Check answers with the whole class.

The company's long-standing presence in the area
Maurice Greenberg's constant focus on the region and persistent lobbying on behalf of the company in China
The company's constant pursuit of close relationships with Asian governments, regulators and powerful businessmen

(E)

- Allow the Ss to read the article again and find answers to the questions.

1 AIG's objective is to get unrestricted access to China's vast insurance market.
2 He sees his role as forging relationships with governments and influential people by representing the company in high-level discussions.
3 Asia is a growth area for insurance and if the company is to continue to grow, it needs to maintain its strength in Asia and increase it by expanding into China.

(F)

- Get the Ss to hunt for these words in pairs. Check answers with the class.

pursue relationships (lines 49–50)
build relationships (line 56)
forge relationships (lines 82–83)

(G)

1 untapped potential
2 long-standing presence
3 unrestricted access
4 affiliated agents
5 emerging markets
6 high-level discussions
7 leading nations

(H)

- Ask the Ss to work in groups to discuss these questions and then give feedback to the whole class.

Language review: Multi-word verbs

Ss look at verbs made up of more than one word, otherwise known as phrasal verbs, and study them being used in context.

(A) 3.4

- Tell the Ss to look through the sections of the conversation. Answer any queries about meaning.
- Get the Ss, in pairs, to put the conversation in the correct order.
- Play recording 3.4 once or twice so that Ss can check their answers.

f c b d g j h e a i

- Ask the Ss to read the conversation in simultaneous pairs. Circulate and monitor, especially for realistic intonation.
- Ask one or two pairs to perform the conversation in front of the whole class.

(B)

- Get the Ss, in pairs, to underline the multi-word verbs in the conversation and then match them to their meanings.

1	get on (really well)	6	sounded out
2	count on	7	let (us) down
3	build up	8	set up
4	hold on to	9	draw up
5	put (it) off	10	call (it) off

- Check the answers with the whole class.
- Point out the separable multi-word verbs, for example *build up something* and *build something up*. Point out that when using *it* as the object, the verbs must be separated; for example, you can say *build it up* but not *build up it*.

- Ask the Ss, in pairs, to rephrase the comments.

> 1 We'll have to *call* the meeting *off* tomorrow. / We'll have to *call off* the meeting tomorrow.
> 2 Let's *put off* the presentation until next week. / Let's *put* the presentation *off* until next week.
> 3 We know our suppliers will never *let* us *down*. / We can *count on* our suppliers to meet their deadlines.
> 4 We have now *set up* a first class distribution network in Europe.
> 5 Could you please *draw up* a contract as soon as possible. / Could you please *draw* a contract *up* as soon as possible.
> 6 Could you *set up* a meeting with them for next week. / Could you *set* a meeting *up* with them for next week.
> 7 We've *held on* to the same market share that we had last year.
> 8 The new sales manager *gets on* very well with his team.

- Check the answers with the whole class.
- Again, point out the separable multi-word verbs, as in 1, 2, 5 and 6. (4 is theoretically separable, but *up* after *network* would be a long way from *set*, and would sound rather odd.)
- If there is time, your Ss could discuss the questions below in pairs. Write them on the board, and invite different pairs to talk about different points. The idea is to use as many multi-word verbs as possible (not just ones from this section) when answering the questions.
- Try to have a phrasal verb dictionary to hand, for example the *Longman Phrasal Verbs Dictionary*.

> 1 How can businesses build up market share?
> 2 How can companies hold on to their most valued employees?
> 3 What preparation should be made before setting up a meeting with an important potential customer?

- Circulate, monitor and assist if necessary. Note how each pair is using multi-word verbs.
- With the whole class, go over the multi-word verbs you have heard, correcting problems where necessary.

> **Possible answer for question 1**
> Of course, before companies can *build up* market share, they have to *get into* the market in the first place. They have to *find out about* how the market works, how distribution is *set up* and so on. When they have *put together* enough information, they can *set out* to attack the market, perhaps *starting off* in just a small area to begin with. They may try to *set themselves apart from* competitors by offering a product with special features, or they may compete on price.

Skills: Networking

Ss look at networking language in a series of networking situations, and use it themselves to role play two situations.

(A) 3.5

- Tell the Ss that they are going to listen to a series of conversations in the context of people networking.
- Ask them to look through the statements as preparation for listening, saying they will have to decide which statements are true and which false.
- Play recording 3.5 and stop at the end of each situation to give time for the Ss to make their choice.
- Ask the Ss for their answers.

> **1 a)** false **b)** true **2 a)** false, **b)** false
> **3 a)** true, **b)** false **4 a)** false, **b)** true

(B) 3.6

- Ask the Ss to look at the questions.
- Play recording 3.6 once or twice and ask for the answers.

> 1 Valentin Perez (A) wants advice on franchising contracts. A friend has given him the name of the person that he calls, saying that they might be able to help. B (whose name we do not learn) is unable to help, but gives Valentin Perez the name of someone who might be able to: Stephanie Grant.
> 2 The call is successful in the sense that Valentin Perez gets Stephanie Grant's name.

(C) 3.6

- Before playing the recording again, ask the Ss to look at items 1–6, and to think briefly about what the missing words might be.
- Play recording 3.6 again, and have the Ss fill in the blanks.

> 1 I hope you don't mind me phoning. Silvana said it would probably be OK.
> 2 Is it a convenient time to ring or could I call you back at a better time?
> 3 Silvana mentioned that you might be able to advise me on franchising contracts.
> 4 Mmm, I don't know. I could maybe give you a little help, but I know someone who's an expert in that area.
> 5 You haven't got her phone number by any chance?
> 6 Can I mention your name when I call her?

(D)

- Before role playing the situations, tell the Ss to look at the Useful language box.
- Get the Ss, in pairs, to practise saying the expressions using friendly intonation.
- Ss take turns to say one of the expressions from the Useful language box, and to make an appropriate reply. For example:

A Haven't we met somewhere before?
B Yes, it was at the group sales conference in Portugal last year.
A Oh yes. Very good conference, wasn't it!
B We both went to that presentation on networking skills.
A That's right! It was one of the most interesting at the conference!

- You can demonstrate with one student to give the Ss the general idea. Then get the Ss to practise in pairs.
- Praise and correct as usual, concentrating on friendly intonation.
- Keep the class in pairs. If you are short of time, some pairs can role play situation 1 and others situation 2.
- For situation 1, encourage the owner to think of a name for their notional colleague, and the contact to think of a typical Russian name, such as Ivan(a) Pavlov(a).
- For situation 2, the Ss can invent names for themselves or use their own names.
- Make sure that the Ss understand the situation they are going to role play before they start.
- Start the activity. Circulate and monitor.
- Praise good points and correct weaker ones, again concentrating on intonation.
- Ask for one or two public performances of each situation.

Case study

Getting to know you

Kimsoong, a Korean car manufacturer, wants to strengthen customer loyalty as a way of dealing with increasing competition.

Stage 1

- Instruct the Ss to read the section on the company's background in pairs.
- Circulate and answer any queries. Discuss common queries with the whole group.
- Quickly put the points in the left-hand column of the table below on the board and elicit information from the group so as to complete the column on the right.
- Make sure the Ss understand the situation by getting individual Ss each to expand orally on a part of the table, using complete sentences.

Background

Company	Kimsoong
Activity	Car manufacturer
Based in	Korea, European HQ near Paris
Structure	◎ Retail franchises in most European countries; also tyre- and exhaust-fitting services
Special features of the company	◎ Reliability at low prices ◎ Basic models include many features that are usually options ◎ Environmentally aware ◎ Social conscience – makes donations to environmental groups – Eco-car under development

- Ask the Ss to read the sections on problems and their possible solutions and elicit the points below.
- As before, invite individual Ss to summarise the situation using complete sentences.

Actions	Hoped-for benefit
◎ Look after existing customers well. Develop better understanding of customers through accurate customer profile. ◎ Customer loyalty programme (cost shared 50/50 with franchises). ◎ To encourage staff to be more active in building up good customer relations.	◎ To build up long-term customer relationships – customers may buy 3 or 4 cars over 10-year period thereby increasing profits.

Stage 2

- Before doing the task itself, Ss should study, in pairs, the Kimsoong customer profile for a couple of minutes.
- Go round the class quickly and ask individual Ss to make statements about different points, for example:
  - Nearly half the buyers of Kimsoong cars are under 30.
  - Less than 1 in 6 buyers buy another Kimsoong.

Stage 3: Task 3.7

- Get the Ss to work in pairs or threes on their ideas for the customer loyalty programme. Then play recording 3.7 and ask the Ss to make notes on the five suggestions made by the directors (discount for existing customers, send company magazine to customers, good deals on trade-ins, free after-sales service for three years, expensive pen for returning questionnaire).
- Invite representatives of the groups to present their ideas to the whole class. The representatives can write key points on the board and explain them briefly.
- Have the whole class discuss the various ideas, including those suggested by the directors, and choose the best ones, perhaps by voting on them. You can run this discussion yourself or ask a student to chair the meeting. (The student should be briefed beforehand on the time available.)

Stage 4: Writing

Ss write to an existing customer of a company in order to make an offer that will increase customer loyalty.

- Go round the class and ask individual Ss which company they might write about and what the special offer might be.
- Ask for possible openings to the letter, for example:
  - Dear Mr Eastwood, You are one of our most valued customers. That's why we're making you this special offer. ...
- The Ss could write letters in pairs collaboratively in class. Circulate, monitor and assist. Alternatively, set the activity as homework.

Writing file page 138

1 to 1

Use these points for the task as the basis for a discussion about existing customers and a possible loyalty programme.

Lesson notes

UNIT 4

Success

At a glance

	Classwork – Course Book	Further work
Lesson 1 *Each lesson (excluding case studies) is about 45–60 minutes. This does not include administration and time spent going through homework.*	**Starting up** Ss look at language for describing successful people and organisations and talk about success symbols in their own culture. **Listening: A successful business** A business woman talks about how she built up a successful electronic watch company. **Discussion: Sole brothers** Ss read about and compare two shoe companies.	
Lesson 2	**Reading: Steve Jobs** Ss read a profile of co-founder of Apple, Steve Jobs, and answer questions. **Language review: Present and past tenses** The tenses are compared and contrasted. Ss look at how they are used in the Jobs article and then use them to write about another company's history.	**Text bank** (pages 144–147) **Practice File** Language review (page 17) **ML Grammar and Usage**
Lesson 3	**Vocabulary: Prefixes** Ss look at how some common prefixes are used with particular verbs. **Skills: Negotiating** The language of signalling, checking understanding and summarising is examined. Ss analyse how it occurs in a negotiating situation and use it themselves to role play a situation.	**Practice File** Vocabulary (page 16) **Resource bank** (page 198)
Lesson 4 *Each case study is about 1½ to 2 hours.*	**Case study: Camden Football Club** Ss take part in the negotiations between a football club and a big media company.	**Practice File** Writing (page 18)

For a fast route through the unit focussing mainly on speaking skills, just use the underlined sections.

For 1 to 1 situations, most parts of the unit lend themselves, with minimal adaptation, to use with individual students. Where this is not the case, alternative procedures are given.

Business brief

People are fascinated by success. Business commentators try to understand the **success factors** that make for successful individuals, products and companies, and for economically successful countries.

People Different types of organisation require different types of leaders. Think of start-ups with their dynamic entrepreneurs, mature companies with their solid but hopefully inspirational CEOs, companies in difficulty with their turnaround specialists. Each also requires managers and employees with different **personality make-ups**. Think of the combination of personality types needed in banks compared to those in advertising agencies.

Products Successful products are notoriously hard to predict. There are subtle combinations of social, cultural and technological circumstances that mean that something will succeed at one time but not another. People talk rightly about a product 'whose time has come'. The technology to meet a particular need may exist for a long time before the product on which it is based **takes off**. In the beginning, cost may be a factor, but after a time, a **critical mass** of users develops, costs come down, and no one 'can understand how they could have done without one'.

Companies Success factors here include **energy**, **vision** and **efficiency**, but many of the companies that were thought to possess these attributes 30 or even five years ago are not those we would think of as having these qualities today. **Management fashions** are a big factor: **gurus** and management books have a lot to answer for. Once something becomes a **mantra**, everyone starts doing it, but objective measures of the relative efficiency of each type of company are hard to find.

Countries Economic success stories such as Japan, Germany and Sweden became models that everyone wanted to imitate. In the 1970s, government experts and academics went to these places by the plane-load looking for the magic ingredients. In the 1980s and early 1990s, they went to the emerging economies of the Asian tigers. Now the US economy is again held up as a model for all to follow. At various times, commitment to **self-improvement**, **entrepreneurial flair**, efficient **access to capital**, vibrant **institutions** and a good **education system** are held to be important factors for success, but the countries mentioned above possess these to very varying degrees. The exact formula for success at a particular time is hard to pin down.

In any case, how do you successfully imitate companies and countries? Companies have a particular **culture** that is the result of their history, short or long. If managers and their consultants change them radically, for example by downsizing them, they may be ripping out the very things that make them tick. On the other hand, change may be really necessary, and companies with cultures and structures that were successful under earlier conditions are very hard to change in a genuine way, even if they go through the motions of adopting the latest management fashion. Unless convinced otherwise by a **charismatic leader**, there will always be a number of **refuseniks**: managers and employees who refuse to change because they can't understand how the things that made the company successful in the past are no longer valuable, and can even be a cause of failure. One reason for developing new products in **start-ups** is that they can develop a culture and a recipe for success from scratch.

With countries, how do you imitate social structures and habits that have evolved over centuries elsewhere, often with an entirely different starting point? The old joke about not wanting to start from here if you're going there is applicable. In any case, by the time the model has been identified as one worth imitating, the world economy has moved on, and your chosen model may no longer be the one to follow.

The ability to **adapt** is key. Here, the US is world leader in adapting old organisations to new technological conditions – Ford and IBM, for example, have had amazing **turnarounds** from earlier difficulties. But radical **innovation** is equally important. The US is also good at generating entirely new companies that quickly become world leaders – witness Microsoft and Intel. The US economy is as dominant as ever.

Read on

Here is a very limited selection of books about managers, companies and countries respectively.

Michael Gershman: *Getting It Right the Second Time: Remarketing Strategies to Turn Failure into Success*, Management Books, 2000

Richard Koch: *The Successful Boss's First 100 Days*, Financial Times/Prentice Hall, 1998

Lesson notes

Warmer

- Ask the Ss to name the most successful business person / people in their own country / countries. (In a multi-country group, this is a good chance for Ss to learn about each other's business heroes.)

Overview

- Tell the Ss that they will be looking at success in business people and in organisations.
- Ask the Ss to look at the Overview section at the beginning of the unit. Tell them a little about the things on the list, using the table on page 32 of this book as a guide. Tell them which points you will be covering in the current lesson and which in later lessons.

Quotation

- Get the Ss to explain the joke in the quotation.
- Ask them if they think it's true. Do they think, for example, that some people are successful by luck, perhaps by being in the right place at the right time?
- Invite some quick comments, but don't anticipate the content of the rest of the unit too much.

Starting up

In this section, the Ss look at the vocabulary for describing successful people and organisations and talk about success symbols in their own culture.

(A)

- Get the Ss to discuss the words in pairs. Tell the Ss that they can add vocabulary that came up during the warmer session to their lists if they want to. Circulate, monitor and assist, for example by explaining *ruthlessness*, *charisma* and *nepotism*, helping with pronunciation, and suggesting words where necessary to describe particular character traits.
- Ask individual pairs to give their five most important characteristics and ask them why they have chosen them.
- Invite comments and encourage discussion. The Ss may say, for example, that the characteristics depend on the type of person. The characteristics of a successful novelist overlap with, but are not identical to, those for a successful chief executive. (Drive and discipline might be common to both.)

(B)

- Ask the Ss, in pairs, to talk about individuals they know, perhaps in relation to the five words they chose in Exercise A, and report their findings to the whole class. Say that they can relate the characteristics to the people that they mentioned in the Warmer activity if they want to.

(C)

- Get the Ss to work on the success symbols in pairs. Ask them also to name the particular cars, jewellery, holiday destinations, leisure activities, etc. that successful people choose at the moment. Invite comments and encourage discussion with the whole group. Where there are different nationalities in the class, treat the status symbols of each culture tactfully, of course.

(D)

- Get the Ss to work again in pairs, this time changing partners. Ask them to complete the statements with the words in the box. Check answers with the whole class.

a) profit **b)** leader **c)** innovation **d)** workforce
e) customer **f)** brand **g)** shares **h)** headquarters
i) subsidiaries **j)** people

- If you have time, get pairs to think of a successful company that they admire, and ask which statements in the exercise apply to this company. (In the case of successful recent start-ups, it may be that not many of the points apply.) Round up the discussion with the whole group.

Listening: A successful business

Ss listen to a business woman talking about the electronic watch company which she founded.

(A) 4.1

- Play recording 4.1 and ask the Ss to listen for the general gist.
- Go through the statements with the class. Then play the recording again, stopping after each key point so that the Ss have time to to decide whether each statement is true or false.
- Play the recording a third time, again stopping after each key point so that the Ss have time to check their answers.

1 false **2** true **3** true **4** false **5** false **6** true

- Go through the answers with the Ss, if necessary playing parts of the recording again if they didn't get something.

(B) 4.2

- Go through the two questions with the class before you play the recording so that they know what information they are listening for.
- Play recording 4.2 and encourage the Ss to take notes. Allow them to compare their answers in pairs before checking with the whole class.

1. Vision and strategic planning; use of management tools such as SWOT analysis; use of the Internet for marketing; development of a customer relationship management system.
2. Be well prepared; seize opportunities which arise; stay open-minded.

Discussion: Sole brothers

Ss read about and compare two shoe companies, Puma and Adidas Saloman.

- Ask the Ss to work in pairs and to decide who is going to read which text. They should both take note of the points so that they can look for information to help them with their summaries. Allow them to take brief notes, but don't let them write summaries and then just read them out.
- The Ss take turns to give their summaries. As they do so, circulate, monitor and assist, noting strong points and those that need correction. Encourage them to ask each other questions at the end of each one.

- Still working in their pairs, the Ss discuss what the two companies have in common and in what ways they are different. When they have finished, have a feedback session with the whole class, writing their ideas on the board.

Here are some similarities and differences between the two companies. The Ss will no doubt think of others!

Similarities

Both companies were founded by members of the Dassler family.
Both companies are successful producers of sports shoes.
Both companies are listed on the Frankfurt stock exchange.
Both companies have had their products worn and endorsed by famous sports stars.
Both companies have had success with providing shoes for the Olympic Games.
Both companies found success and a change of direction after new CEOs were appointed.
Both companies are expanding worldwide.
Both companies have kept sports shoes as their core product but have expanded into clothing and fashion goods.
Both companies have had problems: Adidas in the early days and Puma after it went public.

Differences

Adidas is listed on the Paris stock exchange, whereas Puma is listed on the Munich stock exchange.
Adidas has made an acquisition (Saloman) and changed its name. Puma has not.
Puma has remained a manufacturing and sales company but Adidas has changed into a marketing company and licenses products under the Adidas name.
Puma has had success by using a website to sell its products.
Puma has exploited links with a fashion designer to develop its range of products.
Puma has used product placement in Hollywood movies as a marketing tool.

Reading: Steve Jobs

Ss say what they know about three key figures from the development of computers and the Internet and then read a profile of Steve Jobs, co-founder of Apple and owner of Pixar, the computer animation firm. They answer questions on Jobs's successful career.

- Ask the Ss to work in pairs to pool their knowledge of the three people listed. Then have a class brainstorming session, listing as much information as you can on the board.

Here is some information about the three men. The Ss may know more.

1 **Bill Gates**
Chairman and Chief Software Architect of Microsoft Corporation, the worldwide leader in software. Born October 28 1955. Grew up in Seattle, where his father is a lawyer. Began programming computers at the age of 13. Went to Harvard University, but left before graduating in order to devote his time to Microsoft, a company he began in 1975 with his friend Paul Allen. Married Melinda French Gates in 1994 and has three children. Gives generously to charity through the Bill and Melinda Gates Foundation.

2 **Steve Jobs**
Co-founder of Apple. Now CEO of both Apple Computers and Pixar Animation Studios, famous for computer animated films such as *Toy Story* and *Finding Nemo*. Born February 24 1955 in Wisconsin. Adopted soon after birth by Paul and Clara Jobs and raised in Santa Clara, California. Helped popularise the concept of the home computer with the Apple II. Fired from Apple by John Sculley but later rejoined the company and turned its fortunes around with the iPod. Married Laurene Powell in 1991 and has three children with her. Also has a daughter with Christine Brennan.

2 **Tim Berners-Lee**
Inventor of the World Wide Web and Director of the World Wide Web Consortium, which oversees its continued development. Born in London June 8 1955. Parents both mathematicians who worked on the Manchester Mark I, one of the earliest computers. Graduated from Oxford University in 1976. Created the World Wide Web in 1991 and built the first server and web browser. Currently Chair of Computer Science at Southampton University. Married with two children.

- Tell the Ss to read the article and then discuss the questions in pairs. Circulate, monitor and assist. Then ask the whole class for their answers.

1 **a)** the year Jobs and Wozniak started Apple
b) the year Jobs was fired from Apple by John Sculley
c) the year Jobs rejoined Apple

2 The computer Apple I.

3 **a)** The success of the computers Apple I and Apple II.
b) The success of Pixar.

4 He was fired by John Sculley.

5 When Apple was failing, he was invited back by the company.

6 One year.

7 It will change the way people buy music and will combat the pirating of music which is damaging the music industry.

8 Answers might include his genius, vision, determination and confidence in his own ability and in his products.

Language review: Present and past tenses

The tenses are compared and contrasted. Ss look at how they are used in the Steve Jobs article and then use them to write about another company's history.

- Get the Ss to work, in pairs, on the questions. Circulate, monitor and assist.
- Get individual Ss to make statements about their own company or educational institution using the different tenses.
- Discuss the rules with the whole class and get the Ss to complete the statements.

1 present simple
2 past simple
3 present continuous
4 present perfect

1 Past simple, because these are completed actions which took place at a particular time in the past.
2 *has complained, has been, have followed, have seen, has walked out*
Because these are present results of past actions.
3 *is, does not believe, is*
The present simple is used because these are situations which are generally true.

(B)

- The Ss could do this at home if your classroom does not have access to the Internet.
- Collect the paragraphs and check that the Ss have used the tenses correctly.

(C)

- Go through notes with the whole class, explaining the task and any unfamiliar words (e.g. *flagship*).
- Get individual Ss to come up to the board in turn and write the first sentence of each section, so that they see present simple, past simple and present perfect in context.
- Ask the Ss to use these sentences as the basis for writing the complete article, individually or in pairs in class, or as homework.

The company
TOYS "Я" US is one of the world's largest toy retailers. It sells its merchandise through more than 1,500 outlets, with 685 toy stores in the US, a further 605 toy stores overseas and 216 BABIES "Я" US stores.

How the company started
In 1954 Charles Lazarus began a business for children only and he set up his first baby furniture store in Washington, DC. Lazarus opened his first toy supermarket in 1957 and in 1978 TOYS "Я" US became a public company.

Recent events
In 2001 TOYS "Я" US opened its Times Square flagship store in New York City. Although it has recently lost its number one position in the US to Walmart, it has significantly expanded its video merchandising in its US stores and has evolved into an 11-billion-dollar business.

What it is doing now
TOYS "Я" US is currently trying to regain its number one position from Walmart. Lazarus is now focusing on a new venture, BABIES "Я" US, and is working hard to make it the number one baby product specialist chain store in the world.

Vocabulary: Prefixes

Ss look at how some common prefixes are used with particular verbs.

- Ask the Ss to find the three example words in the article on page 32 (in lines 1, 54, and 79). Ask them to look at the context and say what each word means. Establish that if the prefixes *co-*, *re* and *under* are removed from these words, then words with different meanings are left. Elicit the implications of the prefixes (*co-* means *with:* Jobs didn't found Apple alone, he founded it with Steve Wozniak; *re* means *again:* Pixar was called something else before Jobs bought the company; *under* means *too little:* Jobs doesn't believe in being modest and saying too little about the success of his companies).
- Get the Ss to complete the exercise in pairs. Circulate, monitor and assist.
- Ask the Ss what other words they know that use these prefixes (e.g. *overeat, mismanage, outdo, co-author, rewrite, ultra-generous, ex-wife, decommission, undervalue*).

1 over **2** out **3** mis **4** ultra **5** ex **6** de **7** co-
8 under **9** re

(B)

- Do the first one as an example with the whole class and demonstrate that the odd one out in each group is the word that cannot take the prefix in bold at the beginning of the line. Ask the Ss to complete the exercise in pairs. Circulate, monitor and assist.

1 profit **2** boss **3** decide **4** lose **5** look **6** win
7 big **8** staff **9** grow

(C)

- Get the students to work either individually or in pairs to complete the sentences.
- Check answers with the whole class.

2 co-authors **3** relaunch **4** overestimated
5 mismanaged **6** outbid **7** ultra-modern **8** ex-boss
9 denationalised

Skills: Negotiating

The language of signalling, checking understanding and summarising is covered. Ss analyse how it occurs in a negotiating situation and use it themselves to role play a situation.

(A)

- Go through the Useful language box with the whole class. Get individual Ss to read the expressions, working on intonation.
- Explain briefly the role and importance of these expressions in structuring negotiations.

(B)

- Get the Ss to read the conversation aloud in pairs, and identify signalling, checking understanding and summarising expressions.
- Ask different pairs for their findings and discuss them with the whole class.

Special requirements? What do you mean exactly? (Checking understanding)
Mmm, OK, how about this? (Signalling)
OK, so you're saying you will modify the car if we ask you to? (Checking understanding)
Right then, let's see what we've got. (Summarising)
That's it. OK, let's talk about delivery now. (Signalling)

(C) 4.3

- Play the recording once right through, and then again, stopping after each item.
- Ask the Ss to identify signalling, checking understanding and summarising expressions, so as to eliminate them.

1 checking understanding
2 signalling
3 –
4 checking understanding
5 signalling
6 summarising
7 checking understanding
8 –
So the answer is 3 and 8.

(D)

- Explain the situation.
- Put the Ss into pairs and appoint the Sales Managers and Chief Buyers. Make sure that everyone knows who they are.
- Ask the Sales Managers to turn to page 149 and the Chief Buyers to turn to page 147.
- Ask the Ss to study their information carefully.
- Tell the Ss they should
  - start the negotiation with some small talk
  - get into the negotiation itself, trying to use the expressions for checking understanding, signalling and summarising, and
  - write down what they agree.
- Answer any questions the Ss may have, then tell them to do the negotiation in pairs.
- Circulate, monitor and assist. Note language points for praise and correction, especially in relation to the expressions for signalling, checking understanding and summarising.
- When the pairs have finished their negotiation, ask the different pairs what they decided. Summarise the results on the board, so that Ss can see the range of results.
- Ask one or two pairs to summarise the stages of their negotiations, the tactics each partner was using, particular difficulties and sticking points.
- Do a round-up of language points for praise and those that need correction. Focus on five or six language points, for example, in relation to expressions for signalling, checking understanding and summarising, and get individual Ss to use the correct forms.

1 to 1

This role play can be done between teacher and student. Don't forget to note language points for praise and correction afterwards. Discuss with the student their negotiating plan and the tactics they were using.

Lesson notes

Case study

Camden FC

Ss study information about Camden FC and take part in the negotiations between the club and a big media company about future broadcasting rights and other issues.

Stage 1 4.4

- Divide the whole class into two halves, A and B.
- Get the Ss to read the section on Camden's background.
- Play recording 4.4 and ask the Ss to take notes of the key points.
- Get the Ss to read the section about the current situation.
- Circulate and answer any queries.
- Put the points in the left-hand column of table below on the board. Ask the Ss questions to elicit the information to complete the table, e.g. *What has Camden's recent performance been like on the field?*
- Then, similarly, get the Ss in Group A to elicit information from those in Group B about the current situation.

Background: Camden FC

Recent performance in football	Very successful in UK and Europe
Recent performance in business	Commercially very successful
Footballing success due to	Cristos Sroda, Manager, and his strategy of promoting younger players and buying some international ones
Commercial success due to	Sophie Legrange, Commercial Director, and her strategy of increasing profits through ◎ corporate hospitality ◎ sponsorship ◎ conferences ◎ diversification: travel agency, etc.
One lucrative source of income	TV rights

Current situation

Current sponsorship deal with	Insurance company
Possible new deal with Other income from United Media's interest in Camden due to United Media's	United Media plc other activities Potentially large audiences (advertisers will be interested – not specifically stated)
Key factors in negotiations between Camden and United Media	◎ Camden feel they are in a strong position ◎ Some say Camden rely too much on their star player, Paolo Rosetti. He is now 30, is unreliable, has been getting bad publicity recently, and he has personal problems

- Check that the situation is clear to all the Ss by asking a few quick questions.
- Once you are satisfied that the situation is clear, move on to Stage 2.

Stage 2

- Divide the class into groups of four to six. Within each group, half the Ss will represent Camden FC and the other half, United Media plc: two to three Ss on each side.
- Ask the whole class to look at the agenda for the negotiations and elaborate briefly on each point.
- Before the Ss read their role cards, make it clear that each side will have to work out its objectives, priorities, strategy and tactics, and think carefully about what concessions they are willing to make.
- Camden FC negotiators turn to page 147 and read their role cards.
- United Media negotiators turn to page 154 and read their role cards.
- Get each team to work together to develop an effective strategy for the negotiations. Circulate, monitor and assist.

Stage 3: Task 4.5

- Make sure that each side has a chief negotiator who will be the first to speak. The chief United Media negotiator will outline the purpose of the negotiations and the chief Camden negotiator will reply. The chief negotiators should make sure that the discussions move on smartly, so that participants do not spend too long on each point.
- The negotiations can begin, in parallel where there is more than one group.
- Circulate and monitor, noting strong points and those that need correction. Do not intervene in the negotiations themselves unless the teams are completely stuck.

- Just before the negotiatons seem to be coming to a conclusion, stop the class and tell them that a news report has just come on the radio. Play recording 4.5. Then ask the Ss to continue their negotiation.
- When time is up, ask the Ss on different sides what happened in their particular negotiations: what their objectives were, what tactics they used, whether they achieved their objectives, etc. Ask them what effect the news report had on their negotiations.
- Praise strong language points and correct ones that need correcting, getting individual Ss to rephrase what they said earlier, incorporating the corrections.

Stage 4: Writing

Following the negotiations, the Ss write a press release or a letter depending on the outcome of their particular session.

- This writing exercise can be done as pair work in class or for homework.
- Make sure that each student knows which type of writing they are going to produce: a press release from the point of view of the company they represented, or a letter, if the negotiation was unsuccessful.

Writing file page 141.

1 to 1

This negotiation can be done 1 to 1. Ask the student which side they would prefer to represent. You represent the other side. Don't forget to note language points for praise and correction after. Afterwards, discuss with the student their negotiating plan and the tactics they were using. Highlight some of the language you chose to use as well.

UNIT 5

Job satisfaction

At a glance

	Classwork – Course Book	Further work
Lesson 1 *Each lesson (excluding case studies) is about 45–60 minutes. This does not include administration and time spent going through homework.*	**Starting up** Ss discuss what motivates people at work. **Vocabulary: Synonyms and word building** Ss look at the vocabulary of motivation and job satisfaction. **Discussion: Job satisfaction** Ss discuss their experiences of job satisfaction. **Listening: Staff satisfaction survey** A Human Resources Director talks about how her company creates job satisfaction among its staff.	**Practice File** Vocabulary (page 20)
Lesson 2	**Reading: Perks that work** Ss read an article about the perks that companies offer their workers in order to build company loyalty and retain their staff.	**Text bank** (pages 148–151)
Lesson 3	**Language review: Passives** Ss work on the passive forms of a range of verb tenses. **Skills: Handling difficult situations** Ss look at the language used in tricky situations, and apply it themselves to role play a situation.	**ML Grammar and Usage** **Practice File** Language review (page 21) **Resource bank** (page 198)
Lesson 4 *Each case study is about 1½ to 2 hours.*	**Case study: Office attraction** A Managing Director is worried about close relationships between employees and their effect on the company. Ss suggest what action the company should take.	**Practice File** Writing (page 22)

For a fast route through the unit focussing mainly on speaking skills, just use the underlined sections.

For 1 to 1 situations, most parts of the unit lend themselves, with minimal adaptation, to use with individual students. Where this is not the case, alternative procedures are given.

Business brief

'Happiness is having one's passion for one's profession,' wrote the French novelist (and management thinker) Stendhal. The number of people in this fortunate position is limited, but there are all sorts of aspects of office and factory work that can make it enjoyable. Relations with colleagues can be satisfying and congenial. People may find great pleasure in working in a team, for example. Conversely, bad relations with colleagues can be extremely unpleasant, and lead to great dissatisfaction and distress.

Basic work on what motivates people in organisations was done by Frederick Herzberg in the 1960s. He found that things such as **salary** and **working conditions** were not in themselves enough to make employees satisfied with their work, but that they can cause dissatisfaction if they are not good enough. He called these things **hygiene factors**. Here is a complete list:

- Supervision
- Company policy
- Working conditions
- Salary
- Peer relationships
- Security

Some things can give positive satisfaction. These are the **motivator factors**:

- Achievement
- Recognition
- The work itself
- Responsibility
- Advancement
- Growth

Another classic writer in this area is Douglas McGregor, who talked about **Theory X**, the idea, still held by many managers, that people instinctively dislike work, and **Theory Y**, the more enlightened view that everybody has the potential for development and for taking responsibility.

More recently has come the notion of **empowerment**, the idea that decision-making should be decentralised to employees who are as close as possible to the issues to be resolved: see Units 8 **Team building** and 12 **Management styles**.

But where some employees may like being given responsibility, for others it is a source of **stress**. People talk more about the need for work that gives them **quality of life**, the **work-life balance** and the avoidance of stress. Others argue that **challenge** involves a reasonable and inevitable degree of stress if people are to have the feeling of **achievement**, a necessary outcome of work if it is to give satisfaction. They complain that a **stress industry** is emerging, with its **stress counsellors** and **stress therapists**, when levels of stress are in reality no higher today than they were before.

Read on

Warren Bennis et al.: *Douglas McGregor Revisited – Managing the Human Side of Enterprise*, Wiley, 2000

Wayne Cascio: *Managing Human Resources*, McGraw-Hill, 1997

Harvard Business Review on Work and Life Balance, Harvard Business School Press, 2000

Frederick Herzberg: *Motivation to Work*, Transaction, 1993

Paul Spector: *Job Satisfaction: Application, Assessment, Causes and Consequences*, Sage, 1997

Lesson notes

Warmer

- Write *job satisfaction* and *motivation* on the board. Ask Ss, in pairs, to discuss and define each of them.
- Ask each pair for the results of their discussion, and their definition. Invite comments from the whole class. (The *Longman Dictionary of Contemporary English* defines *satisfaction* as 'a feeling of happiness or pleasure because you have achieved something' and *motivation* as 'eagerness or willingness to do something without needing to be told or forced to do it'.)

Overview

- Tell the Ss that they will be looking at job satisfaction.
- Ask the Ss to look at the Overview section at the beginning of the unit. Tell them a little about the things on the list, using the table on page 40 of this book as a guide. Tell them which points you will be covering in the current lesson and which in later lessons.

Quotation

- Ask the Ss to look at the quotation and say if they agree with it. Ask if they know who Ogden Nash was (an American writer of humorous verse, if they're interested).

Starting up

Ss discuss motivating factors at work, and have the opportunity to do a quiz on professional burnout.

Ⓐ

- Go through the list of words and expressions. Get individual Ss to explain the less obvious ones (there's no need for them to explain *bigger salary* for example). Explain terms that the Ss don't know. Work on pronunciation where necessary.

Ⓑ

- Get the Ss to discuss the questions in pairs or threes. Circulate, monitor and assist. Note language points for praise and correction.
- Get the representatives of the pairs or threes to say what their findings were. Encourage whole-class discussion, comparing the results from each group.
- Praise good language points from the discussion and work on three or four points that need improvement, getting individual Ss to say the correct forms.
- If you have time, get the Ss to look at the 'Are you in danger of burning out' quiz on page 137. They can do it in pairs in class, or for homework. In both cases, ask individual Ss afterwards for their 'profile' and ask if they agree with it. Invite comments and encourage discussion.

Vocabulary: Synonyms and word building

Ss look at the vocabulary of motivation and job satisfaction.

Ⓐ

- Go round the whole class and get the Ss to read out the words and expressions. Correct stress and pronunciation where necessary, for example *auTOnomy*, *burEAUcracy*, but don't explain meanings at this point.
- Get the Ss to do the matching exercise in pairs. Circulate and monitor.
- Check the answers with the whole class.

1 g **2** e **3** f **4** b **5** a **6** c **7** d

Ⓑ

- Ask the Ss to complete the sentences in pairs. Circulate, monitor and assist.
- Go through the answers with the whole class.

1 autonomy **2** bureaucracy **3** burnout **4** pay
5 perks **6** golden handshake **7** appraisal

Ⓒ

- Ask the Ss to complete the exercise in pairs. Circulate, monitor and assist.
- Go through the answers with the whole class.

1	**a)** satisfied	**b)** dissatisfied	**c)** satisfaction
2	**a)** motivating	**b)** demotivated	**c)** motivation (Note: not 'motivator')
3	**a)** frustration	**b)** frustrating	**c)** frustrated

- Point out the negative prefixes underlined above. Tell the Ss that the best thing is to learn these as complete words, rather than get into the 'rules' for forming negatives, which are quite complicated.

Discussion: Job satisfaction

Ss discuss their own feelings of satisfaction and frustration at work and comment on three statements about job satisfaction.

- Ask the Ss to discuss the questions in pairs. Circulate, monitor and assist, noting language points for praise and correction.
- Get pairs to report their responses to the whole class. Invite comments and encourage further discussion.
- Praise good language use from the discussion and work on three or four points that need improvement, getting individual Ss to say the correct forms.

Listening: Staff satisfaction survey

A Human Resources Director talks about her company's annual survey, which is used to create job satisfaction among its staff.

- Find out if any of the Ss work for a company which uses a survey to assess staff job satisfaction. Brainstorm with the whole class two or three questions that might appear on the Procter and Gamble staff survey. Write their suggestions on the board and then ask them to work in small groups and to write down five more questions.
- Get groups to report their questions to the whole class.

B 5.1

- Play recording 5.1. The speaker doesn't quote any of the actual questions on the survey, but she talks about the areas of people's lives that the survey focuses on and gives some examples of more specific topics which the questions address. Ask the Ss to tick any of their question topics which the speaker mentions.

C 5.1

- Play the recording again, pausing to allow the Ss time to write down all the things which the survey asks about.
- When the Ss compare their answers with other members of their groups, you might like to ask them to formulate some of the actual questions on the survey, e.g. *Are you proud of the company and what it does? Do you understand how your work fits in with the company strategy? Are you satisfied with your work–life balance? Does your manager manage you well and help you to develop your career? Do you have a trusted mentor in the company to give you guidance? Do you understand all the benefits and compensation you are entitled to? Do you feel that you are adequately rewarded for your work?*

D 5.2

- Go through the questions with the whole class before you play the recording so that they know what information they are listening for.
- Play recording 5.2 and encourage the Ss to take notes as they listen. Pause the recording at key points to facilitate this. You may need to play the recording more than once.
- Check answers with the whole class.

1. Some people want a reduced work schedule. Some want to work from home instead of commuting to the office. Some want to work hard but would like to have enough energy left to enjoy a social life and to contribute to their communities in their spare time. (Ss might also mention the issue of the environmental impact of a company being a factor in changing priorities.)
2. Part-time work for mothers coming back from maternity leave and also for junior and senior managers who want to undertake some child care duties; flexible working hours to allow people to cope with emergencies and look after relatives, children or pets.
3. The ethical standards of the company and the company's policy on environmental issues.
4. To reduce pollution and to reduce traffic in the local area.

Reading: Perks that work

Ss read about some of the perks offered by companies in an effort to retain staff and build company loyalty. The article discusses whether the provision of generous perks makes sense for companies and what the best ways are of keeping employees happy.

A

- Ask the whole class for examples of perks that they receive in their jobs or which they know of, e.g. company car, canteen, healthcare provision, company pension, etc. Ask them if they know of any unusual perks.
- Ask the Ss to work in pairs and to imagine that they are joining a new company. Tell them to draw up a list of the perks that they would like to have.
- Get the pairs to report back to the whole class on their perks. You might like to ask the class to vote on the best list.

B

- Give the Ss time to read the whole article and then ask them to go back and find the lines in which the ideas are mentioned. Allow them to work in pairs or small groups if they wish. Circulate, monitor and assist with any difficult vocabulary.
- Check answers with the class.

1. lines 88 to 93
2. lines 94 to 107
3. lines 36 to 55
4. lines 58 to 83
5. lines 24 to 32
6. lines 9 to 14

C

- Ask the Ss to find and underline the word partnerships in the article.
- Check answers with the whole class.

1. personal problems (line 13)
2. financial planning (line 14)
3. top performers (line 26)
4. general manager (lines 63–64)
5. common sense (line 69)
6. social responsibility (line 75)
7. corporate culture (line 84)
8. employee loyalty (line 98)

D

- Get the Ss to work either individually or in pairs to complete the sentences.
- Check answers with the whole class.

1. personal problems
2. employee loyalty
3. general manager
4. corporate culture
5. social responsibility
6. top performers
7. common sense

 E

- Ask the Ss to discuss the statements in pairs or threes.
- Circulate and monitor.
- Ask the pairs or threes to present their findings to the whole class. Invite comments and encourage further discussion.
- Praise good language use from the discussion and work on three or four points that need improvement, getting individual Ss to say the correct forms.

Language review: Passives

Ss work on the formation and use of the passive forms of a range of verb tenses.

 A

- Go through the three points in the Language review box with the whole class fairly quickly. Don't spend too much time on them now, but come back to them in relation to later activities in this section: see below.
- Ask the Ss, in pairs, to match the sentences a)–h) with the tenses. Circulate, monitor and assist, reminding them about modal verbs (*must*, *might*, *should*, etc.), and helping with vocabulary, e.g. *hampered*.
- Ask the pairs for their answers.

1 c **2** e **3** h **4** d **5** d **6** g **7** a **8** f

- Discuss the sentences with the whole class, in relation to the first of the three points in the Language review box, for example
  - **a)** We're more interested in the supervisors being trained than in the people training them.
  - **b)** We're more interested in the people being forced to choose than those forcing them to choose.

(B)

- Explain vocabulary from the extracts that you think may be unfamiliar: *conduct*, *perceive*, etc. (without giving the answers, of course).
- Ask the Ss to work in pairs on the extract. Circulate, monitor and assist.
- Ask pairs for the answers.

1 *have been conducted*
2 *be perceived*
3 *are entered*
4 *were given*
5 *were paid*
6 *were paid*
7 *is reduced*

(C)

- Explain that the points form the basis for sentences from a report on an Employee Incentive Scheme.
- Explain any words that require it, for example *incentive*, *canvass*. Explain that a *share option scheme* is one in which employees are given shares in addition to their salaries. If the company performs well, they make money.
- Go round the class quickly and get answers from individual Ss.

Procedure
Questionnaires were distributed to all departments.
All managers were interviewed.
A sample of workers was canvassed.

Present problems
Staff are not being consulted.
Flexitime is not being allowed.

Measures to improve job satisfaction since March
Staff have been consulted properly.
Research into flexitime has been carried out.

Incentive recommendations
A new scheme should be introduced from 1 Nov.
A system of team bonuses should be adopted.
Further research should be carried out into a share option scheme.

- Relate this exercise to the initial point about the passive being used to describe processes and procedures.

Skills: Handling difficult situations

Ss look at and listen to the language used in tricky situations, and discuss what they would say in other difficult circumstances.

 A

- Explain to Ss that they will be looking at language for dealing with tricky situations, and get them to do the exercise in pairs. Circulate and monitor.
- Check the answers with the whole class.

1 h **2** g **3** d **4** e **5** f **6** b **7** a **8** c

- Ss work in pairs to role play the eight situations. Circulate, monitor and assist. Note language points for praise and correction.
- Ask for a few performances of the situations from individual pairs in front of the whole class.
- Praise good language points from the discussion and work on three or four points that need improvement, getting individual Ss to say the correct forms.

1 to 1

These role plays can be done directly between teacher and student. Don't forget to note language points for praise and correction afterwards.

(B) 5.3

- Play recording 5.3, stopping after each conversation to elicit the answers.

Apologising	Ending a conversation
Showing sympathy	Saying 'no' politely

(C) 5.3

- Go through the Language box getting individual Ss to read the expressions with appropriate intonation. Get them to overdo it slightly, but without sounding insincere!

- Play recording 5.3 again. Stop after each conversation and get Ss to match an expression from each conversation to a particular heading in the Language box.

Saying 'no' politely
I'm sorry, I really can't.

Showing sympathy
I know what you mean. You're not the only one who feels like that.

Apologising
I'm really sorry. We're going to have to ...

Ending a conversation
Could we talk about this later?

(D)

- Get the Ss to discuss appropriate expressions for the different situations in pairs. Circulate, monitor and assist.
- With the whole class, ask pairs for their expressions. The expressions below are suggestions. Ss will certainly come up with other ideas.

1. That's really bad luck. I know how you must feel.
2. I don't know how to tell you this but ...
3. I was thinking that it would be good to have a chance to talk about the contract over dinner.
4. I hope you don't mind me saying this, but actually it's not very comfortable. Would it be possible to move?

- As an additional activity, you could ask Ss to do mini role plays incorporating these expressions.

Case study

Office attraction

A managing director is worried about close relationships between employees and their effect on the company. Ss role play members of the Human Resources Department and suggest what action the company should take.

Stage 1

- Get the Ss to read the background section to themselves and meanwhile write the points on the left of the table below on the board. When the Ss have finished reading, elicit adjectives and expressions that describe the points on the left, and write them up.

Working atmosphere preferred by Karl Jansen, MD	relaxed
Staff rule book	slim
Company culture	casual, maybe too casual
Working hours	long
Competition with other companies and its effect	fierce, causing stress among employees
Close relationships between members of staff	increasingly common

- Get the Ss to read the e-mail and meanwhile write the points on the left of the table below on the board. When the Ss have finished reading, elicit information about the points on the left, and write them up.

Subject	Policy on office relationships
Main point	KJ's concern about relationships between members of staff
Result of three recent relationships	Damaged performance of those concerned as well as that of colleagues
Names of those involved and nature of problem	Tania Jordan – appointment John Goodman – re-assignment Derek Hartman – complaints

Stage 2: The details and specific questions 5.4

- Divide the class into groups of four. These groups will later form the basis of the role play groups. They represent members of the Human Resources Department. One person is Jenny Cunningham, its head, and the other three work under her. Each of them will concentrate on a particular case: that of Jordan, Goodman and Hartman, respectively.

Lesson notes

- Assign the roles of Jenny Cunningham and her subordinates in each group, making clear which case each subordinate is going to concentrate on.
- The person in each group playing Jenny Cunningham quickly skims the different cases to get the basic facts and then reads the 'specific questions' in order to prepare for the meeting where the Human Resources Department will decide what to recommend in each case.
- Ask the three 'subordinates' in each group silently to read the information about their particular case and to develop the recommendations they will put forward in the meeting. Circulate, monitor and assist. In preparing the details of each case, you could suggest to your Ss that they complete information under the headings: background; problem identified; action taken; remaining problem; recommendation.
- The student dealing with the Derek Hartman case should leave the group after reading the section about him and come over to one corner of the classroom. In this corner, play recording 5.4, the conversation between Karl and Claudia, once or twice to all the Ss from the different groups specialising in the Hartman case and ask them to take notes. They will need this information in the forthcoming meeting. When they are ready, ask them to rejoin their respective groups.
- Call the whole class to order and answer any queries.

Stage 3: Task

- Write the agenda for all the meetings on the board, explaining as you write up the points.

Agenda

1 Tania Jordan/Marcus Ball: facts of the case and recommendations
2 John Goodman: facts and recommendations
3 Derek Hartman: facts and recommendations
4 Written policy on close relationships at work? Sanctions (= punishments)?
5 How to avoid unfair advantages through close relationships? Specific examples of bad practice to be included in written policy, if we decide to have one?

- Tell the whole class that Jenny Cunningham will chair the meeting in each group. The person playing her will follow the agenda. For agenda items 1–3, tell the person playing Jenny that they should ask the student working on that case to summarise what happened, make their recommendation, and then open the meeting to general discussion. (The student working on Derek Hartman's case should be sure to summarise what they heard in the recording, as well as the other information about him.)
- When the situation is clear to everyone, the meetings can start. Circulate and monitor, but do not intervene except if absolutely necessary. Note language points for later praise and correction.
- At the end of the activity, praise good language points that you heard while you were circulating and monitoring, and work on three or four points that need improvement, getting individual Ss to say the correct forms.
- Ask each group to summarise its recommendations. Compare those of different groups. Invite comments and encourage discussion.

Stage 4: Writing

Ss write a set of guidelines which could be used as a discussion document at the next board meeting, based on the discussion at their particular meeting.

- This writing exercise can be done as pair work in class or for homework.

Writing file page 142.

1 to 1

The student can discuss the different cases directly with you. Don't forget to note language points for praise and correction afterwards.

Risk

At a glance

	Classwork – Course Book	Further work
Lesson 1 *Each lesson (excluding case studies) is about 45–60 minutes. This does not include administration and time spent going through homework.*	**Starting up** Ss look at different types of risk, and listen to a risk advisor talking about the risks faced by businesses. **Vocabulary: Describing risk** Verbs and adjectives used in the context of risk. **Listening: Effective risk management** Ss listen to another expert in risk management talking in detail about different risks, and ways of managing them.	**Practice File** Vocabulary (page 24)
Lesson 2	**Reading: Planning for the future** Ss read an article about the dangers to companies of not having effective strategies and procedures for risk management. **Language review: Adverbs of degree** Ss look at adverbs such as *rather*, *slightly* and *extremely* and use them in a number of situations.	**Text bank** (pages 152–155) **Practice File** Language review (page 25) **ML Grammar and Usage**
Lesson 3	**Skills: Reaching agreement** Ss listen to the language of agreement in the context of a marketing team meeting. They then put this language into action to role play a situation.	**Resource Bank** (page 198)
Lesson 4 *Each case study is about 1½ to 2 hours.*	**Case study: Suprema Cars** A sports car manufacturer is in trouble and has sought the advice of a management consultant. Seven options have been proposed for increasing profitability.	**Practice File** Writing (page 26)

For a fast route through the unit focussing mainly on speaking skills, just use the underlined sections.

For 1 to 1 situations, most parts of the unit lend themselves, with minimal adaptation, to use with individual students. Where this is not the case, alternative procedures are given.

Business brief

All business is built on risk. Operating in politically unstable countries is one of the most extreme examples of this. The dangers may range from **kidnapping** of managers through to **confiscation of assets** by the government. Company managers may have to face **fraud** and **corruption**. But the fact that companies want to work there at all shows that they think the **returns** could be very high. As always, there is a **trade-off** between risk and return: investing in very challenging conditions is a graphic, if extreme, illustration of this trade-off.

Companies do not have to go to unstable countries to be harmed by criminal activity. **Industrial espionage** has existed for as long as there have been industries to spy on, but this can now be carried out at a distance by gaining access to company computer networks. **IT security** specialists may try to protect their company's systems with **firewalls** (technical safeguards against such snooping by **hackers**) and against **computer viruses**.

So far, we have looked at some of the more extreme examples of risk, but even business-as-usual is inherently risky. For example, by putting money into a new venture, investors are taking serious financial risks. Most businesses fail (some put the figure as high as nine out of ten), and as the first **shakeout** of Internet start-ups showed, this can happen increasingly quickly after they are founded. **Venture capitalists** who put money into such businesses **spread their risk** so that the **payback** from one or two successful ventures will hopefully more than compensate for the money lost in the failures. For more on financial risk, see Unit 9 **Raising finance**.

There is also the risk that even apparently **well-established companies** that are seemingly in touch with their customers can easily start to go wrong: we can all think of examples in soft drinks, clothing, cars and retailing, to name a few. Here, the risk is of losing sight of the magic ingredients that make for success. Some companies are able to reinvent themselves, in some cases several times over. Others don't understand what they need to do to survive and thrive again, or if they do understand, are unable to transform themselves in the necessary ways. The things about the company that were formerly strengths can now become sources of weakness and obstacles to change. The financial markets see this, and the company's shares fall in value. Investors are increasingly quick to demand changes in top management if there are not immediate improvements. In some cases, companies that were the leaders in their industry can even go bankrupt: in airlines, think of PanAm.

And then there is the risk of management **complacency**. Take a tyre company. A few weeks of shoddy operations and enough faulty tyres are produced to put the whole future of the company at risk through **product liability claims** following accidents caused by blow-outs. **Product recalls** are the worst possible publicity imaginable for companies, and in the worst cases, their image is so damaged that they never recover. This is a case study in **reputational risk**: the trust that customers put in a company can be thrown away overnight. Another example of a company that destroyed the trust of its clients is the well-known Internet service provider that announced free access at all times, and then immediately withdrew the offer. One commentator described this as **brand suicide**.

Read on

Peter L. Bernstein: *Against the Gods: The Remarkable Story of Risk*, Wiley, 1998

C.B. Chapman, Stephen Ward: *Project Risk Management*, Wiley, 1996

Mark Daniell: *World of Risk*, Wiley, 2000

Lesson notes

Warmer

- Write the word 'risky' on the left of the board and dashes indicating the number of letters in the words that come after it, like this. (The figures in brackets indicate the number of dashes to write up):

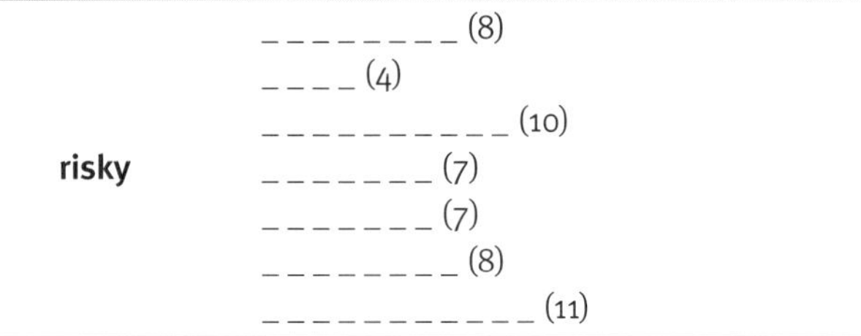

	_ _ _ _ _ _ _ _ (8)
	_ _ _ _ (4)
	_ _ _ _ _ _ _ _ _ _ (10)
risky	_ _ _ _ _ _ _ (7)
	_ _ _ _ _ _ _ (7)
	_ _ _ _ _ _ _ _ (8)
	_ _ _ _ _ _ _ _ _ _ _ (11)

- Tell the Ss that all the missing words are or can be business-related. They have to guess what they are. Tell them to shout out words they think of.
- If they have trouble, give them clues by showing particular letters, for example all the Es in the words, like this:

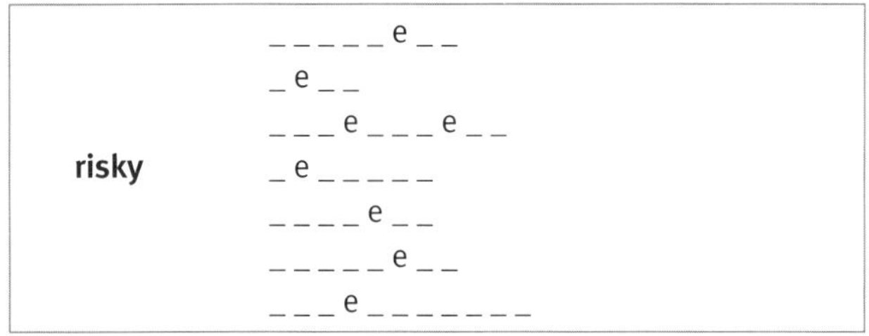

	_ _ _ _ _ e _ _
	_ e _ _
	_ _ _ e _ _ _ e _ _
risky	_ e _ _ _ _ _
	_ _ _ _ e _ _
	_ _ _ _ _ e _ _
	_ _ _ e _ _ _ _ _ _ _

- For words that the Ss still don't get, start giving other letters, or clues to their meaning, for example, the third one means 'when you put money into a business activity, or the amount of money you put in'.
- Ss should eventually end up with seven typical combinations, like this:

	business
	deal
	investment
risky	lending
	project
	strategy
	undertaking

- Point out that the last one has nothing to do with funerals, and means 'project' or 'enterprise'.

Overview

- Tell the Ss that they will be looking at Risk.
- Ask the Ss to look at the Overview section at the beginning of the unit. Tell them a little about the things on the list, using the table on page 48 of this book as a guide. Tell them which points you will be covering in the current lesson and which in later lessons.

Quotation

Ask the Ss to look at the quotation and say what it means (if you don't take risks, you can never succeed at anything). Invite comments and encourage brief discussion.

Starting up

Ss look at different types of risk, and listen to a risk advisor talking about the risks faced by businesses.

A

- Get the Ss to work in pairs on the different types of risk and say which thing is the riskiest in each group. Circulate and assist.
- Ask pairs for their findings. Invite comments and encourage discussion. (In the case of travel, don't get too bogged down in lugubrious statistics!)
- Ask the Ss if anything is done in their country / countries to warn of health risks and of the risks of particular types of investment.
- You could mention health warnings on cigarettes and, on some investment products in the UK, the 'health warning': 'The value of your investment can go down as well as up, and you may not get back the money you invested.' Point out the use of 'health warning' in this financial context.
- Ask if the Ss think such warnings are a) effective, b) necessary. Shouldn't people just be free to indulge in risky behaviour if they want to?

B

- Get the Ss to work in pairs. Suggest students each come up with three risky things they have done. Circulate and monitor.
- With the whole class, ask pairs for their risky activities. Invite comments and encourage discussion. Who are the risk-takers in the class (show of hands)?

C–D 6.1

- Get each student to write down three types of business risk.
- Do a quick round-up of these risks with the whole class.
- Tell the Ss that they will hear a risk advisor from a bank talking about risks faced by businesses.
- Get the Ss to listen to recording 6.1 once or twice and note down the risks mentioned.

1	doing nothing
2	credit or guarantee risk
3	political risk
4	risk of catastrophe or disruption (= the risk of not being able to continue business as usual because of some unforeseen event)

- Ask the Ss for the four risks and ask which of these they had predicted hearing. If necessary, explain *disruption*. Get the Ss to give examples of each type of risk.

Vocabulary: Describing risk

Ss look at verbs and adjectives used in conjunction with *risk*.

(A)

- Do as a whole-class activity. Write the four verbs *predict*, *meet*, *assess* and *manage* on the board and get the Ss to say which heading the other verbs should come under, explaining their meanings if necessary.

Predict	Meet	Assess	Manage
foresee	encounter face	calculate estimate prioritise	eliminate minimise reduce spread

- Ask the Ss to work in pairs on the matching exercise. If they haven't done this type of exercise before, point out clues. For example, if there is *impossible to* at the end of an item on the left, look for an infinitive verb at the beginning of the item on the right. Circulate, monitor and assist. (An actuary (item 6) is a specialist who works for or advises a financial institution. For example, life insurance companies employ actuaries to calculate future mortality rates of policyholders, the payouts that will have to be made, and their timing.)
- Ask the Ss for their answers.

1 e **2** f **3** g **4** d **5** c **6** b **7** a

- Group adjectives on the board under the two headings with the whole class.

High: great; huge; serious; significant; substantial; terrible; tremendous	**Low:** faint; miniscule; negligible; remote; slight

- Work on the stress of words like *sigNIFicant*, *subSTANtial*, *NEGligible* and *treMENdous*.

(D)

- Get the Ss to work in pairs on the three types of risk mentioned. Circulate, monitor and assist. Note language points for praise and correction, especially in relation to the verb and adjective combinations in Exercises A and C above.
- With the whole class, praise good language points from the discussion and work on three or four points that need improvement, getting individual Ss to say the correct forms.

Listening: Effective risk management

Ss listen to another expert on risk management talking about different risks, and ways of managing them.

(A) 6.2

- Go through the instructions with the class so that they know what information they are listening for.
- Play recording 6.2 once or twice and encourage the Ss to take notes as they listen. You may need to pause the recording to allow them to do this.
- Ask the Ss to work in pairs and compare notes on the four types of risk and examples of them.
- Check answers with the whole class. Explain any difficult words.

1. Operational risks – for example: regulatory non-compliance (failing to obey regulations and laws applicable to the industry), supply chain failure, failure of governance within an organisation.
2. Financial risks – for example: cash flow, credit or exchange risks.
3. Hazards – for example: safeguarding employees and the public, natural disasters (fires, floods, etc.) and the interruption in business that these things cause or their environmental impact.
4. Strategic risks – for example: market changes, increased competition, failure of an organisation to adapt or change.

(B) 6.3

- Play recording 6.3 and ask the Ss to take notes of the five key steps to effective risk management that the speaker outlines. Again, you may need to pause the recording at key points to allow them to make notes.
- Ask the Ss to compare their results in pairs before checking with the whole class. Explain any difficult words.

1. Be clear about your organisation's objectives.
2. Identify and describe the risks to those objectives.
3. Evaluate and rank the risks according to the likelihood of occurrence and the potential consequences.
4. Take action to deal with the highest ranking risks.
5. Report on both the inherent and residual risks to the key stakeholders in the organisation.

(C) 6.4

- Play recording 6.4 and ask the Ss to take notes on the three examples of effective risk management the speaker mentions and also the one negative example.
- Check answers with the class and explain any difficult words.

1 The success of companies in responding to the year 2000 computer bug.
2 The survival of those companies affected by the 9/11 attacks who had business continuity arrangements set up and tested beforehand.
3 Coca-Cola's quick withdrawal of its Dasani bottled water from the UK following a contamination scare.

The negative example is Shell's decision to sink its Brent Spa oil platform in the North Sea when there was public opposition to the move.

(D)

- Ask the Ss to discuss in pairs. Circulate, monitor and assist, noting language points for praise and correction.
- Get pairs to report their responses to the whole class. Invite comments and encourage further discussion.
- Praise good language use from the discussion and work on three or four points that need improvement, getting individual Ss to say the correct forms.

Reading: Planning for the future

Ss read an article about the dangers to companies of not having effective risk management strategies and procedures in place.

(A)

- Have a discussion with the whole class on this question. Ask the Ss for any examples they can give of companies that have made successful future plans.

(B)

- Ask the Ss to work in groups to discuss the three risks and decide where in the table they should go. Circulate, monitor and assist, encouraging them to give reasons for their rankings. The answers are given in the reading text, but do not point this out until the Ss have given their own opinions on the rankings.

1 Increased competition
2 Changes in customer demand
3 Loss of productivity due to staff absence/staff turnover

(C)

- Ask the Ss to read the first three paragraphs of the article and to make notes on the types of risk mentioned.

Risks associated with war and terrorism

Business risks associated with globalisation, outsourcing, consolidation, just-in-time delivery and cross-border supply

Traditional risks such as fires, floods, explosions, power failures and natural disasters

(D)

- Ask the Ss to read the whole article and then to discuss the question in pairs. Circulate, monitor and assist, giving help with any difficult words.
- Check answers with the whole class.

Companies are paying more attention to risk management because high-profile risks such as war and terrorism which attract a lot of media coverage have been added to the list of risks businesses have always faced. In addition, changes in the way business is conducted, with new factors such as globalisation, outsourcing, etc. coming into play have made the business world a riskier place.

(E)

- Go through the names with the Ss and then ask them to scan the article to find where they occur. You might suggest that they underline them in the article for ease of reference.
- Ask the Ss to work in pairs to match the people with their beliefs.
- Check answers with the class and ask them to read out the actual words that the people used to express these beliefs.

1 Shivan Subramaniam (lines 11 to 18)
2 Ken Davey (lines 45 to 52)
3 Lord Levene (lines 72 to 75)
4 Neil Irwin (lines 113 to 118)
5 Neil Irwin (lines 121 to 126)
6 Neil Irwin (lines 130 to 132) (also Lord Levene in lines 66 to 71)

(F)

- Encourage the Ss to find and underline the word partnerships in the article so that they can see them in context and quickly refer back to them.

1 business interruptions (lines 56 to 57)
2 recovery plan (lines 32 to 33)
3 decisive action (lines 70 to 71)
4 potential hazards (lines 48 to 49)
5 integrated strategies (line 72)
6 revenue sources (line 50)
7 near-normal operations (line 63)

(G)

- Ask the Ss to work in pairs to match the word partnerships to the verbs.

take decisive action
protect revenue sources
assess potential hazards
develop integrated strategies
implement a recovery plan
resume near-normal operations
prepare for business interruptions

(H)

- Ask the Ss to discuss the questions in small groups. Circulate, monitor and assist, noting language points for praise and correction.
- Get the groups to report their responses to the whole class. Invite comments and encourage further discussion.

- Praise good language use from the discussion and work on three or four points that need improvement, getting individual Ss to say the correct forms.

Language review: Adverbs of degree

Ss look at adverbs such as *rather*, *slightly* and *extremely* and use them in a number of situations.

- Go through the rules with the whole class.

Ⓐ

- Tell the Ss to draw a table with three columns headed *weak*, *moderate* and *strong*. Ask them in pairs to put the adverbs in the table. Circulate and assist.

weak	moderate	strong
a bit slightly	fairly increasingly moderately quite rather reasonably somewhat	entirely exceptionally extremely highly totally very

Ⓑ

- Get the Ss to complete the utterances. Ask them which adverbs are possible in each sentence and which are not. For example, in question 1, *exceptionally*, *extremely* and *very* are possible, but the other adverbs from the same group would be very unlikely. Tell the Ss there are no 'rules' about this: it's a question of learning the typical combinations.

Possible answers

1 exceptionally, extremely, very
2 exceptionally, extremely, highly, totally, very
3 fairly, moderately, quite, rather, somewhat, a bit, slightly
4 entirely, totally
5 fairly, moderately, quite, reasonably

Ⓒ

- Get the Ss to work in pairs, each pair working on four or five phrases. (For example, half the pairs could work on situations for the first five phrases and the other half on situations for the last five.) Each pair should make up mini-conversations like the ones in Exercise B above.

S1: What did you think of the presentation?
S2: Fascinating. And the speaker was incredibly well-prepared. All the equipment worked first time and the handouts were very useful.

- Circulate and monitor, but this time don't make notes of all language points. Concentrate on the intonation of the adverb expressions. Encourage the Ss to exaggerate slightly, but not to go too far over the top!

- Get pairs to give performances of the situations in front of the whole class. One performance for each situation will probably be enough. Work on intonation of adverb expressions as necessary.

Skills: Reaching agreement

Ss listen to the language of agreement in the context of a marketing team meeting. They then put this language into action to role play a situation.

Ⓐ 6.5

- Play recording 6.5 once right through and then once or twice more, pausing at convenient points to explain any unfamiliar vocabulary and allowing the Ss to make notes to complete the table.

Ideas	Approved Yes / No	Comments
On-line promotion	yes	One of the first organisations with a website, cheap form of promotion, must be focussed
TV advertising	no	Expensive, no experience of using it, competitors use it a lot, risky to put so much money into one thing
Sponsorship	no	Could be more easily focussed on target audience, but expensive
Advertisements in journals	yes	As long as it is focussed
Using established contacts	yes	Important to build on these, not expensive
Newspapers / magazines	yes	Know the readership, successful in the past, wide audience

Ⓑ

- Go through the expressions in the Useful language box. Get individual Ss to read them out, completing them as if they were contributing to the meeting they have just listened to, for example *Does anyone have strong feelings about TV advertising?* (They should not use exactly the same expressions as they heard on the recording.)
- Ask the Ss to work in pairs on expressions 1–10. Tell them they can look at the audio script on page 162 to check the context if necessary, and that some expressions go under more than one heading. Circulate and assist.

Lesson notes

1 Disagreeing
2 Giving opinions
3 Giving opinions, Disagreeing
4 Agreeing
5 Agreeing
6 Agreeing, Emphasising
7 Giving opinions, Emphasising
8 Making suggestions
9 Giving opinions
10 Summarising

- Ask pairs for their answers, and to give their reasoning for them. Invite comments and encourage discussion.

- Present the situation to the whole class and make sure they understand it.
- Put the Ss into threes and allocate roles. Tell the Ss to look at the information related to their role. Circulate, monitor and assist.
- When the Ss are clear about their roles, tell them that one of the purposes of the activity is to give them the opportunity to use the expressions they saw in the Useful language box.
- The activity can then begin. Circulate and monitor, noting language points for praise and correction, especially in relation to discussion language.
- When the Ss have completed their meetings, call the class to order. Ask each three what they decided.
- Praise good language points from the discussion and work on three or four points that need improvement, getting individual Ss to say the correct forms, especially for discussion language.

1 to 1

This role play can be done 1 to 1. Ask the student to choose one of the roles. You take one of the others. Don't forget to note language points for praise and correction afterwards.

Case study

Suprema Cars

Suprema Cars, a sports car manufacturer, is having problems, and asks a consultancy for advice on possible strategies. Seven options are proposed.

Stage 1: Background

- Tell the Ss to read the background section to themselves. While they are doing this, write the points on the left in the table below on the board. When the Ss have finished reading, elicit information to complete the table.

Company name	Suprema Cars
Product	classic sports cars
Brand image	quality and craftsmanship (cars are handmade)
Current problems	• factory workers demanding higher wages and better conditions • workforce unhappy because management wants production increased – workers fear quality will suffer • increase in number of cars that have broken down
Current customer perceptions	• love the classic design • believe the cars have excellent performance
Company's current situation	• losing sales and market share • made a loss in the last two years • may be unable to increase prices without losing customers

- Before the Ss read the options offered by the management consultant called in by Suprema Cars, you might like to ask them if they can suggest any solutions to the company's problems.
- Ask the Ss in pairs to read the section headed *A time for taking risks*. Answer any questions about difficult vocabulary.

Stage 2: Task

- Explain to the Ss that they are going to work in groups to discuss the options and identify the risks involved in each one.
- Divide the class into small groups. Explain that one student in each group will be responsible for presenting the group's results to the rest of the class.
- Go through the types of risks outlined in the table and tell the Ss to decide which options involve which risks and to tick the boxes accordingly.

- When they have completed the table, ask them to discuss the levels of risk according to the scale given. They could, perhaps, use coloured pens in the table to indicate the different levels of risk.
- Tell the Ss to continue discussing the various options, considering the advantages and disadvantages of each one. They should then be prepared to discuss their ideas with the other groups and say which of the options they favour at this time.

6.6

- Ask the Ss to listen to a conversation between Jack Dexter and Anita Taylor. Go through the three questions so that they know what information they are listening for.
- Play recording 6.6 and encourage the Ss to take notes. Check answers with the class. Then ask the Ss, in their groups, to decide whether or not they agree with Jack, giving their reasons.

1 Jack is definitely not interested in options 5 and 7.
2 Jack is quite interested in options 1 and 6.
3 Jack favours options 2 and 4

- Get feedback from all the groups.

Stage 3: Feedback

- Praise good language points from the discussion and work on three or four points that need improvement, asking individual Ss to say the correct forms. Refer especially to their use of language from the Skills section if they studied it earlier.
- When the group have made their choice of option, ask each group to make a succinct presentation of its recommendations to the whole class. One way of doing this is to ask a representative from each group to come to the front of the class. Invite comments and encourage discussion after each presentation, but leave time for as many groups as possible to present their findings.

Stage 4: Writing

- Ask the Ss to do this collaboratively in class or as homework. Remind them that they should analyse all the options they considered rather than just informing Jack of their recommendations. Point out the importance of using structuring language, e.g. *On the one hand ..., on the other hand ..., so our recommendation would be to ... .*

Writing file pages 144 and 145.

1 to 1

This case study can be done 1 to 1 as a discussion between teacher and student. Ask the student to make a formal presentation of the options and the best alternatives, as if they were a representative of the Suprema Cars management team.

UNIT 7

e-commerce

At a glance

	Classwork – Course Book	Further work
Lesson 1 *Each lesson (excluding case studies) is about 45–60 minutes. This does not include administration and time spent going through homework.*	**Starting up** Ss talk about their use of the Internet and experiences of e-commerce. **Listening: Success online** The Marketing Director of an online business talks about what makes his company successful. **Vocabulary: Internet terms** Ss look at words related to e-commerce, and use them to describe an e-commerce service company.	**Practice File** Vocabulary (page 28)
Lesson 2	**Reading: Internet shopping** Ss read about how online shopping has changed in recent years and how it continues to develop. **Language review: Conditionals** Ss recap the different types of conditionals and use them to talk about different situations.	**Text bank** (pages 156–159) **ML Grammar and Usage** **Practice File** Language review (page 29)
Lesson 3	**Skills: Presentations** Ss listen to a senior manager of an Internet company making a presentation, and analyse the language he uses.	**Resource bank** (page 199)
Lesson 4 *Each case study is about 1½ to 2 hours.*	**Case study: KGV Europe** A traditional retailer studies the possibility of getting into e-commerce.	**Practice File** Writing (page 30)

For a fast route through the unit focussing mainly on speaking skills, just use the underlined sections.

For 1 to 1 situations, most parts of the unit lend themselves, with minimal adaptation, to use with individual students. Where this is not the case, alternative procedures are given.

Business brief

Six months in e-commerce is like six years in any other business. At least, that's the way it seems at the time of writing (mid-2005). The e-commerce landscape is still very much in its formation. Let's look at three e-commerce operations that illustrate the fluidity of the situation.

Amazon is prehistoric by Internet standards. Using its vast accumulated expertise, it has gone beyond books to sell CDs, videos and other things as well, and its site acts as a 'host' for other suppliers, too. It benefits from a very good reputation for service, especially in delivery: the massive investments in warehouse automation and dispatch seem to have paid off.

Lastminute.com was founded on the original and attractive idea of catering for people who'd like to do something at the last minute, even if you can buy tickets for flights, etc. several weeks ahead. Its founders are famous and feted, at least in the UK, and there has been some clever PR to build the hype. However, when it sold shares to outside investors for the first time, the timing was bad. There was increasing scepticism about the real value of companies like Lastminute.com: the multi-billion valuation implied in the share issue bore no relation to the money it actually made. Its income (commissions from selling tickets, etc.) in 1999 was less than £1 million: peanuts. People who bought its shares presumably hoped to get in early on a company that might one day be very profitable, even if no profits are forecast for several years to come.

Boo.com was one of the first major casualties of e-commerce. It sold sports goods. Development of its site took much longer than planned, because its founders 'wanted everything to be perfect'. The launch was late, and meanwhile the company had used up all its capital.

At the time you read this, how are Amazon and Lastminute doing? Are they among the major players in e-commerce? Do people remember boo.com, perhaps as an object lesson in things that can go wrong, and as a victim of one of the first **shakeouts** in the industry?

Some of the key issues for e-commerce are:

- Physical delivery of goods. Parcel-delivery companies (**old-economy** organisations par excellence) have benefited enormously from companies like Amazon, where goods have to be **physically delivered** to homes. (They are even planning to deliver in the evenings, when people might actually be at home!)
- The future of services. Some think that the real growth in consumer e-commerce is going to be in services like travel and financial products, where the value of each transaction is quite high, and goods do not have to be physically delivered. On some airlines, two-thirds of bookings are being made on the Internet.
- The frustration of using **e-commerce sites**. A recent report found that, on average, 30 per cent of purchases on the Internet are not completed. It conjured up the spectacle of hordes of **virtual shopping carts** abandoned in the **virtual aisles** of these sites – an **e-tailer**'s nightmare! This, of course, has a very negative effect on the company's brand image, and the report even found that some people who had bad experiences on a company's website then avoided its **bricks and mortar** stores. This is one of the problems for traditional retailers who are trying to develop an **e-tail** operation, part of the more general question of how the two types of operation are going to relate to each other.
- **Business-to-business (B2B) e-commerce.** Some say that the biggest impact of the Internet is going to be in business-to-business applications, where suppliers can competitively bid for orders. Competing companies, for example in the car industry, have set up networks where they can get suppliers to do this. Orders are placed and processed, and payment made, over the Internet, hopefully with massive cost reductions through the elimination of processing on paper.

We live in exciting times. Things will develop in ways that are difficult to anticipate. E-commerce will **mature**, settling into more established patterns. What these patterns will be like, it's too early to say. Fortunes will be made by guessing future trends. Luck will no doubt play a big role.

Read on

Because of its fast-moving nature, books are not a good source of up-to-date information on e-commerce. The *Financial Times* runs regular features on the subject under the heading 'E-business Europe'. Search for articles on the *Financial Times* archive: www.ft.com.

Lesson notes

Lesson notes

Warmer

- Write the letter *e-* on the left of the board. On the right put the word *commerce*, and the initial letters of the second part of other words.

e-	1	commerce
	2	m________
	3	b________
	4	c________
	5	t________
	6	f________

- Ask the Ss if they know other words beginning with *e-* (which of course stands for *electronic*). The Ss can work in pairs to find them.
- Depending on the Ss' knowledge of the Internet, give them clues about the words.
  2 – the sending and receiving of messages on the Internet.
  3 – commercial activity on the Internet, not just buying and selling.
  4 – is used to talk about the 'new' economy that depends on the Internet.
  5 – selling goods on the Internet. (It is short for 'e-retailing').
  6 – the activity of sending goods that have been ordered on the Internet. (This one is difficult.)
- Ask the Ss for their answers and write them on the board.

> 2 e-mail
> 3 e-business
> 4 e-conomy
> 5 e-tailing
> 6 e-fulfilment

- For spelling enthusiasts, point out that 6 can be spelt with two 'l's in AmE.

Overview

- Tell the Ss that in this unit they will be looking particularly at e-commerce.
- Ask the Ss to look at the Overview section at the beginning of the unit. Tell them a little about the things on the list, using the table on page 56 of this book as a guide. Tell them which points you will be covering in the current lesson and in later lessons.

Quotation

- Ask the Ss to look at the quotation and say if they agree with it. Invite comments and encourage discussion, but do not pre-empt the topics of the unit too much.

Starting up

Ss talk about their use of the Internet and experiences of e-commerce.

- If necessary, adapt the questions in relation to the Ss' knowledge of the Internet. Even if they haven't used it to buy things, they will have ideas about it.
- Ask the Ss to work on the questions in pairs. Circulate and assist.
- With the whole class, ask pairs for their answers. Invite comments and encourage discussion.

> 1 Perhaps Ss have bought things by mail order, e.g. clothes, investment products. Would they buy them over the Internet?
> 3 Some say that travel and financial products are the best things to sell on the Net. (See Business brief.)
> 5 Ss may talk about fraud, and the danger of giving your credit card number.

Listening: Success online

The Marketing Director of an online business talks about what makes his company successful.

A 7.1

- Ask the Ss to look at the gapped sentences and invite them to think of ways in which they could be completed.
- Play recording 7.1 and ask the Ss to complete the sentences. Ask if they guessed any of them correctly. Ss may ask what Jeff means by 'we don't sell through the channel'. If so, tell them that by 'the channel' he means a company's normal methods of distribution.

> 1 direct relationship
> 2 distributors
> 3 information, purchasing design
> 4 online

B 7.2

- Play recording 7.2 and ask the Ss to take notes on the reasons why Dell has been successful doing business online. You may need to pause the recording at key points to allow them to do this.
- Check answers with the whole class.

> They have direct relationships with their customers.
>
> They hear first-hand from their customers about what information they want and how they want to interact with Dell.
>
> They provide information enabling customers to compare different technologies and give information about promotional offers.
>
> They have developed customised webpages for large corporate customers offering a customised service and customised prices.

C 7.3

- Go through the statements with the class before you play the recording.
- Play recording 7.3 and ask the Ss to mark the statements true or false according to what Jeff Kimbell says.

> **1** true
> **2** false
> **3** true

D

- Ask the Ss to discuss the statements in pairs and decide whether or not they agree with them.
- Get the pairs to report back to the class on their discussion. Encourage them to give reasons for their decisions.

Vocabulary: Internet terms

Ss look at words related to e-commerce, and use them to describe an e-commerce service company.

A

- Get the Ss to work on the words in pairs, using monolingual or bilingual dictionaries. Circulate, monitor and assist.
- Ask pairs for their answers.

> **browse:** to look through a series of web pages, perhaps those of a particular site, or ones found by a search engine relating to a particular topic.
> **directories:** lists of sites of similar organisations, or of sites with information on particular topics.
> **hits:** the number of visits that a particular site receives or the sites found by a search engine that contain the key word you entered.
> **key word:** a word that you enter into a search engine in order to find sites with web pages that contain this word.
> **locate:** find information, a site, etc. that you are looking for.
> **Net:** another word for Internet.
> **online:** used as an adjective or adverb to talk about activities related to the Internet.
> **search:** to look for particular information or a particular site, or the act of looking for it.
> **search engines:** sites like Google, Yahoo, AltaVista, etc. that allow you to find other sites with the information you are looking for by entering key words or expressions.
> **site:** a series of related screens with information about a subject, organisation, etc.
> **surfers:** people who go and look at different sites, perhaps in a random way with no particular purpose in mind.
> **traffic:** the number of people looking at a site in a particular period.

B

- Ask the Ss to look through the *Topsite* description and then complete it in pairs, using words from the box. Circulate and assist.
- Go through the answers with the whole class.

> **1** Net
> **2** search engines
> **3** traffic
> **4** site
> **5** search
> **6** key word
> **7** hits
> **8** surfers
> **9** online
> **10** directories
> **11** browse
> **12** locate

C

- Ask the Ss to discuss the questions in pairs. Circulate, monitor and assist, noting language points for praise and correction.
- Get pairs to report their responses to the whole class. Invite comments and encourage further discussion.
- Praise good language use from the discussion and work on three or four points that need improvement, getting individual Ss to say the correct forms.

Reading: Internet shopping

Ss read about how online shopping has changed in recent years and how it continues to develop.

- Elicit the answer to the question from the whole class. Brainstorm as many examples of each as you can.

> A 'bricks and mortar retailer' is a traditional business with a shop (perhaps on the high street or in a shopping centre) which customers can visit in person in order to choose and buy the goods they want. Examples would include any high-street store which doesn't sell online.
>
> An 'online retailer' sells goods through a website on the Internet. Increasingly many business have both high-street shops and websites through which they sell their goods. However, Amazon and Dell are examples of pure online retailers which have no shops.

- Put the Ss into groups and give them a time-limit, perhaps five minutes, to come up with as much information as they can about the three companies. When the time is up, see which group has the most information.

Amazon is an online retailer, best known for selling books, videos and DVDs. Since it was launched in 1995, Amazon has become the biggest online retailer in the world, with a customer base of over 10 million. The company has revenues of over $4 billion, growing by more than 20% a year. It is now diversifying into other areas, including electronic goods, food and clothing.

eBay is an extremely popular online auction house. People register with eBay to buy and sell goods online. Goods can be bought by posting the highest bid within a set period of time or sometimes by paying the asking price up front. Sellers can display photographs of the things they want to sell on the website and buyers can ask questions of the sellers about the goods on offer. Both new and second-hand goods are sold on eBay.

Sears Roebuck is a large American department store with branches in major cities throughout the United States. It was founded in 1886 by Richard Sears who decided to sell watches in order to supplement his income as a station agent. To begin with the company only sold watches and jewellery from its store in Chicago. It is now one of the best-known department stores in the world and sells a wide range of products from clothing and housewares to electronic goods and computers.

Ⓒ

- Ask the Ss to read the first six paragraphs of the article. Give assistance with any difficult words.
- Ask them to match the summaries with the paragraphs. Allow them to compare their results in pairs before checking answers with the class.

a) Paragraph 3
b) Paragraph 1
c) Paragraph 6
d) Paragraph 2
e) Paragraph 5
f) Paragraph 4

Ⓓ

- Go through the three questions with the class and explain any difficult words. Then ask the Ss to read the rest of the article and look for the answers.

1) Online selling requires heavy investment. Choices need to be made about whether to run the operations themselves or whether to outsource them. They need to decide whether to use the same sourcing model from the same factories and whether to have different distribution centres.
2) Tesco's online grocery business is the biggest in the world and it has helped another supermarket chain to set up an Internet operation. Rakuten is the biggest e-commerce site in Japan. The number of its shops has increased from 13 to over 10,000. Its share of the e-commerce market is three times bigger than that of its nearest rival.
3) They need to get the technology and the orders right, but also have to provide fun and entertainment, making shopping online a nice experience for the customer. They always have to be doing something interesting and something different to attract customers.

Ⓔ

- These word partnerships are all in the article, but encourage the Ss to match them without looking them up there.

1 distribution centre (lines 106 to 107)
2 online retailing (lines 2 to 3)
3 designer labels (line 142)
4 delivery charge (lines 78 to 79)
5 supermarket chains (lines 112 to 113
6 shopping mall (line 123)
7 auction houses (lines 15 to 16)
8 mail-order catalogue (lines 31 to 32)

Ⓕ

- Ask the Ss to use the word partnerships to complete the sentences. Check answers with the class.

1 delivery charge
2 auction houses
3 shopping mall
4 online retailing
5 supermarket chains
6 designer labels
7 distribution centre
8 mail-order catalogue

Ⓖ

- Ask the Ss to discuss the questions in pairs. Circulate, monitor and assist, noting language points for praise and correction.
- Get pairs to report their responses to the whole class. Invite comments and encourage further discussion.
- Praise good language use from the discussion and work on three or four points that need improvement, getting individual Ss to say the correct forms.

Language review: Conditionals

Ss recap the different types of conditionals and use them to talk about different situations.

- Go through the first set of conditional sentences with the whole class.
- Point out the fact that the first two are 'possible' conditions, in the sense that they describe situations that are possible in the future, whereas the third conditional is 'impossible': it describes a situation in the past that it is impossible to do anything about now. The zero conditional describes a 'general truth'.
- In pairs, get the Ss to change the form of each sentence in the second section so it is like one of the ones in the first section. Write the first sentence on the board as an example to give them the idea.

If you (or we) lose that password, we'll never be able to access that file again.
If you tell us what you need to get the job done, you'll have it.
If you need any further information, please contact our helpline.
If the market conditions had been better, the share offer would have been a success.
If we are given time, our factory can meet all those orders.

- Go through the new forms of the sentences with the whole class.

Ⓐ

- Go through the different categories with the whole class, explaining where necessary.
- Ask the Ss to categorise the sentences. Circulate, monitor and assist.

1 reflecting on the past
2 advice
3 promise
4 speculating about the future
5 bargaining
6 promise
7 speculating about the future
8 invitation / request
9 promise / bargaining
10 advice / warning / threat
11 reflecting on the past
12 request

- Go through the answers with the whole class. Invite comments and encourage discussion.

Ⓑ

- Write the following two sentences on the board as examples of different conditionals. Point out which you would use if you thought the situation was likely to happen or which if you thought it was not. Then tell the Ss to work on the situations in pairs. Circulate, monitor and assist.

If I get a pay rise next year, I'll buy a yacht.
If I got a pay rise next year, I'd buy a yacht.

- Go through the answers with the whole class.

Ⓒ

- Write the sentence 'If they'd set up the site properly, they wouldn't have had so many complaints.' Tell the Ss that this is an 'impossible' condition like 'If we'd prepared properly, we wouldn't have lost the contract', which they saw at the beginning of this section. Write this second sentence on the board under the first one, to show that their structures are the same.
- Ask the Ss to work in pairs on what went wrong with ClickShop.com. Circulate, monitor and assist.
- Go through the answers with the whole class.

Example answers:
If they'd set up the site properly, they wouldn't have had so many complaints.
If they'd planned more carefully, they wouldn't have had so many problems.
If they'd used an expert, their site would have been better.
If they hadn't tried to cut corners, they wouldn't have ended up in this situation.
If they'd allocated a bigger budget, they would have saved money in the end.
If they'd recognised the problems earlier, they would have been able to correct them.
If they'd listened to customer feedback, they would have some customers left today.
If they'd done more research, they wouldn't have made all these mistakes.

Skills: Presentations

Ss listen to a senior manager of an online business services company making a presentation, and analyse the language he uses.

Ⓐ 7.4

- Tell the Ss that they are going to listen to a manager of an online business services company giving a presentation to potential customers. Ask them to look quickly through questions 1–3.
- Play the first extract right through and then play it again, as far as '... a sort of quality-controlled environment', explaining anything that causes general problems. Ask the Ss for the answers to questions 1 and 2.

1 Smarterwork connects small business customers with providers of particular services.
2 **a)** the number of months Smarterwork has been in existence
b) the number of registered users of its site
c) the number of employees that it has

- Play the rest of the recording, explain any general problems and ask for the answer to question 3.

3 Clients, typically small businesses, and suppliers: service-providers who have been pre-screened.

- Ask the Ss to explain *pre-screened* (checked to make sure that they are competent and reliable).

Ⓑ 7.5

- Ask the Ss to look at the stages. Discuss with them what the missing stages might be, before playing the recording.
- Play the second extract two or three times, answer any general queries, and get the Ss to complete the stages. Check their answers with them.

The missing stages are:
The client evaluates the bids (with the help of one of Smarterwork's account managers).
The client assigns the project to a supplier.
The client and supplier develop the project.
The money is paid to the supplier.

Ⓒ 7.4

- Ask the Ss to look at the questions and then play recording 7.4 again.
- Get Ss to shout out the answers.

1 a b d
2 1 I'm going to
 2 begin by giving you
 3 I'll go on to tell
 4 I'll explain

Ⓓ 7.5

- Ask the Ss to listen out for ways that the speaker signals stages of the process and play recording 7.5 again.
- Ask the Ss for the phrases that they noted.

Firstly, the client posts a project, ...
Then the suppliers visit the site ...
After that the client evaluates the bids.
At the next stage, the client assigns the project to a supplier and *then* the client transfers ...
The client and supplier *then* develop the project.
Finally, the client signs off ...

Ⓔ

- With the whole class, look at the expressions given and the headings in the Useful language box. Get them to match the two. You could also ask them to suggest one or two more possible expressions of each type.

1 Involving the audience
2 Emphasising
3 Commenting
4 Changing subject
5 Referring to visuals

Ⓕ

- Ask the Ss to prepare a three-minute presentation. The content should be interesting, but it's also important to recycle the language, structure the presentation correctly and stick to the time limit.
- Ss can prepare the presentation in pairs or threes, with one member responsible for actually giving it. Circulate, monitor and assist. Each group should prepare a list of key points that the presentation will contain. They can also prepare visuals, for example organigrams, maps, etc. If you have transparencies and overhead pens, hand them out and get the Ss to prepare their presentations using them.
- Ask the Ss to give their presentations. Note language points for praise and correction. If there are a lot of Ss, keep some presentations for a later session to avoid presentation fatigue setting in!
- Praise good language points from the presentations and work on three or four points that need improvement, getting individual Ss to say the correct forms. Concentrate on structuring language, but also comment on other points.

Case study

KGV Europe

A traditional retailer studies the possibility of getting into e-commerce.

Stage 1: Background

- Get the Ss to read the background section. Meanwhile write the points in the first column of the table below on the board. When the Ss have finished reading, elicit information to complete the table.

Company type	High-street music retailer
Stores	12 in the Netherlands, of which 3 are megastores; 65 in Europe, of which 8 are megastores
Profits	Down 35% in three years
Megastore sales	Up 8% (heavy expenditure on advertising): 55% of total turnover
Problems / Weaknesses	Fierce competition, narrow product range, lack of innovation, not exploiting Internet opportunities

Stage 2: Market study 7.6

- Ask the Ss to go through the findings of the Market study in pairs. All pairs look at the six main findings of the study, but also specialise in the different areas. Ask half the pairs to look also at Chart 1 and the other half to look at Chart 2, in addition to Chart 3 and the six main findings.
- With the whole class, ask different pairs to summarise the information that they studied.
- Say who the people are that the Ss will hear on the recording: Michael, a director, and Hanna, the newly-recruited Financial Director. Get the Ss to listen to their conversation once or twice, explaining any difficulties. They should note down the key points.

Michael
- serious problems need radical solution
- leave high-street retailing
- sell stores and use money to set up Internet operation
- Internet: lower costs
- can't stay as they are: ageing client base, falling share price

Hanna
- no experience in e-commerce
- e-commerce businesses not doing well and not the whole answer
- must improve promotion
- outsource advertising: use agency
- learn lessons from market study and commission another on product range

Stage 3: Task

- Divide the class into threes or fours. Get the whole class to look at the questions and go through them quickly. Say that the overall purpose of the presentation is to outline the issues surrounding KGV's future strategy and that each group will have to make a strategy presentation to the whole class.
- When the groups have prepared their presentations, ask one member of each group to give the presentation to the rest of the class.
- In the same groups, the Ss hold a meeting as members of KGV's management team. They should discuss each of the options, decide what KGV's future strategy should be and work out an action plan for the next year.
- Ask one representative from each group to report the group's decision and describe their action plan to the rest of the class.

1 to 1

The task can be done as a discussion between teacher and student, looking at the different options. Don't forget to note language points for praise and correction afterwards.

Writing

- Ss can do this as homework or collaboratively in class. Explain the writing task. Point out that the e-mail should:
  - give a summary of the discussion at the meeting
  - give the decisions that were made
  - ask the director for their comments.

Writing file page 139

UNIT A Revision

This unit revises and reinforces some of the key language points from Units 1–7, and links with those units are clearly shown. You can point out these links to the Ss if you think that would be useful. This revision unit, like Revision Unit B, concentrates on reading and writing activities. Some of the exercise types are similar to those in the Reading and Writing section of levels 2 and 3 of the Business English Certificate examination organised by the University of Cambridge ESOL Examinations.
For more speaking practice, see the Resource Bank section of this book beginning on page 196.
The exercises in this unit can be done in class individually or collaboratively, or for homework.

1 Communication

Vocabulary

Ⓐ–Ⓒ

- These exercises look again at the vocabulary describing good communicators (page 7).

A		B		C	
1	persuasive	1	reserved	1	digressed
2	eloquent	2	focussed	2	clarify
3	succint	3	articulate, coherent	3	confuse
4	responsive	4	extrovert	4	interrupted
5	fluent	5	inhibited	5	engage
6	hesitant	6	sensitive	6	explain
				7	ramble, listening

Writing

- Ss practise replying to an e-mail, relating to the Case study activity on page 13.

Model answer

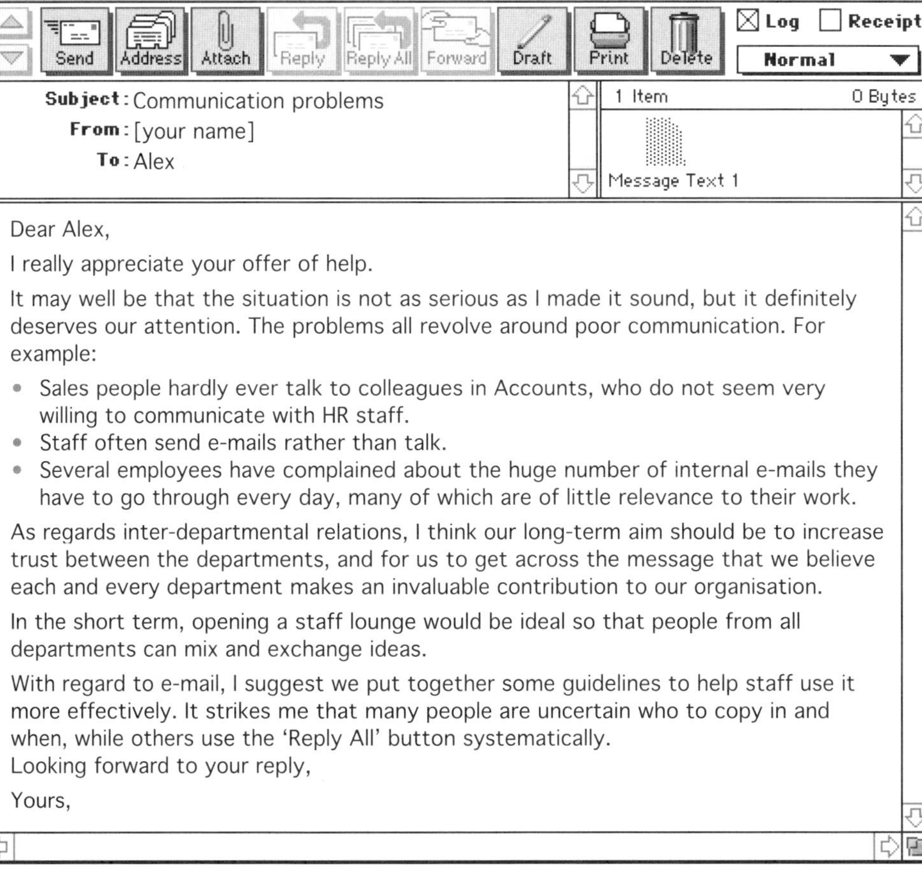

Subject: Communication problems
From: [your name]
To: Alex

Dear Alex,

I really appreciate your offer of help.

It may well be that the situation is not as serious as I made it sound, but it definitely deserves our attention. The problems all revolve around poor communication. For example:

- Sales people hardly ever talk to colleagues in Accounts, who do not seem very willing to communicate with HR staff.
- Staff often send e-mails rather than talk.
- Several employees have complained about the huge number of internal e-mails they have to go through every day, many of which are of little relevance to their work.

As regards inter-departmental relations, I think our long-term aim should be to increase trust between the departments, and for us to get across the message that we believe each and every department makes an invaluable contribution to our organisation.

In the short term, opening a staff lounge would be ideal so that people from all departments can mix and exchange ideas.

With regard to e-mail, I suggest we put together some guidelines to help staff use it more effectively. It strikes me that many people are uncertain who to copy in and when, while others use the 'Reply All' button systematically.
Looking forward to your reply,

Yours,

2 International marketing

Collocations and compounds

◎ These exercises look again at the vocabulary of international marketing.

A

1 expanding 2 launch 3 overseas 4 get a foothold in 5 retreat from

B

1 marketing strategy, marketing consultancy 2 market segment, market leader
3 sales figures, sales targets 4 product range, product design
5 brand loyalty, brand image 6 price range, price rise

Reading

◎ This reading text fits into the general theme of international marketing.

1 b 2 a 3 b 4 c 5 a 6 d 7 b 8 a 9 c 10 c 11 a
12 d 13 b 14 c

3 Building relationships

Multi-word verbs

◎ This exercise practises the multi-word verbs from the Language review section on page 26.

1 look into
2 hold on
3 hand in
4 call it off
5 tied up
6 sound her out
7 turn up
8 called it off

Writing

◎ Ss write a formal letter relating to the general theme of the unit.

Model answer

Dear Mr Stawowy,

It was a great pleasure to meet you at the Kraków trade fair last Saturday, and I would like to thank you for your interest in our range of office furniture.

As you already know, we have an unrivalled reputation for quality and innovative designs, and we export to eight different countries.

We are seeking to break into Eastern Europe, and we are aware that your business would provide an excellent distribution channel and help us gain a foothold in the growing Polish market, and possibly in neighbouring countries as well. On the other hand, there is no doubt that the quality and the unique design of our products would appeal to a large segment of your market.

With a view to discussing this and other areas of common interest, we would like to invite you to spend a few days with us. You could visit our production facility in Zaventem and our head office in Ixelles, which is right in the centre of Brussels. Ms Lina Debacker, our Sales Manager, would also be delighted to meet you.

With regard to possible dates, we would like to suggest tentatively early next month, and would be grateful if you could let us know whether this is suitable for you.

We very much look forward to hearing from you soon.

Yours sincerely,

4 Success

Prefixes

More practice on common prefixes from the Vocabulary section (page 34).

1 overcharged
2 deregulated
3 outbid
4 misinterpreted
5 overspent
6 mismanaged
7 relaunch
8 out-voted
9 relocated
10 underestimated

Reading

Ss read and complete a text about success in negotiation.

1 h 2 a 3 c 4 g 5 e 6 b 7 f

5 Job satisfaction

Passives

Ss look again at passives, dealt with in the Language review section on page 42.

1 was given
2 is currently being revised
3 be avoided, are reduced
4 have only been appraised
5 had been given
6 are being introduced
7 be reduced
8 is selected, will be offered

Writing

Model answer

When we noticed that staff retention showed sign of deteriorating, two other managers and I decided to talk informally to our employees. The three of us then discussed the findings of our survey.

Overall, the level of job satisfaction at our company is relatively high. However, it seems that quite a few employees do not really identify with our company and are ignorant of the values that we hold. Furthermore, the vast majority of staff declared that at one point or other they had felt they personally did not benefit from the perks we offer and had felt demotivated as a result. The two fringe benefits that came in for criticism most often were company cars and company holidays. Company cars are perceived as a privilege for a handful of high performers, mostly in Sales, while the holidays we offer are generally considered unsuitable for people with children, i.e. the majority.

In view of these observations, we feel that perks such as private health insurance, help with child care, and a new leave policy would have wider appeal and would benefit many more employees than our current system.

A flexible leave policy would be particularly well received, as it would enable staff to take time off when they need it, for example in order to be with their children more. In addition, showing that we do care for their life–work balance is very likely to increase employee loyalty and help them identify with our culture.

6 Risk

Adverbs of degree

◎ Ss revise the adverbs of degree presented in the Language review section on page 50.

A

Small: **1** slight **2** negligible **3** faint **5** remote
Big: **1** huge **2** great **3** substantial **4** significant

B

1 slightly damaged
2 badly misjudged
3 superbly presented
4 severely criticised
5 thoroughly enjoyed
6 deeply disappointed
7 incredibly well-prepared

Proof-reading

◎ This type of exercise can be quite tricky, so spend some time explaining it to the Ss before asking them to do it.

3 one **4** as **5** who **6** ✓ **7** it **8** ✓ **9** and **10** up

7 e-commerce

Conditionals

◎ More work on the conditionals from the Language review section on page 58.

A

1 f **2** a **3** c **4** b **5** d **6** e

B

1 owned **2** wouldn't have taken off **3** will get **4** were
5 would have expanded **6** order

Proof-reading

◎ Again, spend some time explaining this exercise to the Ss before asking them to do it.

3 there (their) **4** follows (following) **5** were (are) **6** most (more)
7 awareness (aware) **8** had (have) **9** for (on) **10** him (them)

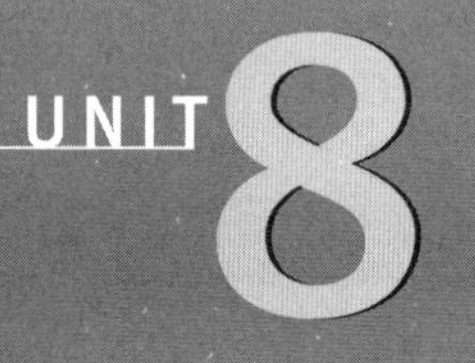

Team building

At a glance

	Classwork – Course Book	Further work
Lesson 1 *Each lesson (excluding case studies) is about 45–60 minutes. This does not include administration and time spent going through homework.*	**Starting up** Ss talk about their experiences of the teams they have been in, and do a quiz about different types of team members. **Listening: Building successful teams** A specialist in Human Resources talks about the key factors in team building. **Vocabulary: Prefixes** Ss look at a number of prefixes and use them in context to talk about people they have worked with and teams they have been in.	**Practice File** Vocabulary (page 32)
Lesson 2	**Reading: The key to successful team building** Ss read about why it is important for people in business to be team players. **Language review: Modal perfect** Ss look at how modal perfect verbs such as *needn't have*, *may have*, *might have*, *must have*, *could have*, *should have* and *would have* are used.	**Text bank** (pages 160–163) **ML Grammar and Usage** **Practice File** Language review (page 33)
Lesson 3	**Skills: Resolving conflict** Techniques for dealing with disagreements: Ss apply the language for this to role play a situation in which one member of a team is causing problems.	**Resource bank** (page 200)
Lesson 4 *Each case study is about 1½ to 2 hours.*	**Case study: The new boss** There are problems when a new manager takes over a sales team. Ss role play the directors of the company in their efforts to resolve them.	**Practice File** Writing (page 34)

For a fast route through the unit focussing mainly on speaking skills, just use the underlined sections.

For 1 to 1 situations, most parts of the unit lend themselves, with minimal adaptation, to use with individual students. Where this is not the case, alternative procedures are given.

Business brief

In constructing teams, it's important not just to get talented people, but the right combination of talents. In the famous phrase, 'it's important to have a great team of minds, rather than a team of great minds'. Meredith Belbin sees these types as necessary in teams, whether in business or elsewhere:

- The **Implementer**, who converts the team's plan into something achievable.
- The **Co-ordinator**, who sets agendas, defines team-members' roles and keeps the objectives in view.
- The **Shaper**, who defines issues, shapes ideas and leads the action.
- The **Plant**, who provides the original ideas and finds new approaches when the team is stuck.
- The **Resource Investigator**, who communicates with the outside world and finds new ways to get things done.
- The **Monitor Evaluator**, who evaluates information objectively and draws accurate conclusions from it.
- The **Team Worker**, who builds the team, supports others and reduces conflict.
- The **Completer Finisher**, who gets the deadlines right.

This model lends itself better to some business situations than others, but the idea of roles and competencies in a team is important, whatever form these take in particular situations. Some organisations are more **hierarchical** and less **democratic** than others, and team members are obviously expected to behave more deferentially in the former. Senior managers there have the traditional leader's role: what they say goes. In other organisations, power is more **devolved**, and managers talk about, or at least pay lip-service to, the **empowerment** of those under them: the idea that decision-making should be decentralised to members of their teams.

In addition to the traditional organisation, we increasingly find **virtual organisations** and virtual teams. People are brought together for a particular project and then disbanded. Here, in addition to Belbin's types above, the role of the **selector/facilitator** is crucial.

Stages of team life

The typical team is said to go through a number of stages during its existence.

1 **Forming**. The group is anxious and feels dependent on a leader. The group will be attempting to discover how it is going to operate, what the 'normal' behaviours will be: how supportive, how critical, how serious and how humorous the group will be.
2 **Storming**. The atmosphere may be one of conflict, with rebellion against the leader, conflict between sub-groups and resistance to control. There is likely to be resistance to the task, and even the sense that the task is impossible.
3 **Norming**. At this stage, members of the group feel closer together and the conflicts are settled, or at least forgotten. Members of the group will start to support each other. There is increasingly the feeling that the task is possible to achieve.
4 **Performing**. The group is carrying out the task for which it was formed. Roles within the group are flexible, with people willing to do the work normally done by others. Members feel safe enough to express differences of opinion in relation to others.
5 **Mourning**. The group is disbanded; its members begin to feel nostalgic about its activities and achievements. Perhaps they go for a drink or a meal to celebrate.

All this may be familiar from the groups we encounter, and play our role in managing, in language training!

Read on

Meredith Belbin: *Management Teams: Why they Succeed or Fail*, Butterworth Heinemann, 1981

Ron Johnson, David Redmond, Meredith Belbin: *The Art of Empowerment*, Prentice Hall, 1998

The first four stages of team life above were suggested by B.W. Tuckman, as quoted in Michael Argyle: *Social Interaction*, Tavistock, 1969

Business brief

Lesson notes

Warmer

- Write the word 'TEAMS' in big letters on the board. Ask Ss in pairs or threes to brainstorm all the types of team they can think of, in the business world and outside. (Point out that you are not looking particularly for words that come in front of *team*.) Circulate and monitor.
- After a few minutes, ask pairs and threes to say what they came up with. Invite comments and encourage discussion.

Examples:
sports teams
project development teams
sales teams
medical teams doing operations
management teams
teams of ministers with their political advisers and civil servants

Overview

- Tell Ss that in this unit they will be looking at team building.
- Ask Ss to look at the Overview section at the beginning of the unit. Tell them a little about the things on the list, using the table on page 68 of this book as a guide. Tell them which points you will be covering in the current lesson and in later lessons.

Quotation

- Ask the whole class what they understand by the quotation and if they agree with it.

Ss may be familiar with the saying 'A camel is a horse designed by committee', attributed to British engineer Alec Issigonis, designer of the Mini. The implication is that a committee has members working towards their own agendas, whereas a team works together for the common good.

Starting up

Ss talk about their experiences of the teams they have been in, and do a quiz about different types of team members to see what profile they themselves have.

- Ask Ss to discuss in pairs. Circulate, monitor and assist.
- Get pairs to report their findings to the whole class.

Possible issues

Advantages	**Disadvantages**
• Things can be achieved by a team that can't be achieved by individuals working separately – some things can only be achieved by teams. • Some people prefer working with others rather than on their own. • Team-working allows everyone to feel they have something to contribute.	• Explaining and organising the task can take so much time that it's easier and quicker to do it yourself. • Communication breakdowns can lead to severe problems in achieving the task. • Conflict between team members can be very destructive.

B – C

- Go through the quiz with the whole class and explain any difficulties.
- Divide the class into threes or fours. Appoint someone in each group who will record members' responses but also do the quiz themselves.
- Tell the notetakers that after the activity, they will have to give a mini-presentation about the group members' profiles as team players. Read out the text in the box below to give them the idea.

Anita is a creative type who values original ideas over detailed planning. Bertil, on the other hand, is more interested in clear thinking. Catherine found that the quiz told her that she is more interested in details and clear planning, and she was a bit surprised by this. The quiz told me I'm more of a creative person, which I tend to agree with.

- Ss in each group do the quiz individually, finding what sort of team player they are by looking at the key on page 152 of the Course Book. Ss then tell the other members of the group what sort of team player they are and the notetaker records this. Notetakers should also record if the other Ss agree with what the quiz tells them.
- Circulate, monitor and assist. Note language points for praise and correction.
- When Ss have finished the quiz, the notetaker summarises the profile of each group member as you did in the example above.
- Praise good language points from the discussion and work on three or four points that need improvement, getting individual Ss to say the correct forms.
- Ask your Ss to work on Questions 1 and 2 in Exercise C in threes or fours. Circulate and monitor.
- Ask the groups for their answers. Invite comments and encourage discussion.

Listening: Building successful teams

A specialist in Human Resources talks about the key factors in team building.

Ⓐ 8.1

- Tell Ss they are going to listen to Janet Greenfield, an expert on team building. Ask Ss to look through the headings to prepare them for what they are going to hear.
- Play the recording once or twice, explaining anything that is unclear.
- Play the recording again, stopping where key points occur so as to give time to Ss to write them down.
- Elicit the Ss' answers about the key points.

The corporate culture must encourage teamwork. All the members of the team must have clear personal objectives and must understand how these relate to the objectives of the company. All the members of the team must feel that their contribution is recognised and valued by the management.

Ⓑ 8.2

- Play recording 8.2 once or twice, helping with any difficulties.
- Play the recording again and ask the Ss to make two sets of notes: one on Lombardi's ideas about football and one on how his ideas can be applied to business.
- Ask the Ss to compare their notes in pairs or small groups.
- Ask Ss for their answers.

Sport

Every player must know exactly how to play his position well – discipline.
Every player should be treated the same as the others.
Every player should care about the others.

Business

Every employee must know the basics of their job and be trained to perform well.
There should be discipline in the company so everyone knows how to behave.
There should be team spirit, fostered by events, activities, schemes, etc. that bring people together so they get on better and care for each other.

Ⓒ

- Ask the Ss to discuss the questions in pairs or small groups. Circulate, monitor and assist, noting language points for praise and correction.
- Get pairs or groups to report their responses to the whole class. Invite comments and encourage further discussion.
- Praise good language use from the discussion and work on three or four points that need improvement, getting individual Ss to say the correct forms.

Vocabulary: Prefixes

Ss look at a number of prefixes and use them in context in a written exercise, and to talk about people they have worked with and teams they have been in.

Ⓐ

- Go quickly through the prefixes with the whole class. Get Ss to read the words with the correct stress patterns, e.g. *misMANage*, *pro-EuroPEan*. Point out the pronunciation of *bi-* as in *buy*, not as in *bee*.
- Get Ss, in pairs, to match the prefixes to their meanings.
- With the whole class, go quickly through the answers.

1 b	**2** b	**3** c	**4** a	**5** c	**6** b
7 c	**8** a	**9** b	**10** b		

- With the whole class, get Ss to give typical combinations containing the words with prefixes. Give them one or two possible combinations from the list below as examples. Do as a quick-fire activity.

mismanage a company, the economy
pro-European voters, politicians
predict events, the future
post-merger problems
dishonest behaviour, politicians
my ex-boss, Mr Smith
bilateral trade agreements
reconsider the decision
irresponsible actions, behaviour
hypercritical employers

Ⓑ

- Get Ss to work in pairs on the text. Circulate and assist.
- Check the answers with the whole class.

1 mismanaged
2 post-merger
3 pro-European
4 ex-boss
5 dishonest
6 irresponsible
7 hypercritical
8 reconsider

Ⓒ

- Do add-the-prefixes as a quick-fire activity with the whole class.

uncommunicative	indecisive	inefficient
unenthusiastic	inflexible	unfocussed
unimaginative	disloyal	disorganised
impractical	unsociable	unstable
intolerant		

Lesson notes

- Get Ss to work, in pairs, on the questions. Circulate, monitor and assist. Treat Question 1 tactfully. Tell Ss they don't have to name the people involved.
- When reporting back to the class, each member of the pair talks about the other member's colleagues in relation to Question 1. For Question 2, one member of the pair talks about their general findings.

Reading: They key to successful team building

Ss read about why it is important for people in business to be team players.

(A)

- Ask the whole class what they understand by the title of the article (a Japanese proverb) and if they agree with it. (Do they have a similar proverb in their own language(s)?)

> Ss might mention that a team brings together a combination of different skills and talents: see Business brief on page 69. If they don't raise this point, you might want to introduce it yourself.

(B)

- Ask the Ss to read the article quickly. Then go through the first four questions with them and ask them to read the first three paragraphs again and try to find the answers. Allow them to work in pairs or small groups if they wish.

> 1 In the past individual attributes such as intelligence and toughness were the key to success and employees worked in competition with each other. Now personal strengths are less important than a person's ability to work in a team and share knowledge and skills with colleagues so they can work together in competition with other companies.
> 2 Competition today should be against commercial competitors rather than between colleagues.
> 3 You need to be able to compromise your own views for the good of the team. You need to have a belief in the way the team works and in its strength. You need to recognise where your own strengths and contribution fit in with the team. You have to be honest with yourself and with the rest of the team. You have to be able to control conflict within the team. You have to care about the development of your team mates.
> 4 Effective teams are able to solve problems more easily than one person can. All teams must be managed well by a capable facilitator with an understanding of the way teams develop and change. Teams grow and develop and are more productive and efficient at some stages of their development than at others.

- Go through the remaining questions with the class. Ask the Ss to read the rest of the article and find the answers.

> 5 According to the writer, they should have attitudes a), b) and c).
> 6 Because essentially, whatever their nationality, most members of a team have the same basic objectives in life.
> 7 Thai team members place greater emphasis on personal relationships whereas Western team members place greater value on personal achievement.

(C)

- Ask the Ss to discuss the statements in pairs or small groups. Circulate, monitor and assist, noting language points for praise and correction.
- Get pairs or groups to report their responses to the whole class. Invite comments and encourage further discussion.
- Praise good language use from the discussion and work on three or four points that need improvement, getting individual Ss to say the correct forms.

(D)

- Check answers with the class before asking Ss to own up to which of the qualities they possess. You could also ask them to rank them in order of importance in a team situation.

1 patience	2 foresight	3 creativity
4 organisation	5 intuition	6 toughness
7 stamina	8 diplomacy	9 honesty

(E)

- Ask the Ss to discuss the questions in pairs. Circulate, monitor and assist, noting language points for praise and correction.
- Get one member of each pair to report their findings to the whole class. Invite comments and encourage further discussion.
- Praise good language use from the discussion and work on three or four points that need improvement, getting individual Ss to say the correct forms.

Language review: Modal perfect

Ss look at how modal perfect verbs such as *needn't have*, *may have*, *might have*, *must have*, *could have* and *should have* and *would have* are used and what they mean.

- Go through the points in the Language review box with the whole class, inviting and answering queries.

(A)

- Ask individual Ss to read out the sentences in italics, without doing the exercise. Concentrate on stress and the correct pronunciation of contractions like *needn't* and *couldn't*.
- Do the exercise as a whole-class activity, elaborating where necessary.

1	no
2	yes
3	yes
4	no
5	no
6	not sure
7	not sure
8	no

(B)

- Ask Ss to work on the questions in pairs. Circulate, monitor and assist.
- Go through the answers with the whole class, pointing out the subtleties mentioned below, but don't make it too complicated for the Ss' level.

1 should (But you didn't and now it's too late.)
2 might or could (But it wasn't.)
3 Correct. Point out to Ss that it means the same as 'might have destroyed'. (But it didn't.) And if you say 'may have destroyed', you don't know yet whether the merchandise was destroyed or not, because you haven't found out yet.)
4 must (We don't know for sure, but we think this is the case.)
5 Correct. (We don't know for sure what the reason was. 'He must have been delayed' would show more certainty.)
6 Correct. (You couldn't have seen him a) even if you had wanted to see him, or b) even if you thought you had seen him, mistaking someone else for Mr Lebeau.)
7 must (We're assuming he had a bad flight. 'He might have had a bad flight' would mean we are less sure about this.)
8 should (But we didn't. 'We could have ...' or 'We might have made him leader' implies that this was possible to do, but lacks the idea that it would have been the right thing to do.)

(C)

- Go through the situation quickly with the whole class.
- Divide the class into pairs, appointing a Financial Director and a sales rep in each pair.
- To show the class what to do, take the part of the Financial Director and ask one of the Ss to be the sales rep. Say: 'You shouldn't have stayed in a five-star hotel', to which the sales rep should reply something like: 'There was no alternative. There was a big conference on and it was the only place I could get a room.'
- Continue with one or two of the other points, emphasising that the sales rep should find convincing excuses each time and vary the formula, so they don't say 'There was no alternative' every time, but use sentences like 'I had no choice', and 'There was nothing else I could do.'
- When the whole class has understood the idea, ask them to role play the situation. Circulate, monitor and assist, especially with the modal perfect. Note language points for praise and correction.
- Praise good language points from the discussion and work on three or four points that need improvement, especially with the modal perfect, getting individual Ss to say the correct forms.
- Ask for one or two public performances of the situation for the whole class.

1 to 1

This role play can be done 1 to 1. Ask your student to be the sales rep and you take the role of Financial Director. Then change roles. Encourage imagination. Don't forget to note language points for praise and correction, especially in relation to the modal perfect.

Skills: Resolving conflict

Ss look at techniques for dealing with disagreements in teams. They work on the language for this and apply it to role play a situation in which one member of a team is causing problems.

- Go through the suggestions with the whole class.

Do	Don't
Try to see the problem from the point of view of the team. Be truthful about how you see the situation. Encourage open and frank discussion. Bring potential conflict and disagreement into the open. Persist with 'impossible people' – you may win them over. Try to find 'win–win' solutions.	Delay taking action, if possible. Get angry from time to time with difficult members. Try to ignore tensions within the team. Give special attention to team members who are creating problems.

- Ask Ss to categorise the statements with a show of hands for each one.
- Invite comments and encourage discussion. The above division is for illustration only: there may be disagreements: for example, there are those who say that there is no point in trying to win over impossible people, and that energy is best expended elsewhere. Some may say that anger also has its place.

(B) 8.3

- Play recording 8.3 and ask the Ss to put a tick next to the suggestions in Exercise A that Karen uses. You will probably have to play the recording several times.
- Allow the Ss to compare answers in pairs before checking with the class.

Karen uses suggestions 1, 3, 4, 5, 7 and 10.

Lesson notes

- Go through the expressions already in the Useful language box and ask Ss, in pairs, to add one more expression from the transcript on page 164 under each heading.

Expressing your feelings
I'm really fed up with her.
Making suggestions
Maybe you should ...
Why don't we ...
Expressing satisfaction
All right, we'll see if that works. Thanks for listening.
Expressing dissatisfaction
How would that help?
Showing sympathy
I understand your feelings.
Identifying the real problem
What you're saying is ...
Resolving the conflict
I'll have a quiet word in her ear.
Reviewing the situation
Let's talk about this in a few weeks' time.

- Divide the class into pairs, appointing the team leader and team member in each pair.
- Tell Ss to turn to their particular role description. Get them to read it silently. Circulate, monitor and assist.
- If you think it's necessary, do a demonstration in front of the whole class of the beginning of the situation, with you as the team member and an outgoing student as team leader.
- When all the Ss are clear about their roles and about the situation, start the activity.
- Circulate and monitor but do not intervene except if absolutely necessary. Note language points for praise and correction, especially in the area of conflict-resolving language.
- When Ss have finished, call the whole class to order. Praise good language points and work on three or four points that need improvement, getting individual Ss to say the correct forms.
- Ask one of the pairs to give a public performance in front of the whole group.

Case study

The new boss

There are problems when a new manager takes over a sales team. Ss role play the directors of the company in their efforts to resolve them.

Stage 1: Background 8.4

- Get Ss to read the background section and the notes on Nigel Fraser and the members of the sales team. Meanwhile write the points in the first column of the table below on the board. When Ss have finished reading, elicit information to complete the first five sections of the table.
- Tell the Ss that they are going to listen to a meeting chaired by Nigel Fraser and that they should make notes on what they learn about the team's problems.
- Play recording 8.4, pausing it at key points to allow the Ss to take notes.
- Ask the Ss to read the section headed 'Additional problems in the sales team' and elicit the information to complete the final section of the table.

Activity	Selling fax machines, data projectors and slim plasma screens
Sales Manager until 18 months ago	Vanessa Bryant
Present Sales Manager	Nigel Fraser
Sales targets	Increase turnover by 10%; create dynamic sales team
Sales performance	20% below target; low morale since NF arrived
Problems	NF wants more meetings, but most of the staff don't; present meetings are dominated by one or two people: some don't turn up Staff blame each other or other departments for problems Staff don't help each other; rivalry and dislike between some members Unable to accept criticism and become aggressive NF happier in his previous job; staff talk about the 'good old days' under Vanessa Bryant

Stage 2: Task preparation

- Divide the class into groups of four and ask them to choose one role card each. Establish that they are all directors of BES and that they are going to have a meeting to discuss the situation and decide what to do. Make sure that they realise that Director 1 leads the meetings.
- Tell them that each of the directors has thought about the company's problems and has different opinions and suggestions about what they should do. The Ss should read their role cards carefully (without showing them to other members of the group) and prepare to represent their views at the meeting. If their role cards mention any of the members of the sales team specifically, they should read the descriptions of those people carefully. Circulate, monitor and assist with anything the Ss don't understand. Discuss any problems that cause particular difficulty with the whole class.
- Go through the three points (points 2, 3 and 4) that will form the basis of the discussion with the whole class and answer any queries.

Stage 3: Task

- When the situation is clear, the discussions can begin. Circulate and monitor. Do not intervene unless it's necessary. Note language points for praise and correction, especially in the area of team building.
- When the groups have finished, with the whole class praise good language points from the discussion and work on three or four points that need improvement, getting individual Ss to say the correct forms.
- Ask the groups for the conclusions they have come to and the action they have decided to take. Note them on the board under the respective headings.
- Invite comments and encourage discussion, comparing the findings of the different groups.

1 to 1

This discussion can be done 1 to 1. Give the student plenty of time to read and absorb the background information, the profiles of the different salespeople and the points for discussion. Discuss the issues with your student as if you are both directors of BES.

Writing

- For the writing task you can
  – tell Ss which one to do
  – ask half to do one task and the other half the other
  – or let Ss choose for themselves.
- Tell Ss to look at the writing task you have assigned them. Or, if you are letting them choose, tell them to look at both tasks and ask them which one they are going to do.
- For the first task, say that the letter should come in the form of a report to the MD of BES, who was not present at the discussion.
- For the second task, say that this should be a personal letter from the sales manager to a member of the sales team. Point out that they can do this in the context of BES, i.e. a letter from Nigel Fraser to one of his sales team, or in the context of another company.

Writing file page 138.

Lesson notes

Raising finance

At a glance

	Classwork – Course Book	Further work
Lesson 1 *Each lesson (excluding case studies) is about 45–60 minutes. This does not include administration and time spent going through homework.*	**Starting up** Ss compare sources of personal borrowing and discuss some common sayings about money. **Listening: Getting a bank loan** A specialist in finance talks about how to get a loan from a financial institution. **Vocabulary: Idioms** Ss study idiomatic language about money.	**Practice File** Vocabulary (page 36)
Lesson 2	**Reading: Raising finance** Ss read about the different ways of raising new business finance. **Language review: Dependent prepositions** Ss look at the prepositions that can follow certain verbs, adjectives and nouns and use them in context.	**Text bank** pages (164–167) **ML Grammar and Usage** **Practice File** Language review (page 37)
Lesson 3	**Skills: Negotiating** Ss discuss negotiating tips, look at different techniques used in negotiations and put them into action to role play a situation.	**Resource bank** (page 200)
Lesson 4 *Each case study is about 1½ to 2 hours.*	**Case study: Vision Film Company** A film company negotiates for finance to make a feature film.	**Practice File** Writing (page 38)

For a fast route through the unit focussing mainly on speaking skills, just use the underlined sections.

For 1 to 1 situations, most parts of the unit lend themselves, with minimal adaptation, to use with individual students. Where this is not the case, alternative procedures are given.

Business brief

You have a brilliant but unusual business idea. You could put all your life savings into it, and ask friends and family to invest in it as well. But this may not be enough. Or your friends may, perhaps wisely, refuse to lend you money. You go to your local bank, but they don't understand your idea and suggest you look elsewhere.

You go to a **venture capitalist**. Venture capitalists are used to looking at new ideas, especially in hi-tech industries, and they see the potential in your brilliant idea. The venture capitalist also recommends it to some **business angels**, private investors looking for new **start-ups** to invest in. They provide you with **seed capital** to set up your business.

You launch your business, and it's a great success. But the amount of money it generates from sales is not enough to invest in it further: it's not **self-financing**, so you decide to raise more capital in an **initial public offering** or **IPO**: your company is **floated** and you issue shares on a stock market for the first time, perhaps a market or a section of one that specialises in shares in hi-tech companies.

You wait anxiously for the day of the **issue** or **float**. Interest from investors is high, and all the shares are sold. Over the next few weeks, there is a stream of favourable news from your company about its sales, new products and the brilliant new people it has managed to recruit. The shares increase steadily in value.

Now look at this process from the point of view of investors. The venture capitalists and business angels, for example, know most new businesses will fail, but that a few will do reasonably well and one or two will, with luck, hit the jackpot, paying back all the money they lost on unprofitable projects and much more. This exemplifies the classic trade-off between **risk and return**, the idea that the riskier an investment is, the more profit you require from it.

In your IPO, there may be investors who think that your company might be a future IBM or Microsoft, and they want to get in on the ground floor, hold on to the shares as they increase inexorably in value. They make large **capital gains** that can be **realised** when they sell the shares. Or they may anticipate selling quickly and making a quick profit.

Other investors may prefer to avoid the unpredictable world of **tech stocks** altogether and go for steady but unspectacular returns from established, well-known companies. These are the **blue chips** that form the basis of many conservative investment **portfolios**. One day in a few years' time, when your company is **mature** and growing at five or ten per cent a year, rather than doubling in size every six months, your brilliant business idea may have become a blue-chip company itself.

Governments increasingly depend on investment from the private sector in public projects. These **public–private partnerships** are financed by a combination of commercial investment and public money from taxation and government borrowing.

Read on

Michael Brett: *How to Read the Financial Pages*, Century Business paperback, 5th edition, 2000

Graham Bannock, William Manser: *International Dictionary of Finance*, Economist Books/Hutchinson, 1999

Mastering Finance, FT Pitman, 1997

Pocket Finance, Economist Books/Hamish Hamilton, 1994

Lesson notes

Lesson notes

Warmer

- Introduce the unit to Ss by saying that you can talk about *raising finance*, *raising capital* or *raising money* for a project. They are all used to talk about obtaining money through borrowing of different kinds. (Even issuing shares in your company is a form of borrowing: the company is in effect borrowing money from shareholders.)
- Write the word *money* in big letters on the right side of the board, with the word *raise* on the left.
- Ask Ss to brainstorm in small groups the different verbs that can come in front of money. Each group should think of as many verbs as possible.
- With the whole class, ask how many verbs each group has found. Get Ss to shout them out and write them on the left.

> Possible verbs include:
> borrow, donate, earn, invest, lend, lose, make, obtain, provide, save, spend, transfer, waste, win

Overview

- Tell Ss that in this unit they will be looking specifically at borrowing, especially by businesses raising finance in order to develop.
- Ask Ss to look at the Overview section at the beginning of the unit. Tell them a little about the things on the list, using the table on page 76 of this book as a guide. Tell them which points you will be covering in the current lesson, and which in later lessons.

Quotation

- Ask the whole class what they understand by the proverb and ask if they agree with it.

Starting up

Ss compare sources of personal borrowing and talk about and discuss some common sayings about money.

Ⓐ

- Explain *loan shark* (someone who lends money at very high rates of interest to people who aren't able to borrow from banks, and may threaten violence if it is not repaid).
- Get Ss to discuss the advantages and disadvantages of the different sources in pairs. Circulate and monitor. Note language points for praise and correction.
- When pairs have finished their discussion, call the class to order and praise good language points from the discussion and work on three or four points that need improvement, especially in relation to this topic, getting individual Ss to say the correct forms.
- Ask pairs what they came up with. Invite comments and encourage whole-class discussion.

> Possible issues:
>
> **a)** Bank: Advantages include: it's a business transaction that doesn't involve friends.
> Disadvantages include high rates of interest which mean it can be expensive; all sorts of problems if you can't repay the loan such as your credit rating (explain) will be affected and it might be difficult to get loans in future.
>
> **b)** Friend or colleague: Advantages include the fact that it is unlikely that interest will be charged. Disadvantages include possible damage to the relationship, particularly if the loan is not repaid promptly.
>
> **c)** Member of family: Families are often the main source of borrowing for many business start-ups but they might be less willing to lend for other purposes.
>
> **d)** Loan shark: The advantage is that people with no credit history (because they have never had bank accounts or credit cards) can borrow money, but the downside is that interest rates are extortionate and they might be harmed if they don't repay.
>
> **e)** Credit card company: Easy to do (explain *cash advance*) but interest rates are very high and a bank loan would be cheaper.

Ⓑ

- Ask the Ss to discuss the items and the sources of finance they would use in pairs or threes.
- Circulate and monitor.
- Ask the pairs or threes to present their findings to the whole class. Invite comments and encourage further discussion.
- Praise good language use from the discussion and work on three or four points that need improvement, getting individual Ss to say the correct forms.

Ⓒ

- Do this with the whole class, inviting individual students to give their explanations of the sayings.
- Have a show of hands to determine who agrees with which sayings.

Listening: Getting a bank loan

A finance specialist talks about how to get a loan from a financial institution. Ss complete a chart and answer questions about the best way to raise finance.

Ⓐ

- Do this as a whole-class brainstorming activity. Either concentrate solely on a business loan or divide the board into two halves and write up ideas for what you would need to give the bank for a personal loan on one side and what you would need to offer for a business loan on the other.

Here are some ideas. Your Ss may come up with others.

Personal loan
An explanation of what you want the money for
A recent bank statement
Some form of ID, e.g. a passport
An indication of how you intend to pay the money back.

Business loan
A business plan showing projections of future profits
Recent financial statements
Something, e.g. property as collateral (security for the loan)
A plan for repaying the money

B 9.1

- Play the first part of recording 9.1 and ask the Ss to make notes of the four things Patrick says you will need to give the bank. Check answers with the class before going on to listen to the rest of the recording.

- A good business plan (including future projections)
- Recent financial statements
- A repayment plan
- Collateral

- Explain the words *collateral* and *security* (something of value belonging to the person seeking the loan that will pass into the ownership of the bank if the loan is not repaid). Play the next part of the recording and ask the Ss to note down the types of security the speaker mentions. You may need to play the recording several times and pause it at key points to enable them to do this.

real estate (e.g. house, apartment, business premises), hard goods such as business equipment, stocks and shares in the company, personal assets, personal guarantee

- Go through the chart with the class. Then play the rest of recording 9.1 and ask them to complete it. You may need to play the recording several times to allow them to do this.

Type of loan	Purpose of loan	Length of loan
Short-term	to set up a business	a year or less
Intermediate-term	to buy equipment and cover the expenses in the early stages of development of a business	one to three years
Long-term	to help a business grow; for furniture, equipment, buying a long lease, etc.	three to seven years

C 9.2

- Go through the questions with the class. Then play recording 9.2 and ask the Ss to take notes. You may need to play the recording several times.

- Ask the Ss to compare their notes in pairs and to try to answer the questions.
- Check the answers with the whole class.

1 Go to a different lender and make the same request with the same business plan and the other documents. If several lenders turn you down, make changes to make your business plan more convincing and improve your credit rating, or consider buying the land for the business at a later date.
2 You could negotiate the terms of the loan, perhaps a lower interest rate, the way in which the money is to be repaid, the date for the repayments and the date for the final payment.
3 Get a lawyer to check the loan agreement and find out if any of the terms are negotiable.

Vocabulary: Idioms

Ss study idiomatic language about money.

- Tell Ss they are going to work on some finance-related idioms.
- Do this exercise as a quick-fire activity with the whole class.

1 rope **2** trees **3** muck **4** licence **5** fool **6** object

B

- Ask Ss to work on the exercise in pairs. Circulate, monitor and assist.
- With the whole class, elicit answers from the pairs.

a) 2 **b)** 1 and 4 **c)** 3 **d)** 5 **e)** 6

C

- Ask the Ss to work in pairs and to take turns to read a situation and respond to it. Encourage them to add a few words linking the idioms to the situation, rather than just reading them out. Circulate, monitor and assist.
- To check answers, ask individual pairs to perform their exchanges to the rest of the class.

1 As they say, 'A fool and his money are soon parted'.
2 Money is no object to her, then.
3 Well, they do say that where there's muck, there's money.
4 Oh, I know. Children think that money grows on trees, don't they?

Reading: Raising finance

Ss read about different ways of raising new business finance.

- Ask the Ss to work on the exercise in pairs. They can use a dictionary, preferably a specialised one such as the *Longman Business English Dictionary*. Circulate, monitor and assist.
- With the whole class, elicit answers from the pairs. Also get the Ss to discuss the meanings of the distractors and why they do not fit.

1 a	**2** b	**3** b	**4** c	**5** a	**6** c

- Go through the questions with the whole class so that they know what information they are looking for. Then ask them to read the first 64 lines of the text and find the answers.

> **1** Few growing companies are able to finance expansion from cash flow alone. They need to raise finance from external sources.
> **2** It is really important to strike a balance between equity and debt.
> **3** With debt, the bank giving the loan requires interest payments and capital repayments and the business assets or personal assets of the shareholders and directors can be at risk if these are not met. The bank can put the business into administration or bankruptcy if it defaults on the loan or if business is not going well. With equity, the institution lending the money has a stake in the business and, therefore, a greater incentive to see the business succeed as it takes the risk of failure along with all the other shareholders. If the company is successful, the lender benefits and makes profits on the eventual sale of the equity stake.
> **4** The main aim is to keep the financial risk of the company at an optimal level so that it isn't exposed to excessively high borrowings, but neither is the share capital diluted unnecessarily.

Lesson notes

(C)

- Ask the Ss to read lines 65–133 and to match the words and definitions.

1 c	**2** g	**3** a	**4** b	**5** f	**6** e	**7** d

(D)

- Ask the Ss to work in pairs or small groups and to discuss the situations and match them with a suitable source of finance. Circulate, monitor and assist.
- Ask a representative of each pair or group to report their decisions to the class, giving reasons for their choice.

> **1** lease **2** grant **3** invoice discounting **4** venture capital

(E)

- Ask the Ss to discuss the two statements in pairs. They should then report back to the class, giving reasons for agreeing or disagreeing.

Language review: Dependent prepositions

Ss look at the prepositions that can follow certain verbs, adjectives and nouns and use them in context.

(A)

- Tell Ss that they are going to look at prepositions following verbs, adjectives and nouns. Read out and comment on the examples in the Language review box. (These patterns are often shown in dictionaries. For example, in *Longman Dictionary of Contemporary English*, the pattern *investment in* is shown by *(in)* in front of the example. Get Ss to refer to their dictionaries if they have one.
- Get Ss to read the article again and do the exercise in pairs. Circulate, monitor and assist.
- Check and discuss the answers with the whole class.

> **1** consideration in, balance between
> **2** defaults on
> **3** risk of, benefit from

(B)

- Prepare Ss for this exercise by saying that they should try to anticipate the preposition that will occur at the beginning of the second half of each sentence. For example in question 1, they should be looking for *in*, thereby eliminating everything except parts d) and f). The sense tells you that part f) must be the right answer.
- Get Ss to do the exercise in pairs. Circulate, monitor and assist.
- Check and discuss the answers with the whole class, asking pairs how they came to their conclusions.

1 f	**2** g	**3** d	**4** h	**5** e	**6** c	**7** b
8 a	**9** j	**10** i				

Skills: Negotiating

Ss discuss negotiating tips, look at different techniques used in negotiations and put them into action to role play a situation.

- Tell Ss they are going to look at a number of negotiating tips, which they will discuss in pairs or threes. Tell them there are no right or wrong answers, and that the statements are designed to encourage thought and discussion.
- Circulate and monitor. Intervene only if necessary. Note language points for praise and correction, especially in relation to the subject of negotiation.
- With the whole class, praise good language points from the discussion and work on three or four points that need improvement, getting individual Ss to say the correct forms.
- Ask the Ss for their findings. Invite comments and encourage whole-class discussion.

1 May depend on the complexity of the negotiation. Above all, you must listen carefully to the answers. (See the Skills section of Unit 10 on active listening.)
2 Presumably there will be a point where the other side becomes irritated if they are interrupted too much.
3 This one is in a lot of text books on negotiating. Some people think that giving something away can produce a good atmosphere. Others say that it shows weakness.
4 This is really two separate points. Simple language is probably a good idea, but some might say that it's important to underplay one's high-priority objectives and over-emphasise low-priority ones.
5 Again, there will come a point where too much of this becomes irritating.
6 On the whole, negotiators probably do not do this enough, so it's worth emphasising.
7 Some might argue that this is true in an ideal world, but in practice assertiveness (rather than aggressiveness) can have its place.
8 Some people will be more comfortable with this than others. Some negotiators are good at exploiting the feelings of the other side. Showing emotions is more acceptable in some cultures than others.

(B)

- Ask Ss to look at expressions in the Useful language box. Go through the expressions and ask Ss to match the headings with the definitions given.

1 d 2 e 3 b 4 a 5 c

(C) 9.3

- Explain what Ss have to do, and then get them to work in pairs. Play recording 9.3 and pause it after each expression.
- Go through the answers with the whole class.
- Point out that Open questions often begin with *wh-* words like *what*, *why*, *when*, etc. *How* is also an honorary member of this group. Closed questions can often be answered *yes* or *no*. Point out that *seems to be* is a good softening phrase.

1 Closed question
2 Softening phrase
3 Summarising
4 Open question
5 Signalling phrase

(D) 9.4

- Play recording 9.4 all the way through once. Then go through the expressions and see if any of the Ss can complete them.
- Play the recording again, pausing at key points to allow the Ss to complete any expressions they haven't already identified.
- Check answers with the class and then ask the Ss to place each expression under the correct heading in the Useful language box.

1 Could I ask you ... (Open questions, but the word *Could* might be interpreted as softening the tone)
2 ... if I may ask (Closed questions, but again, *if I may ask* could be seen as softening the tone)
3 ... to make a suggestion (Signalling phrases)
4 Could I ask ... (Open questions)
5 Let me clarify what you've just said (Signalling phrases)
6 Let me sum up ... (Summarising)

(E)

- Explain the situation. Divide the class into threes: each three contains a business owner, a business angel and an observer. The job of the observer will be to note the different stages in the negotiation and the techniques and language used by each side.
- Make sure everyone knows which role they are taking.
- Give time for Ss to absorb the information needed for their role. Get the observer to skim the information for both roles. Circulate, monitor and assist.
- When all Ss are clear about their role and what they have to do, the activity can begin. Circulate and monitor, but do not intervene unless it's necessary. Make sure that the observer in each three is taking notes.
- Note language points for praise and correction, especially ones relating to the language of negotiation.
- When Ss have finished their negotiation, praise good language points from the discussion and work on three or four points that need improvement, getting individual Ss to say the correct forms.

- Ask the observer from each three to recap the different stages and point out the techniques and language used by each side in the situation they were observing. Ask the Ss playing the roles in each three to say if this is a good summary of what happened.
- Recap again the key negotiating phrases, and relate them, if appropriate, to those in the Useful language box.

1 to 1

This negotiation can be done 1 to 1. Ask your student which side they would prefer to represent. You represent the other side. Don't forget to note language points for praise and correction. Afterwards, ask the student about their negotiating plan, the tactics they were using, etc.

Case study

Vision Film Company

A film company negotiates for finance to make a feature film.

Stage 1: Background

With the whole class, get Ss to read the background section. Meanwhile write the points in the first column of the table below on the board. When Ss have finished reading, elicit information to complete the table.

Activity	Film making
Based	Kraków, Poland
Founded	15 years ago
Output so far	commercials and documentaries, some award-winning
Personnel	production staff plus freelancers
Current project	feature film set in post-war Europe
Finance source	European Finance Associates
Provisional finance package	$10 million
Stage in negotiations	second meeting next month to finalise
Usual investment return	sum invested + interest + share of profits

Stage 2: Executive Summary

- Divide the class into threes. Each three contains: a scriptwriter, an accountant and a project manager
- Each person independently runs through the information that is relevant to them and should be ready to comment on it to the whole class.
  - The scriptwriter will summarise and comment, in their own words, on the story line of the film and the target audience, target market and proposed promotion.
  - The accountant will go through the budget and projected revenues, and be ready to explain the different figures.
  - The project manager will talk about the different stages of the project.
- Circulate, monitor and assist.
- When the Ss are ready, ask one scriptwriter to present their information to the whole class, one accountant to do the same with theirs, and one project manager to present theirs.

Stage 3: Task

- Divide the class into fours. In each four, there are two representatives of VFC and two from EFA, the finance company. Make sure that everyone knows who is who. (These fours have nothing to do with the threes in Stage 2 opposite.)
- Give time for Ss to read and absorb their respective information. Circulate and assist.
- Before the negotiation begins, get each side to confer about their negotiation objectives and tactics: what do they hope to get out of the negotiations and how do they hope to achieve this?
- When everyone is clear about their information, objectives and tactics, the negotiations can begin. Circulate and assist but do not intervene unless necessary.
- Note language points for praise and correction, especially in relation to negotiation language.
- When the negotiations are complete, praise good language points from the discussion and work on three or four points that need improvement, getting individual Ss to say the correct forms.
- Ask a member of each group to summarise briefly what happened and what was decided. Invite comments and encourage discussion.

1 to 1

This negotiation can be done 1 to 1. Ask your student which side they would prefer to represent. You represent the other side. While doing the negotiation, note language points for praise and correction. Afterwards, ask the student about their negotiating plan and the tactics they were using.

Writing

- Ss can do the writing task collaboratively in class, or for homework.

Writing file page 139.

UNIT 10

Customer service

At a glance

	Classwork – Course Book	Further work
Lesson 1 *Each lesson (excluding case studies) is about 45–60 minutes. This does not include administration and time spent going through homework.*	**Starting up** Ss talk about what irritates them and about the place of customer care in a company's success. **Listening: Customer service** The Retail Sales Director of Harrods talks about good customer service and how best to achieve it. **Discussion: Customer complaints** Ss look at suggestions for ways of dealing with customer complaints and draw up a list of the best techniques for doing this.	
Lesson 2	**Vocabulary: Handling complaints** Ss look at words related to customer service and some common idioms, using them in context. **Reading: Customers first** Ss read about the decline in standards of customer service in the UK and why customers should be a company's first priority.	**Practice File** Vocabulary (page 40) **Text bank** (pages 168–171)
Lesson 3	**Language review: Gerunds** Ss study gerund formation and the way that gerunds are used. Ss then use them in drawing up guidelines about customer service. **Skills: Active listening** Ss look at listening skills in the context of customer service. They listen to interviews with satisfied and angry customers and learn some key expressions.	**Practice File** Language review (page 41) **ML Grammar and Usage** **Resource bank** (page 201)
Lesson 4 *Each case study is about 1½ to 2 hours.*	**Case study: Hermes Communications** Ss role play the handling of a range of customer complaints at a phone company.	**Practice File** Writing (page 42)

For a fast route through the unit focussing mainly on speaking skills, just use the underlined sections.

For 1 to 1 situations, most parts of the unit lend themselves, with minimal adaptation, to use with individual students. Where this is not the case, alternative procedures are given.

Business brief

Philip Kotler defines **customer service** as 'all the activities involved in making it easy for customers to reach the right parties within the company and receive quick and satisfactory service, answers and resolution of problems'.

Customers have **expectations**, and when these are met, there is **customer satisfaction**. When they are exceeded, there may be **delight**, but this depends on the degree of **involvement** in the purchase. There is a scale between the chore of the weekly shop at the supermarket and the purchase of something expensive such as a car that, for many people, only takes place once every few years. The scope for delight and, conversely, **dissatisfaction** is greater in the latter situation.

The telephone can be used to sell some services, such as banking or insurance, entirely replacing face-to-face contact. The **customer helpline** can be a channel of communication to complement face-to-face contact. Or it can be used before or after buying goods as a source of information or channel of complaint.

The figures are familiar: 95 per cent of dissatisfied customers don't complain, but just change suppliers. It is estimated that customers receiving good service create new business by telling up to 12 other people. Those treated badly will tell up to 20 people. Eighty per cent of those who feel their complaints are handled fairly will stay **loyal**, and **customer allegiance** will be built. **Customer retention** is key: studies show that getting **repeat business** is five times cheaper than finding new customers. **Customer defection** must, of course, be reduced as much as possible, but a company can learn a lot from the ones who do leave through **lost customer analysis**: getting customers to give the reasons why they have defected, and changing the way it does things.

Service providers, such as mobile phone or cable TV companies, have to deal with **churn**, the number of customers who go to another provider or stop using the service altogether each year.

In many services, satisfaction is hard to achieve because the **customer interaction** is difficult to control, which is why service organisations like airlines, banks and legal firms create high levels of dissatisfaction. If a product or service breaks down, fixing the problem may build **customer loyalty**, but it will also eat into the **profit margin**. Customers must be satisfied or delighted, but **at a profit**. If salespeople or call-centre staff or hotel receptionists are over-zealous, there may be lots of satisfied customers, but the business may be operating at a loss.

Kotler says that it is not companies that compete, but **marketing networks** comprising a number of companies. For example, a PC is assembled from components made by several manufacturers, sold through a call centre which may be a subcontractor, delivered by a transport company and perhaps **serviced** by yet another organisation as part of the manufacturer's **product support**. It is the customer's total experience that counts. Making the computer is just one part of this. The **logistics** of selling and organising the services needed by each customer becomes key.

Read on

Philip Kotler: *Marketing Management*, Prentice Hall, 1999 edition, ch. 2: 'Building Customer Satisfaction, Value, and Retention'

Adrian Palmer: *Principles of Services Marketing,* McGraw-Hill, 1998

Ron Zemke, John A. Woods: *Best Practices in Customer Service*, Amacom, 1999

Lesson notes

Warmer

- Write 'CUSTOMER SERVICE' in big letters on the board. Ask the Ss, in threes, to brainstorm briefly
  – what they understand by this term
  – what their own organisation or educational institution does in this area.

> There is this definition of customer service quoted at the beginning of the Business brief on page 86: 'all the activities involved in making it easy for customers to reach the right parties within the company and receive quick and satisfactory service, answers, and resolution of problems'. This relates mainly to situations where things have gone wrong.
> Customer service is also used in a neutral sense to talk about normal dealings when customers are buying products or services. Ss may refer to both these senses in their brainstorming sessions.
> Ss working in business will have something to say about customer service, whoever their customers are, whether business-to-business or business-to-consumer. It could be interesting to see how those working for government organisations view their 'customers' and what they understand by customer service. In the case of educational institutions, do they view their students as 'customers'? How are 'customer complaints' dealt with?

Overview

- Tell the Ss that in this unit they will be looking particularly at customer service.
- Ask the Ss to look at the Overview section at the beginning of the unit. Tell them a little about the things on the list, using the table on page 84 of this book. Tell them which points you will be covering in the current lesson and in later lessons.

Quotation

- Ask the Ss to look at the quotation. Can they think of other queuing situations that can be annoying (such as supermarket checkouts, buying tickets)? Do they have particularly bad incidents to recount?

Starting up

Ss talk about what irritates them and about the place of customer care in a company's success.

Ⓐ–Ⓑ

- Get the Ss to discuss the different points in both exercises in pairs. Say that there is some overlap between the items, e.g. unhelpful and indifferent service personnel. The main idea is to encourage Ss to think of specific incidents they have encountered, even ones of too much customer care, for example the waiter who asks three times during the meal if everything is alright.
- Pairs report back to the whole class. Invite comments and encourage discussion.

Listening: Customer service

The Retail Sales Director of Harrods talks about good customer service and how best to achieve it.

- Don't spend too much time on this but have a quick brainstorming session to find out what the Ss know about Harrods.

> Harrods is a large upmarket department store on Brompton Road in Knightsbridge, London. The Harrods motto is *Omni Omnibus Ubique*, which means *All things, for all people everywhere* and refers to its claim that absolutely anything can be bought there. It is particularly famous for the range of goods available in the seasonal Christmas department and the food hall. The present owner is an Egyptian, Mohamed Fayed (whose son Dodi was killed in the same car crash as Princess Diana). He bought the store in 1985 for £615 million.

Ⓑ 10.1

- Go through the statements with the Ss and explain any difficult words so that they know what information they are listening for.
- Play recording 10.1 once or twice and ask the Ss to decide if the statements are true, false or not given (if the speaker says nothing about it).
- Check the answers with the whole class. Encourage them to give reasons why some of the statements are false.

> 1 false (it is about *exceeding* customer expectations)
> 2 false (they expect a level of service that is *better* than other retailers)
> 3 true
> 4 true
> 5 not given (the speaker says nothing about how often feedback is given)
> 5 false (they are given a certificate from the chairman and £50 in vouchers to spend in the store)

Ⓒ 10.2

- Ask the Ss to look at the sentences and think about how they could be completed.
- Then play the first question and answer on recording 10.2 once or twice and ask the Ss to complete the sentences. Explain to them that they won't hear these sentences in the recording. They will need to understand the meaning of what the speaker says and paraphrase it to complete the sentences.

- Check answers with the whole class, accepting any which are grammatically correct and match the speaker's meaning.

Example answers
1 establish/build consumer loyalty
2 are the same as those available in other stores/are no different from those in other outlets
3 seriously are likely to lose their customers/seriously don't build customer loyalty and their customers may move to other retailers

(D)

- Play the second question and answer on recording 10.2 and ask the Ss to take notes on how the speaker thinks technology can contribute to improved customer service and whether she thinks this is useful for Harrods. You may need to play the recording several times.
- Check answers with the class.

Sarah mentions a new device at another store, which monitors customer service by having customers press buttons to indicate their levels of satisfaction, but she isn't sure how effective this is and she doesn't think it would be useful for Harrods. The other technology she refers to is that related to store cards. Through these they can monitor how often customers return to the store and this, she thinks, is a good way of getting feedback on how satisfied customers are.

(E) 10.3

- Go through the seven steps with the Ss and ask them to try to predict what the missing verbs might be.
- Play recording 10.3 and ask the Ss to complete the seven steps.
- Check answers with the class and find out how many correct predictions there were concerning the missing verbs.

1 Welcome
2 Approach, initiate
3 Ask, establish
4 Use, select, meet
5 Highlight
6 Offer, maximise
7 Thank, invite

(F)

- Put the Ss in pairs and give them time to prepare their dialogues. Circulate, monitor and assist.
- Ask the Ss to practise their role plays in their pairs before asking some of the pairs to perform their role plays for the rest of the class.

Discussion: Customer complaints

Ss look at suggestions for ways of dealing with customer complaints and draw up a list of the best techniques for doing this.

- Tell the Ss that they will be drawing up a shortlist of suggestions for dealing with customer complaints, and then compiling a list of the most useful ones.
- Get Ss to work in threes. Half the threes in the class are As, and the other half are Bs. The As discuss the list of ways of dealing with customer complaints for Group A and the Bs those for Group B. Say that each group has to decide on the five most useful suggestions in its particular list.
- Circulate and monitor. Do not intervene unless necessary. Note language points for praise and correction.
- When the groups have made their shortlists, praise good language points from the discussion and work on three or four points that need improvement, getting individual Ss to say the correct forms.
- Match each Group A with a Group B, getting the Ss to change places if necessary. Tell them that each group of six (three As and three Bs) has to negotiate a final list of six suggestions from the ten suggestions that they have chosen between them.
- Circulate and monitor again. Do not intervene unless necessary. Note language points for praise and correction.
- When the groups have made their final list, praise good language points from the discussion and work on three or four points that need improvement, getting individual Ss to say the correct forms.
- Ask each group of six for its final list. Compare the lists from different groups, invite comments and encourage discussion, perhaps comparing the customer service suggestions that are suitable in different contexts and with different cultures. (For example, putting things in writing might be seen as essential in some cultures, but just an extra burden on the already irritated customer in others.)

1 to 1
This discussion can be done 1 to 1. Ask the student to look at and discuss each list separately, choosing five points from each list. Ask them to explain the reasons for their choice. Then ask them to choose the six most important ones from the ten they have selected and, again, to explain their reasons.

Vocabulary: Handling complaints

Ss look at words related to customer service and some common idioms, using them in context.

- Tell the Ss to look through the sentence parts. Ask them to match them as a quick-fire activity. Point out the pronunciation of *rapport* with its silent *t*.

1 complaints – e)
2 rapport – d)
3 reassure – a)
4 standards – b)
5 products – c)

- Ask the Ss to work on matching the idioms in pairs. Circulate, monitor and assist.
- With the whole class, do a round-up of the answers and explain any difficulties.

1 c 2 d 3 f 4 e 5 a 6 b 7 g

- Do this as a quick-fire activity with the whole class. Explain any difficulties.

1 get to the bottom of the problem
2 pass the buck
3 ripped off
4 slipped my mind
5 talking at cross purposes
6 it was the last straw
7 got straight to the point

Reading: Customers first

Ss read about the decline in standards of customer service in the UK and why customers should be a company's first priority.

(A)

- Go through the questions with the class so that they know what information to look for when they read the article.
- Ask the Ss to read the article and allow them to work in pairs to decide on the answers to the questions. Circulate, monitor and assist with any difficult words.
- Check the answers with the class.

1 It took weeks to sort out the problems with his new printer-scanner-copier. He couldn't get through to the Powergen 24-hour helpline and had to call them from work.
2 Not turning up at the appointed time. Falsely claiming to have rung the doorbell and found no one in.
3 Customers are the most vital part of any business, they are its reason for existing and they are the people upon whom all success depends. Keeping them satisfied is the most important thing a company can do.
4 Competition may force a company to move jobs to low-wage countries (thus having fewer people on hand to give good customer service). The bigger a business is, the more widespread its suppliers and customers become and delivering good service to them becomes more difficult. You may have to invest in IT systems to keep track of orders.

(B)

- Go through the points with the whole class so that the Ss know what they are looking for, then ask them to read the article again.
- Get the Ss to compare answers in pairs and then report back to the class on their results.

1 He says the opposite of this in lines 40 to 50.
2 He makes this point in lines 51 to 57 by lamenting the fact that some companies have cut back on their customer service training.
3 He makes this point in lines 79 to 84. By saying that outsourcing is not on its own responsible for deteriorating customer service, he suggests that it is one cause.
4 He doesn't make this point. He says in lines 84 to 90 that the fact that some companies seem to believe this is a problem.
5 He makes this point in lines 73 to 76.

(C)

- Ask the Ss to discuss in pairs any examples of good and bad customer service they have experienced and then to report back to the class.

Language review: Gerunds

Ss study gerund formation and the way that gerunds are used. The Ss then use them in drawing up guidelines about customer service.

(A)

- Go through the gerunds in the Language review box with the whole class. Refer back to Exercise A in the Starting up Section where this is mentioned, even if the Ss haven't done this.
- Get the Ss to look at the article on page 87 in pairs and find gerunds. Circulate and assist.

a) But making a profit ... (line 96); Carrying this out ... (line 129)
b) including not turning up at the appointed time and then claiming to have rung the doorbell; I am not attacking outsourcing as such ... (lines 79 to 81)
c) without jamming (lines 15 to 16); about cutting costs ... (lines 77 to 78); a way of providing the same goods ... (line 132)

(B)–(C)

- Ss can work on these exercises in pairs. Circulate and assist.
- With the whole class, elicit the answers from the pairs.

B

1 b **2** b **3** d **4** c **5** e **6** f

C

Possible answers. Ss may suggest others.

1 returning
2 giving
3 doing / undertaking / commissioning
4 organising / running
5 drawing up / establishing / setting up
6 drawing up / establishing / setting
7 checking / examining / monitoring
8 dealing
9 ensuring / making sure
10 learning

Check your Ss' own ideas for improving customer service.

Skills: Active listening

Ss look at listening skills in the context of customer service. They listen to interviews with satisfied and angry customers and learn some key expressions.

- With the whole class, ask about the points here. Invite comments and encourage discussion.

- Divide the class into pairs or threes. Circulate, monitor and assist. Note language points for praise and correction, especially in relation to this topic.
- With the whole class, praise good language points from the discussion and work on three or four points that need improvement, getting individual Ss to say the correct forms.
- Ask the Ss for their suggestions. Invite comments and encourage discussion. Some interesting cultural issues should emerge here.

- *Look people directly in the eye at all times.* But don't overdo it. It will make them feel uncomfortable. How much eye contact is appropriate in your Ss' culture(s) a) between people of the same status, b) between people of differing status?
- *Nod your head often to show interest.* Again, don't overdo it. Ask your Ss about nodding in general: in their culture(s) does it indicate interest, agreement, something else, or nothing at all?
- *Repeat what the speaker has said in your own words.* Can be useful as a way of checking key points. Another useful technique is to repeat *exactly* some of the expressions the speaker has used.
- *Be aware of the speaker's body language.* People will be aware of this whether they try to be or not.
- *Interrupt the speaker often to show you are listening.* It's good to make some 'phatic' noises such as *aha, mmm, I see, right.* Ask your Ss how much it's normal to do this in their own language, and what the equivalent of *aha* is in their own language(s).
- *Think about what you are going to say while the speaker is talking.* Yes, but pay attention to what they are saying as well. Some cultures, such as Japan and Finland, allow the other person time for reflecting on what the first person has said before they are expected to respond. Ask the Ss if this is the case in their culture(s).
- *Use body language to show you are attentive.* Again, don't overdo it. It can be intimidating.
- *Try to predict what they are going to say next.* But don't jump to conclusions.
- *Ask questions if you do not understand.* Yes, but try to avoid questions that result from not having listened properly. If someone has to answer too many questions about what they said earlier, it will undermine rapport.
- *Say nothing until you are absolutely sure that the speaker has finished.* Butting in is the usual habit in some places. Ask your Ss what they think about this.

(C) **10.4**

- Tell the Ss that they are going to hear three customers talking about their experiences. Ask your Ss to look at Question 1.
- Play the recording once right through, and then once again, stopping at the end of each conversation to allow the Ss to take notes.

1

Product/service	Why good/bad
1 Wine	The customer took back some wine to the shop because they and a guest hadn't liked it. The salesman told the customer to choose two other bottles to replace it, even if they were more expensive.
2 Flight	The speaker flew to Spain with their family on a no frills airline. The service was very friendly and helpful (the speaker has small children) and the flight was punctual.
3 Printer	This customer waited in all day for a new printer to be delivered, but it never arrived. The service on the phone was very friendly and helpful, but the printer didn't turn up for the rest of the week.

- With the whole class, ask individual Ss to summarise each incident. Use this as an opportunity to practise summarising skills. Say they should not get sidetracked by details such as what exactly was wrong with the wine, the fact there were no meals on the plane.
- Ask the Ss to look at the expressions in the Useful language box. Go through them in detail, practising intonation.
- Play recording 10.4 again, pausing where necessary. Get your Ss to underline the expressions from the language box that they hear.
- Check the answers with the whole class. Then get the Ss, in pairs, to add one or two expressions of their own under each heading.
- Check the suggestions with the whole class.

2

Expressions heard in the recording are underlined. One other expression is suggested for each heading in italics, but your Ss may have thought of others.

Showing interest
Really?
OK / *I see*

Showing empathy
How awful!
That must have been terrible!

Asking for details
What did you do?
Tell me more!

Clarifying
When you say ..., what are you thinking of?

Summarising
(So) if I understand you correctly ...

Repetition / Question tags
See 'Fruit juice?' in conversation 1.

A *Customer satisfaction levels are increasing.*
B *Increasing? / Are they?*

- Ask your Ss to talk about excellent and poor experiences in pairs. You can show the whole class the sort of thing you are looking for by asking an individual student for one of their experiences, and using some of the expressions in the Useful language box to ask them about it.
- When the class has understood the idea, start the discussions.
- Circulate, monitor and assist if necessary. Note language points for praise and correction, especially in relation to the language in this section.
- With the whole class, praise good language points from the discussion and work on three or four points that need improvement, getting individual Ss to say the correct forms.
- Ask for one or two public performances of the situations that the Ss just talked about so that the whole class can listen.
- Invite comments and encourage discussion about the situations.

Case study

Hermes Communications

Ss role play the handling of a range of customer complaints at a phone company.

Stage 1: Background 10.5

- Read the background information with the whole class and get one student to paraphrase it in their own words.
- Divide the class into pairs, ask them to choose their roles and read the five written complaints.
- Then play recording 10.5 and ask them to make notes.
- Tell the Ss that they should summarise the information in each complaint. Go through complaint 1 with the whole class to give them the idea.

Communi-cation type	Brief details of complaint	Anger level*	Action/ requested response / compensation	Priority**
1 e-mail	Query on bill, but can't get through on helpline.	2	Customer will call at regional office on Monday.	
2 e-mail	Mobile phone loses power very quickly. Believes there is design fault with screen.	2	Wants to know what the company is going to do about this problem.	
3 e-mail	Topped up mobile phone with credit card, but account not credited. Unable to call an important client.	3	Wants to know how he will be compensated.	
4 Fax	Subscribed to cheap rate calls to US for six months, but we discontinued service after three months and requested an extra £30 to continue.	3	None requested.	
5 Letter	Uses phone for up to three hours a day and gets headaches.	1	Would like us to comment.	
6 Helpline	Over-pushy sales staff in one of our shops.	2	Did not want to name member of staff. Says we should look at our training methods.	
7 Voice-mail	Bought new phone but can't understand how to use it as very complicated and manual too big. Felt pressured to buy this model by sales staff.	2	Wants someone to call her back.	

* Score out of 3, where 1 = unhappy, 2 = cross and 3 = furious.

** This will be judged by each pair when it has looked at all the complaints. 1 = top priority, 4 = not urgent.

Stage 2: Task

- When the Ss have summarised all the complaints (including those they heard on the recording), ask them to decide which ones are top priority and which ones less urgent. They should number them 1 to 4, with 1 as top priority and 4 as not urgent. Ask them to discuss the ones that they have judged to be top priority and to decide how they are going to deal with them.
- Circulate, monitor and assist if necessary.
- When the pairs have finished, get them to report back to the whole class on their discussions and decisions. Then ask the whole class to discuss ways in which customer service could be improved in the company. Write their ideas on the board.

1 to 1

These activities can be done 1 to 1, with the student analysing the information and then discussing it with you. Don't forget to note language points for praise and correction afterwards. Highlight some of the language you chose to use as well.

Writing

- Ss can do the writing task collaboratively in class, or for homework.

Writing file page 144.

UNIT 11 Crisis management

At a glance

	Classwork – Course Book	Further work
Lesson 1 *Each lesson (excluding case studies) is about 45–60 minutes. This does not include administration and time spent going through homework.*	**Starting up** Ss discuss the difference between a problem and a crisis, and look at the steps to take in crisis situations. **Listening: Managing crises** An expert talks about how to deal with crisis situations, and gives some examples.	
Lesson 2	**Reading: Keeping your client relationship afloat** Ss read an article in which a major problem with a luxury cruise liner is used to demonstrate how to deal effectively with a crisis. **Vocabulary: Noun phrases with and without *of*** Ss look at these types of noun phrases and use them in context.	**Text bank** pages (172–175) **Practice File** Vocabulary (page 44)
Lesson 3	**Language review: Contrast and addition** Ss study the language for contrasting things and adding extra information. **Skills: Asking and answering difficult questions** A chief executive answers difficult questions from journalists. Ss listen to the language used, and apply it themselves in a similar situation.	**Practice File** Language review (page 45) **ML Grammar and Usage** **Resource bank** (page 201)
Lesson 4 *Each case study is about 1½ to 2 hours.*	**Case study: Game over** Titan Stores is accused of selling pirated software. Ss analyse the related information and role play Titan's directors and media representatives at a press conference.	**Practice File** Writing (page 46)

For a fast route through the unit focussing mainly on speaking skills, just use the underlined sections.

For 1 to 1 situations, most parts of the unit lend themselves, with minimal adaptation, to use with individual students. Where this is not the case, alternative procedures are given.

Business brief

A crisis may well be an opportunity to test a company's capabilities, but it is an opportunity that most companies would prefer to do without. Some businesses never recover from disasters involving loss of life, such as these:

- PanAm and the Lockerbie bomb: terrorist attack;
- Townsend Thoresen and its capsized ferry off Zeebrugge, Belgium;
- Union Carbide and the Bhopal disaster: plant explosion.

Presumably, no amount of crisis management or **damage limitation** would have saved these organisations.

There are entire industries that live under a permanent cloud of crisis. For example, accidents and incidents around the world, small and large, have **discredited** the nuclear power industry and given it a permanently negative image. People perceive it as **secretive** and **defensive**. Its long-term future is uncertain.

In Britain, the beef industry has been severely damaged by the 'mad cow' crisis. This has also had repercussions for some state institutions. In future food crises, people will be less willing to believe the **reassurances** of the Ministry of Agriculture. The UK government has set up a Food Standards Agency to try to regain **credibility** in this area, but the crisis has only served to undermine confidence in the overall competence of the state.

Food and drink is a very sensitive issue. The mineral water and soft drinks companies that distribute contaminated products because of mistakes in their bottling plants know this all too well.

Even in disasters where there is no loss of life, the results can be dire, because they are situations that everyone can understand and relate to.

The new cruise ship that breaks down on its maiden voyage, or the liner that leaves on a cruise with workmen still on board because refurbishment is not finished, with passengers filming the chaos on their video cameras, scenes then shown on television, are **public relations nightmares**.

All the examples so far relate to the effect of crises on companies' external audiences: customers and potential customers. But businesses are also increasingly being judged on how well they treat their internal audience: their staff in crisis situations. Companies may offer **employee assistance programmes** to help them through difficult situations or **traumatic incidents**. For example, bank staff may be offered counselling after a bank robbery. This is part of the wider picture of how companies treat their people in general. A reputation for **caring** in this area can reduce **staff turnover** and enhance a company's overall **image** in society as a whole. This makes commercial sense too: high staff turnover is costly, and an image as a caring employer may have a positive effect on sales.

Read on

Michael Bland: *Communicating Out of a Crisis*, Macmillan, 1998

Harvard Business Review on Crisis Management, Harvard Business School Press, 2000

Robert Heath: *Crisis Management for Executives*, Prentice Hall, 1998

Mike Seymour, Simon Moore: *Effective Crisis Management*, Continuum, 1999

Lesson notes

Warmer

- Write the word 'CRISIS' in big letters on the right of the board. Ask the Ss what the plural is, and write up 'CRISES' in big letters. Practise the pronunciation of both words.
- Then draw seven lines to the left of 'crisis' to represent words that can come in front of it, with the first letter of each word.
- Tell the Ss that some of the words relate to people, some to countries, and others to both. Say that you are going to give examples of each type of crisis situation, and the Ss must guess the related word.
- Read example 1 below and ask the Ss to guess the word.
- Continue with the other examples in the same way. If the Ss have trouble guessing the word, give the next letter and, if they still don't get it, one letter at a time until they do.

1. A child is ill and its parents are very worried and unable to go to work.
2. A country's money is fast losing its value in relation to the money of other countries, and the government wants to stop this.
3. A country has high unemployment, falling production and so on.
4. A country has problems in its banking system.
5. There is a border dispute between two countries, and they may go to war with each other.
6. Someone in their late 40s has feelings of uncertainty about their life and career.
7. A government cannot win votes in the country's parliament, and there may have to be an election.

1 domestic
2 currency
3 economic
4 financial
5 international
6 mid-life
7 political

Overview

- Tell the Ss that in this unit they will be looking particularly at crisis management.

  Ask the Ss to look at the Overview section at the beginning of the unit. Tell them a little about the things on the list, using the table on page 94 of this book as a guide. Tell them which points you will be covering in the current lesson and in later lessons.

Quotation

- Ask the Ss to look at the quotation. Discuss it with the whole class. If you have Chinese-speaking Ss, they may be able to write, explain and comment on the characters.
- Ask the Ss the questions:
  – What does it mean to say that a crisis can be an opportunity?
  – Is every crisis an opportunity?
- Invite quick comments and encourage brief discussion.

Starting up

Ss discuss the difference between a problem and a crisis, and look at the steps to take in crisis situations.

- With the whole class, ask the first question to one or two individual Ss to get the discussion going. Then ask the Ss to discuss Question 1 and the other questions in pairs.
- Circulate, monitor and assist if necessary. Note language points for praise and correction, especially ones relating to the pronunciation of *crisis* and *crises* and crisis language in general.
- Praise good language points from the discussion and work on three or four points that need improvement, getting individual Ss to say the correct forms.
- With the whole class, ask pairs for their answers. Invite comments and encourage discussion.

(B)

- Ask the Ss to discuss the points and complete the table in pairs. Say that they should find a logical order of presentation within each step.
- Circulate, monitor and assist.
- With the whole class, ask the pairs for their answers and write them on the board.

Before the crisis	During the crisis	After the crisis
◎ Write down and circulate your crisis management programme ◎ Try to predict what crises could occur ◎ Practise making decisions under stress ◎ Role play a potential crisis	◎ Set up a crisis management team* ◎ Inform the directors ◎ Disclose as much information as you can	◎ Find out what happened and how it happened ◎ Analyse the actions you took to deal with the situation ◎ Work out an action plan to ensure the crisis does not happen again

*Say that this step could also be done before the crisis, if the company decides to have a permanent team.

Listening: Managing crises

A crisis management expert talks about how to deal with crisis situations, and gives some examples.

(A) 11.1

- Tell the Ss that they are going to listen to a crisis management expert. What do they think a crisis management expert does? What do they think he will say?

> Very large organisations employ crisis management experts to plan for possible crises, give training to managers in dealing with them, etc.
> There are also consultancies that specialise in this. Firms without their own crisis management specialists go to such consultancies for advice, or bring them in to handle a particular crisis if one occurs.

- Play recording 11.1 and elicit from the Ss the three crisis areas that the speaker mentions.

> Failure of, or a perceived problem with, a product or brand.
> The perception that management or corporate behaviour has not been up to the required standard.
> Problems highlighted by interest or activist groups.

(B) 11.2

- Play the second part of the interview, recording 11.2, and ask the Ss to take notes on the three things the speaker thinks companies should do to prepare themselves for managing crises.
- Check answers with the whole class.

> - Accept that crises might happen.
> - Identify all the people and groups who might take an interest when a crisis occurs.
> - Prepare, test and validate plans for dealing with crises.

(C) 11.3

- Go through the company names with the Ss and ask them what, if anything, they already know about these companies, either generally or in the context of crises.
- Play recording 11.3 and ask the Ss to take notes on the crisis that hit each company. You may need to play the recording several times and pause it at key points to allow the Ss to do this.
- Allow them to compare notes in pairs. Then choose four pairs to report their findings to the rest of the class. Encourage the others to add any missing information.

> **Johnson and Johnson:** Tylenol headache pills were spiked with cyanide and some people died. The company were open about the crisis and clear about what they were doing. They were successful in bringing the brand back to the market.
> **Heineken:** 17 million bottles of their beer had glass in them. They had to recall the bottles from 152 markets but they were open and pro-active and successfully recalled the product and maintained confidence in their brand.
> **Union Carbide:** A leak from a chemical plant in Bhopal in India killed many people in the local community. The company was secretive and slow to respond. They were perceived as having handled the crisis badly. There are still legal cases going on.
> **Mercedes:** Their new small car, the Baby-B, was found to be unstable. In spite of video evidence, Mercedes continued to deny that anything was wrong for three days. People became very cynical about the car and it took some time to win back confidence.

- Play recording 11.3 again and ask the Ss to say what the characteristics of good crisis management and bad crisis management are.

> **a)** Good crisis management: openness in admitting that there is a problem; explaining clearly what you are doing about it; being pro-active and quick in recalling faulty goods.
> **b)** Bad crisis management: secrecy; being slow to respond; denying the problem or responsibility for the problem.

Reading: Keeping your client relationship afloat

Ss read an article in which a major problem with a luxury cruise liner is used to demonstrate how to deal effectively with a crisis.

(A)

- Have a whole-class brainstorming session on this question and write the Ss' suggestions on the board.

(B)

- Go through the questions with the class so that they know what information to look for as they read the article. Get them to read the article. Circulate, monitor and assist with any difficult vocabulary.
- Ask them to work in pairs to formulate their answers to the questions.
- Check answers with the class.

Lesson notes

Lesson notes

1 It had persistent engine problems and was unable to leave on a very expensive round-the-world cruise.
2 They were disappointed that they didn't get their cruise, but they remained calm and cheerful and were not hostile towards the ship's operators. This was because the crisis had been well handled. The company was open about the problem and senior P & O managers were there to provide information to passengers. The passengers were offered good compensation: a full refund of their money and a discount on their next booking. Many of them reported that they would travel on a P & O cruise in future.
3 Your company can suffer from bad public relations. You can lose customers. You could be taken to court.
4 Dissatisfied customers in the US tend to tell around ten other people of their bad experience. In the worst cases they may tell the press.
5 Early recognition of the problem, accepting responsibility, transparency in communication with customers, adequate compensation.
6 They both offered the same degree of compensation to dissatisfied customers: a full refund and a discount on their next booking.
7 That many of the passengers on the *Aurora* said they intended to travel on a P & O cruise in future.

(C)

- Do this with the whole class, inviting individuals to call out the correct verbs.

1 ensure	2 encourage	3 deal
4 take	5 listen	6 concede
7 communicate	8 compensate	

(D)

- Ask the Ss to work in small groups to think of some crises they know of which were either well or badly managed. Encourage them to use the language from Exercise C to describe the action that was or wasn't taken in each case.
- Get a representative from each group to present the group's findings to the rest of the class.

Vocabulary: Noun phrases with and without *of*

Ss look at these types of noun phrases and use them in context.

(A)–(B)

- Talk through the two types of noun phrases with the whole class. Look at the nouns and, where necessary, their pronunciation (*e.g. contingency*). Get Ss to do the two exercises in pairs.
- Circulate, monitor and assist.
- With the whole class, ask for the answers and discuss any difficulties.

Noun phrases with *of*	Noun phrases without *of*
admission of liability flow of information loss of confidence speed of response	action plan contingency plan damage limitation legal action press conference press release

1 speed of response
2 press conference
3 press release
4 flow of information
5 action plan
6 contingency plan
7 legal action
8 admission of liability
9 loss of confidence
10 damage limitation

- With the whole class, get individual Ss to recap the *Aurora* crisis in the article in the reading section, using the expressions from this section.

(C)

- Ask the Ss to work in pairs to categorise the word partnerships according to their timing in a crisis. Then ask them to discuss question 2 and report their opinions to the class.

1 **a)** action plan, contingency plan
b) speed of response, press conference, press release, flow of information, admission of liability, loss of confidence, damage limitation
c) legal action, loss of confidence

Language review: Contrast and addition

Ss study the language for contrasting things and adding extra information.

- Go through the expressions in the Language review box.

(A)

- Ask the Ss to look through the article on page 94 and underline any examples of addition and contrast that they find. You may need to point out 'while' in line 10 (While the ship was held off the south coast on England) is a time reference and not used for contrast.

Addition

Although there are no examples of the use of *furthermore*, *moreover* and *in addition* in the text, Ss will find these examples of addition: ... and even cheerful (line 13) ... and even lawsuits (line 29) even worse, they can ... (line 56)

Contrast

Though many expressed regret ... (line 14)
While high-profile cases are still relatively rare ... (line 34)
Although every service failure will be different ... (line 61)
Although there are limits to the responsibilities companies should accept ... (line 83)

- Point out that some of the alternatives are grammatically impossible, for example, *While* in question 1. Others may be grammatically possible, but don't fit with the meaning, for example *However* in question 5. Ask the Ss to work on the exercise in pairs.
- Circulate, monitor and assist. Then with the whole class, ask pairs for their answers, discussing how they reached them.

1 However	**2** Although	**3** In spite of
4 whereas	**5** Moreover	

- Ask the Ss to complete the article in pairs. Circulate, monitor and assist.
- Check answers with the whole class.

1 Furthermore/Moreover		**2** Although/While
3 However	**4** Despite	**5** Moreover/Furthermore

Skills: Asking and answering difficult questions

A chief executive answers difficult questions from journalists. Ss listen to the language used, and apply it themselves in a similar situation.

- Present the situation described, and tell your Ss that they are going to listen to a series of questions from journalists. Read through the questions with the whole class, explaining any difficulties. Ask if anything strikes them in the written version as being
  a) neutral / polite b) forceful / aggressive?
  Emphasise that it may be difficult to judge until they hear the recording: words like *please* and *sorry* can be used quite aggressively.
- Write Ss' ideas on the board in note form to refer to later.

Possible answers

1. Seems to imply that the question was not answered the first time, and may indicate forcefulness
2. *Please* in the middle of a question rather than at the beginning or end can imply irritation or impatience.
3. Like 1, seems to imply that the question was not answered the first time, and may indicate forcefulness.
4. Too early to say: all depends on intonation.
5. May be aggressive. The form *Do you deny that* ... may be designed to trip the speaker up.
6. Too early to say: all depends on intonation.
7. The form seems polite, but it might be used ironically.
8. The form seems polite, but again it might be used ironically: all depends on the intonation.
9. The double negative might trip the speaker up, as in 5.
10. Form seems polite, but there may be irony.
11. Another double negative. *Surely* is forceful.
12. Too early to say: all depends on intonation.

- Play recording 11.4 once right through, getting the Ss to listen particularly to the stress and intonation. Then play it again, pausing after each utterance and discussing its tone with the whole class. Compare these reactions with comments that you and the Ss made and noted on the board before hearing the recording.

1 a	**2** b	**3** b	**4** a	**5** b	**6** a	**7** a
8 b	**9** b	**10** a	**11** b	**12** a		

- Go through the answers with the whole class. Note comments on the board. A lot depends on the intonation and also on the skill of the speaker in handling difficult questions.

1. Could sound defensive in context implying that the question was aggressive.
2. Neutral / polite
3. Could be defensive, so question could have been forceful.
4. Seems neutral / but might sound defensive in context.
5. Seems neutral / but might sound defensive in context.
6. Forceful / aggressive.
7. Neutral / polite unless speaker is very skilled at handling difficult questions.
8. Speaker may genuinely not know or question was forceful / aggressive.
9. Neutral / polite.
10. Neutral / polite.
11. Seems defensive so question was probably forceful / aggressive.
12. Seems defensive so question was probably forceful / aggressive.

Lesson notes

Ⓓ

- Give the Ss the general background to the situation. Divide the class into managers from the mobile phone company and journalists.
- Ask the journalists to read their information on page 153 of the Course Book, and the managers theirs on page 148.
- Circulate and assist in the preparation of roles. Explain any difficulties.
- When the Ss have absorbed the basic information, in the managers' group, appoint a 'chief executive' who will lead the press conference. Explain to the managers that under the leadership of the chief executive, they must prepare a coherent strategy for the press conference: when to apologise, when to be defensive, etc.
- Among the journalists, appoint a senior journalist who will start the questioning. Tell all the journalists to take notes to record what the company managers say at the press conference, so as to be able to write an article about it.
- When each side has prepared, ask the managers to leave the room and come in together, sitting at the front of the room, as if at a press conference.
- Tell the lead journalist to start the questioning and then encourage the other journalists to put their questions.

- Note language points for praise and correction, especially in relation to the question-and-answer types above. Only intervene if the questioning falters.
- When the press conference runs out of steam, ask the Chief Executive to wind it up and thank the journalists for attending.
- Praise good language points from the press conference and work on three or four points that need improvement, getting individual Ss to say the correct forms.
- Ask the managers and the journalists about their relative strategies and methods. Invite comments and encourage discussion.
- As a written follow-up, you could ask
  - the journalists to write an article based on the press conference.
  - the managers to write an internal memo about what happened at the press conference and about how successful they thought their strategy was.

1 to 1

This press conference can be done as a 1 to 1 interview. Ask your student which side they would prefer to represent. You represent the other side. Give the student plenty of time to prepare and absorb the information. Afterwards, ask the student about their strategy for the press conference and the tactics they were using.

Case study

Game over

Titan Stores is accused of selling pirated software. Ss analyse the related information and role play Titan's directors and media representatives at a press conference.

Stage 1: Background

- Ask the Ss to read the *Euronews* article about Titan Stores. Meanwhile, write the points in the first column of the table on the board.
- With the whole class, elicit the information to complete the table.

Activity	Retailing
Accusation made against the organisation	Selling pirated computer games
Number of units involved	50,000
Price	Very low
CEO's reaction	Can't be true, company known for its integrity and high ethical standards
One employee's comment	Problems in buying department recently, high staff turnover, low morale

- Ask the Ss to look at the company profile while you write the points in the first column of the next table on the board.
- Elicit information from the Ss to complete the table.

Based in	Dublin
Store locations	Most European cities
History	Started by selling stationery and books, then magazines and music products
Main product Customers	Computer games and other software Teens and young adults
Image	Quality products at affordable prices, high ethical standards
Slogan	'We put people first.'

- Ask the Ss to quickly look through the sales figures.
- With the whole class, ask individual Ss to summarise the information in full sentences, for example
  - Titan Stores has a workforce of 8,000.
  - It had sales of 720 million euros and last year it made a profit of 90 million euros.
  - Computer software and games make up 30% of Titan's sales revenue, followed by stationery and cards, with 24% ... etc.

Stage 2: Listening 11.5

- Play recording 11.5 once right through.
- Explain any difficult language.
- Play the recording again, stopping frequently to ask quick-fire questions. For example, play as far as *Well, yes there is unfortunately* and ask if the accusation is true. Elicit the answer. Play the recording as far as *wouldn't accept any responsibility for them* and ask if the supplier knew the games were pirated, etc.
- Put the Ss in small groups and ask them to discuss the information they received about the three items listed. Then ask a representative of each group to summarise the information on one of the items.
- Finally, elicit what Hugo Stern's advice to Carla Davis is.

The supplier of *Race against Time*: based in the Netherlands; got the games from an 'unusual' source 30% cheaper than the manufacturer; aware they could be illegal copies; claims to have bought the games in good faith; bought them from a firm that has gone bankrupt; won't accept any responsibility for them.

The manufacturer of the game: relations with Titan generally good; has a long-standing relationship with Titan who supported the company when it started up; had several products that no one was interested in except Titan, so a little in Titan's debt; upset about pirating of their games.

Stocks of *Race against Time*: most of original consignment has been sold, but they bought 50,000 last month and they are in the distribution centre; these stocks cannot now be sold.

Hugo advises Carla to form a crisis management team and bring in an outside expert to advise them.

Stage 3: Press conference preparation

- Divide the class into two groups. Explain that there will be a press conference where journalists will question Titan's management of the situation. Two to six students will role play Titan's management team (see below). The other Ss will play journalists. The two groups will prepare for the role play separately.
- Ask the journalists to look at their information on page 149 of the Course Book, looking at their objectives and then the results of their enquiries. If there are more than about four journalists, ask them to prepare questions for the press conference in sub-groups, afterwards choosing the best questions to ask in one group.
- Ss who will role play Titan's management team include
  - Chief Executive
  - Director of Public Relations
  - Director of Human Resources
  - Head of Legal Department
  - Marketing Director
  - an outside consultant from a crisis management firm.

  (It's enough to have Ss playing the first two or three roles if the class is small.)
- Ask the Ss role playing the management team to look at their information on page 146 of the Course Book, looking at their objectives a–c and then the results of their enquiries.
- Circulate, monitor and assist with both groups if necessary. Tell Titan's Chief Executive that he / she will make a brief opening statement about why the press conference has been called and then invite questions from the journalists.

Stage 4: The press conference

- When the Ss are ready, the press conference can begin. Ask the managers to go out of the room and then come in again and sit at the front of the class. The Chief Executive makes the opening statement and then invites questions.
- Note language points for praise and correction.
- Do not intervene unless necessary, but make sure that journalists are asking follow-up questions if the answers to their original questions are not satisfactory.
- Give yourself enough time to discuss the language and other points arising at the end of the session, and ask Titan's Chief Executive to wind up the press conference.
- Praise good language points from the role play and work on three or four points that need improvement, getting individual Ss to say the correct forms.
- Ask Titan's management team and the journalists how they thought the press conference went.

1 to 1

This case study can be done 1 to 1. Instead of the press conference, you can be a journalist interviewing Titan's CEO. Don't forget to note language points for praise and correction afterwards. Highlight some of the language you chose to use as well.

Writing

- Go through the information with the Ss, making clear what they have to do.
- Ask the Ss to write their report collaboratively in class or as homework.

Writing file pages 144 and 145.

Lesson notes

UNIT 12 Management styles

At a glance

	Classwork – Course Book	Further work
Lesson 1 *Each lesson (excluding case studies) is about 45–60 minutes. This does not include administration and time spent going through homework.*	**Starting up** Ss comment on some statements about management style and talk about the role of a manager. **Vocabulary: Management qualities** Ss look at vocabulary relating to management qualities and use it to discuss different management styles. **Listening: Successful managers** Ss listen to an expert talking about the qualities of good managers and the management style that gets the best results.	**Practice File** Vocabulary (page 48)
Lesson 2	**Reading: Management styles** Ss read an article about three key management styles, and say which style they prefer. **Language review: Text reference** Ss look at the ways texts are held together by words like *it*, *this* and *they*.	**Text bank** pages (176–179) **Practice File** Language review (page 49) **ML Grammar and Usage**
Lesson 3	**Skills: Putting people at ease** Ss look at the language for small talk and use it in a number of situations.	**Resource bank** (page 202)
Lesson 4 *Each case study is about 1½ to 2 hours.*	**Case study: Zenova** Ss analyse an international group where management style is causing problems, and assess the candidates being considered to take over management of a project team.	**Practice file** Writing (page 50)

For a fast route through the unit focussing mainly on speaking skills, just use the underlined sections.

For 1 to 1 situations, most parts of the unit lend themselves, with minimal adaptation, to use with individual students. Where this is not the case, alternative procedures are given.

Business brief

Traditionally, the model for **leadership** in business has been the army. Managers and army officers give orders, and their **subordinates** carry them out. Managers, like army officers, may be sent on leadership courses to develop their **leadership skills**. But some would say that leaders are born, not made, and no amount of training can change this. The greatest leaders have **charisma**, a powerful, attractive quality that makes other people admire them and want to follow them. A leader like this may be seen as a **visionary**. Leaders are often described as having **drive**, **dynamism** and **energy** to inspire the people under them, and we recognise these qualities in many famous business and political leaders. The leadership style of a company's boss can influence the management styles of all the managers in the organisation.

In some Asian cultures, there is management by **consensus**: decisions are not **imposed** from above in a **top-down approach**, but arrived at in a process of **consultation**, asking all employees to contribute to decision making, and many western companies have tried to adopt these ideas. Some commentators say that women will become more important as managers, because they have the power to build consensus in a way that the traditional **authoritarian** male manager does not.

One recent development in consensual management has been **coaching** and **mentoring**. Future senior managers are 'groomed' by existing managers, in regular one-to-one sessions, where they discuss the skills and qualities required in their particular **organisational culture**.

Another recent trend has been to encourage employees to use their own **initiative**: the right to take decisions and act on their own without asking managers first. This is **empowerment**. **Decision making** becomes more **decentralised** and less **bureaucratic**, less dependent on managers and complex formal management systems. This has often been necessary where the number of management levels is reduced. This is related to the ability of managers to **delegate**, to give other people responsibility for work rather than doing it all themselves. Of course, with empowerment and delegation, the problem is keeping control of your operations, and keeping the operations profitable and on course. This is one of the key issues of modern management style.

Empowerment is related to the wider issue of company **ownership**. Managers and employees increasingly have shares in the firms they work for. This of course makes them more **motivated** and **committed** to the firm, and encourages new patterns of more responsible behaviour.

Read on

Robert Benfari: *Understanding and Changing Your Management Style*, Jossey-Bass, 1999

Gareth Lewis: *The Mentoring Manager*, Financial Times Prentice Hall, 1999

Eric Parsloe: *The Manager as Coach and Mentor*, Chartered Institute of Personnel and Development, 1999

Role of the Manager, Financial Times Prentice Hall (Heriot-Watt BA course), 1998

John Wilson: *Management Style*, Hodder & Stoughton, 2000

Lesson notes

Warmer

- Write 'MANAGEMENT STYLE' in big letters on the board. Ask the Ss to brainstorm what they understand by this term.
- Ask them for their definition ('the way that managers relate to and deal with the people under them' or something similar, if your Ss are stuck). Invite comments and encourage brief discussion to arouse interest, without pre-empting the topics in the unit.

Overview

- Ask the Ss to look at the Overview section at the beginning of the unit. Tell them a little about the things on the list, using the table on page 102 of this book as a guide. Tell them which points you will be covering in the current lesson and in later lessons.

Quotation

- Read out the quotation and ask the Ss to comment. (This quotation should not be too controversial!)
- Write 'MANAGEMENT IS ...' on the board, adding 'tasks' and 'discipline' one above the other on the right of the board. As a quick-fire, whole-class activity, get the Ss to give you other words that could follow 'Management is ...'. Ss might say 'structure' and 'organisation' but also encourage more unexpected words like 'imagination', 'vision' and 'creativity'.

Starting up

Ss comment on some statements about management style and talk about the role of manager.

- Ask the Ss to comment on the statements in pairs. Circulate and assist with any difficulties.
- With the whole class, discuss the pairs' findings. If there are Ss from more than one country, obviously be tactful and do not disparage any particular style. However, there should be some interesting material for cross-cultural comparisons, even if the Ss are from the same country, but thinking about different companies with different management styles.

Emphasise that there are no 'right' answers, but here are some ideas:

1. A good idea if the department is small enough (but be careful with people who dislike mixing their personal and professional lives).
2. This could seem intrusive, but was for a long time seen as a manager's prerogative, and may still be in some places.
3. Most people enjoy occasional praise. Criticism must be constructive, and not degenerate into bullying.
4. Most employees would probably like managers to arbitrate in at least some disputes.
5. People with specific, hard-earned skills may be happy to be able to do things that their managers are unable to do.
6. Some companies have an 'open-door' policy, and encourage employees to take comments and pursue grievances to the highest level. Others would not encourage this. 'At all times' might mean being able to phone your manager at home until late in the evening, but in many places there is a strict division between home and work and you would not be able to do this.
7. There are probably two basic types of manager here, those who do get involved in socialising with staff, and those that find it easier to manage by staying clear. Again, this can be a cultural issue.
8. Probably a good idea in theory, but many organisations are known for profane language between employees when away from customers with, at times, highly-developed in-house slang. Racist or sexist comments should not be tolerated, of course.
9. True in many, if not most cultures. But there are managers who pride themselves on finishing the day on time, for example by refusing to be distracted from the tasks at hand, and gain the admiration of their less organised employees for being able to do this.
10. Staff with customer contact would probably expect to be commented on if their appearance is not up to scratch. Others might find it more difficult to accept this. There are many employer–employee disputes in this area, of course.

- Ask the Ss to choose their top three roles in pairs and then ask the pairs to report to the whole class. Invite comments and encourage discussion.

Vocabulary: Management qualities

Ss look at vocabulary relating to management qualities and use it to discuss different management styles.

- Ask your Ss to work in pairs to complete the table. Point out that in some places there can be more than one form. Circulate and assist with the meanings and pronunciation of unfamiliar words. You could ask the Ss to use a dictionary such as the *Longman Dictionary of Contemporary English*.

1 Adjective	2 Opposite adjective	3 Noun form
considerate	inconsiderate	consideration / considerateness
creative	uncreative	creativity / creativeness
decisive	indecisive	decisiveness
diplomatic	undiplomatic	diplomacy
efficient	inefficient	efficiency
flexible	inflexible	flexibility
inspiring	uninspiring	inspiration
interested	disinterested / uninterested	interest
logical	illogical	logic / logicality
organised	disorganised	organisation
rational	irrational	rationality
responsible	irresponsible	responsibility
sociable	unsociable	sociability
supportive	unsupportive	support

Where there is more than one form:
Disinterested means 'able to judge a situation fairly because you will not gain any advantage from it'. But tell the Ss that it is now also being used with the same meaning as *uninterested* and, even if some native speakers disapprove of this, they will certainly hear or see it being used this way.
Where there are alternative forms for nouns, say that they are more or less interchangeable when talking about people, though some forms (such as *creativity*) are more frequently used than the other.

- Discuss the answers with the whole class, but don't get bogged down talking about the alternative forms.

B–C

- First of all, check that your Ss have understood the words by going round the class and getting the Ss to start sentences with 'A manager should be ...' followed by the different adjective forms and a potted definition. For example
  - A manager should be inspiring. They (avoid clumsy *He or she*) should give people energy and the feeling that they can achieve something.
  - A manager should be sociable. They should be friendly and easy to talk to.
- When you have done one or two as examples, ask your Ss to prepare the remaining words in pairs.
- With the whole class, ask the Ss to read out their definitions and correct any misunderstandings.
- Then ask the Ss to work in pairs on their four top qualities and their four worst ones, adding one more quality and weakness of their own. Circulate and monitor.
- With the whole class, write up the scores given by each pair to each quality and each weakness, and calculate scores to find the most 'popular' qualities and weaknesses. Invite comments and encourage discussion.

D

- Do as a quick-fire activity with the whole class. Explain the meanings of unfamiliar words and practise pronunciations.

1 d 2 d 3 a 4 b 5 f 6 e

E

- Rather than discussing this topic in the abstract, get the Ss to talk in pairs or threes about particular work situations in their organisation and the appropriate style for each situation. With the whole class, ask the pairs and threes for their comments and encourage discussion. (If your Ss are pre-work, they may find it difficult to talk about this. If so, move on to the next exercise.)

F

- Get Ss to talk about these points in pairs and threes and then report back to the whole class. The answers to this will depend to a certain extent on cultural expectations. Treat tactfully.

Listening: Successful managers

Ss listen to an expert talking about the qualities of good managers and the management style that gets the best results.

A

- Have a whole-class discussion of this question and write the Ss' suggestions on the board.

B 12.1

- Go through the questions with the class so that they know what information they are listening for.
- Play recording 12.1 once or twice. You may need to pause it at key points to allow the Ss to make notes.
- Check the answers with the class.

1 Listen and ask questions.
2 He asks his local personnel or a friend or contact in that country to brief him on the customs of that country with regard to business meetings and social and travel situations.

Ⓒ

- Put the Ss in pairs and ask them to think of five ways in which managers can get the best out of people. Then ask the pairs to join another pair, making a group of four, and pool their ideas.
- Get a representative of each group to report their ideas to the class.

Ⓓ 12.2

- Ask the Ss to take notes on Niall's five key points. You may need to play recording 12.2 several times and pause it at key points in order to allow them to do this.

1. Show recognition of their work and compliment them publicly.
2. Communicate decisions clearly and take ownership of them.
3. Give specific reasons why decisions have been taken and make sure all managers are giving the same reasons.
4. Explain clearly the benefits of decisions to the individuals, the organisation and its customers.
5. Ask for people's commitment to working with the management to achieve the company's objectives.

Reading: Management styles

Ss read an article about three key management styles, and say which style they prefer.

Ⓐ

- Tell the Ss that they are going to read an article about three different management styles.
- Before they read the article, ask them to choose one of the questions and to think about how they would answer it.
- Put them in pairs and ask them to tell each other the answer to the question they have chosen.
- Ask each member of a pair to report back to the class on what their partner's answer was.

Ⓑ

- Read the first section of the text with the whole class, explaining any difficulties and eliciting from the Ss what they understand by the various styles listed.
- Put the Ss into groups of three and ask them to choose one of the management styles focussed on in the article. Go through the statements with the whole class, then ask the Ss to read their chosen sections and decide which of the statements is true for that management style.

1 Delegating	**2** Directing	**3** Discussing
4 Discussing	**5** Discussing	**6** Directing
7 Delegating	**8** Directing	**9** Delegating

Ⓒ

- Back in their groups, the Ss summarise for each other the main features of the styles they read about. Circulate, monitor and assist.

Ⓓ

- Ask the Ss, still in their same groups, to discuss these questions.
- Ask a representative of each group to report their findings to the class.

Ⓔ

- The Ss can do this activity individually or in pairs. When they check their answers in the text, encourage them to underline the word partnerships for ease of reference afterwards and so that they can see the contexts and ways in which they are used.

Group 1

1. establish goals (*Directing* lines 21 to 22; *Discussing* lines 31 to 32; *Delegating* lines 26 to 27)
2. monitor performance (*Directing* lines 40 to 41; Discussing line 47; *Delegating* line 49)
3. provide feedback (*Directing* lines 44 to 45; *Discussing* lines 6 to 7 and line 48; *Delegating* line 50)
4. set standards (*Directing* lines 5 to 6)
5. make decisions (*Directing* line 34; *Discussing* line 42 and line 46; *Delegating* line 38)
6. assign roles (*Directing* line 4)

Group 2

1. present ideas (*Discussing* line 5)
2. achieve goals (*Discussing* lines 35 to 36)
3. direct employees (*Directing* lines 34 to 35)
4. take action (*Directing* lines 35 to 36; *Delegating* lines 42 to 43)
5. improve performance (*Directing* lines 46 to 47)

Ⓕ

- Ask the Ss to do this exercise in pairs. Then go round the class asking for answers from different pairs.

1 look	**2** make	**3** do	**4** get	**5** make
6 deliver	**7** make	**8** achieve		

Language review: Text reference

Ss look at the ways texts are held together by words like *it*, *this* and *they*.

- Go through the points in the Language review box with the whole class, explaining any difficulties.

Ⓐ

- Do question 1a) with the whole class to give the Ss the idea.
- Then ask them to answer the rest of question 1 and question 2 in pairs.

1 a) managers b) discussing
c) managers d) employees'
e) monitoring performance and discussing what actions need to be taken

2 It's important to make sure ideas are fully discussed and debated. (*Discussing style* lines 9 to 11)

- Point out that the extract is a continuation of the article on page 103. Ask the Ss to work in pairs to find all the references. Suggest that they underline them in different colours in the text.
- Check answers with the class.

> **1** I (lines 1, 10, 14, 15, 20, 27, 28, 34, 36), me (lines 6, 10, 26, 30), my (lines 20, 31)
> **2** One (line 5), she (lines 6, 10)
> **3** The other person (line 12), his (line 15, 38), he (lines 18, 24, 30, 32), him (lines 21, 28, 30)
> **4** it's important to pay attention ... (lines 39 to 40)

(C)

- Ask the Ss to write the article in pairs, or individually for homework. If they are writing it in class, circulate, monitor and assist. Note any strong points and any problems in writing, perhaps ones common to more than one pair.
- Praise good language use in the writing and work on three or four points that need improvement, getting individual Ss to say the correct forms.
- Get one or two pairs to read out their articles for the whole class (choose at least one agreeing with the statement and one disagreeing with it). If they do the exercise for homework, they can read them out in the next lesson.
- Encourage further discussion generated by the Ss' articles.

Skills: Putting people at ease

Ss look at the language for small talk and use it in a number of situations.

- Discuss question 1 with the whole class. Ask the Ss if there is an expression in their own language(s) for *small talk* and ask them to translate it literally into English.
- Go round the whole class and get lists of suitable and unsuitable topics from the Ss and write them up on the board. If your Ss are from more than one country, write up the different lists.
- Treat the subject tactfully, especially the hot potatoes of politics and religion. (You might want to teach the expression *hot potato*.)

(B)

- Ask the Ss to work on the possible questions in pairs. Circulate and monitor.
- Then get the pairs to integrate the questions and answers into a longer, natural-sounding conversation. Point out that the phrases do not have to be used in the same order as in the Course Book, and can be adapted. The Ss can use extra phrases as well. Circulate, monitor and assist, especially with intonation.
- Ask one or two pairs to give performances for the whole class.

> **Example conversation** (with expressions from the Course Book underlined):
> Host: How was the flight from London?
> Visitor: Terrible. There was a lot of turbulence and several people were sick. It was a nightmare. Anyway, I'm here now. Good to be here!
> Host: Have you been to Rome before?
> Visitor: Yes, several times. I've been on a couple of business trips. And I came on a school trip back in 1968. A long time ago, but very memorable!
> Host: Really! That was quite a year here! What's it like being back?
> Visitor: I'm really impressed. The architecture is fascinating. I hope I have time to take it all in. I want to go back to all the old sites: the Pantheon, the Coliseum, the Vatican ... I'm going to stay on here over the weekend and do a bit of sightseeing!
> Host: Excellent! Where's your hotel?
> Visitor: Right in the centre. The Grand.
> Host: What's it like? Not too much noise from the traffic I hope. Rome's a very noisy city, as you probably remember.
> Visitor: No, actually my room's very quiet. The Grand's very comfortable, and the service is first class.
> Host: How's business?
> Visitor: We're doing very well, thank you.
> Host: You must be very busy. Had time to do any sport recently?
> Visitor: I enjoy tennis, when I get the time. But you know the problem with time!
> Host: Yes, everyone's working harder and harder these days. It's the same everywhere! Anyway, would you like to go for a coffee before we start work.
> Visitor: I'd love to.

(C) 12.3

- Play recording 12.3 once or twice all the way through and ask the Ss to note down the questions.
- Find out if any of the Ss' questions were the same as those on the recording.

(D)

- Ask the Ss to discuss the questions in pairs or threes. Circulate, monitor and assist.
- With the whole class, ask the pairs or threes to talk about their conclusions.
- Invite comments and encourage discussion with the whole class.

1 The Ss may mention it themselves, but you could bring up ways of socialising in specific parts of the world, for example being taken to restaurants for long lunches in Paris, sporting events or concerts in the UK (corporate hospitality) or karaoke bars in Japan. You could discuss whether or not business visitors and colleagues are invited to people's homes.
2 Ask your Ss about the acceptance (or otherwise) of silence in their own cultures. They may refer to the importance of silence in meetings in places such as Finland and Japan as a sign of respect, showing that you are giving thought to what the other person has said.
3 Answers to this question will be more personal, but there may be cultural differences between Ss from different places. If so, treat with tact.

Ⓔ–Ⓕ

- Do Exercise E as a quick-fire activity with the whole class.

1 c 2 e 3 a 4 b 5 d

- Ask the whole class what they think about this advice and about what they would say themselves to put people at their ease.

One of the issues here will be the use of names. Ask the Ss about what is usual and acceptable in their own countries. Ask them whether the situation is changing.
The appropriateness of asking about personal problems and family could also be discussed.

Ⓖ

- Underline that the idea here is that the Ss are meeting someone for the first time. They have to choose four subjects to talk about.
- Say that for the purposes of this activity, they are in a culture where silences are embarrassing and to be avoided, and tell the Ss that they should try to make graceful transitions between the subjects!
- Circulate, monitor and assist only if necessary. Note language points for praise and correction, especially in relation to small talk.
- Praise good language points from the activity and work on three or four points that need improvement, getting individual Ss to say the correct forms.
- Ask one or two pairs to give performances for the whole class.

Case study

Zenova

Ss analyse an international group where management style is causing problems, and assess the candidates being considered to take over management of a project team.

Stage 1: Background

- Ask the Ss to read the background information about Zenova. Meanwhile, write the points in the first column of the table on the board.
- With the whole class, elicit the information to complete the table.

Activity of company	Multinational health and beauty products manufacturer
Project team working on	Major survey of job satisfaction in all subsidiaries
Current approach	Project team – 16 members from different subsidiaries in Europe, America, Asia and the Middle East – working on interviewing staff, administering surveys, analysing results, producing report
Structure of team	16 members managed by Ryan Douglas
Current problems caused by	Bad management
State of staff	Unhappy; low morale
Risk	Project won't be completed on time
Current solution	Replace Ryan Douglas

Stage 2: Analysing the management style of Ryan Douglas 12.4

- Go through the instructions with the class before you play the recording. Ensure that everyone understands that they are taking the role of directors of Zenova and that they should take notes on what the project team members say about Ryan Douglas's management style. Go through the headings with them and encourage them to use these headings to structure their notes.
- Play recording 12.4. You may need to play it more than once and pause it at appropriate points to allow the Ss to complete their notes. Explain any difficulties.
- When the Ss have finished, ask them to compare their notes in pairs or small groups.
- Have a whole-class feedback session on the strengths and weaknesses of Ryan Douglas's management style.

Stage 3: Replacing the Project Manager

- Ask the Ss to read the description that each of the candidates to replace Ryan Douglas has written about their own particular management style.
- Circulate, monitor and assist. If there are questions about vocabulary, make sure the whole class can hear your answers.

Stage 4: Task

- Divide the class into small groups and go through the instructions with them. Get each group to appoint someone to take notes about who says what. These notes must be particularly clear if you are going to ask the Ss to do the follow-up writing task.
- When the Ss are clear what they have to do, the first part of the meeting, during which they discuss the four candidates and analyse their strengths and weaknesses, can begin.
- Circulate and monitor, but do not intervene unless necessary.
- Note language points for praise and correction, especially in relation to management styles.
- When the groups have finished, call the class to order.
- Praise good language points from the discussion and work on three or four points that need improvement, getting individual Ss to say the correct forms.
- Ask the Ss to return to their groups and to rank the four candidates in terms of their suitability for the position of project manager. Make sure that they use the numbering system suggested in the Course Book and ensure that clear notes are taken in each group about their discussion and their decision.
- Bring the whole class together again and ask one representative from each group to report back to the class on what they discussed and how they ranked the candidates. Write their recommendations on the board.
- Working as a whole class, the Ss choose one candidate to be offered the position of project manager.

1 to 1

This case study can be done 1 to 1, with the student analysing the information and then discussing the candidates and choosing one of them for the position. Don't forget to note language points for praise and correction afterwards. Highlight some of the language you chose to use as well.

Writing

- Ask the Ss to base their writing on the notes taken in their group during the simulated meeting.
- The writing can be done collaboratively in class or as homework.
- If your Ss are doing the writing task individually for homework, you may want to photocopy the notes made by the notetaker in each group so that each student has a record of what was said and decided in their group.

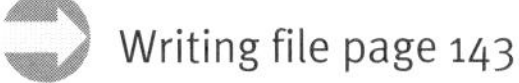

Writing file page 143.

Takeovers and mergers

At a glance

At a glance

	Classwork – Course Book	Further work
Lesson 1 *Each lesson (excluding case studies) is about 45–60 minutes. This does not include administration and time spent going through homework.*	**Starting up** Ss talk about takeovers and mergers, the reasons for them and examples that they know of. **Vocabulary: Describing takeovers and mergers** Ss study words and expressions related to different types of takeover and merger. **Listening: Making acquisitions** Ss listen to a Financial Director talking about acquisitions and their results.	**Practice File** Vocabulary (page 52)
Lesson 2	**Reading: Making a corporate marriage work** Ss read an article on how to make a business merger successful. **Language review: Headlines** Ss look at the particular features and vocabulary of newspaper headlines.	**Text bank** pages (180–183) **Practice File** Language review (page 53) **ML Grammar and Usage**
Lesson 3	**Skills: Summarising in presentations** Ss analyse different ways of summarising the points of a presentation, and put them into action.	**Resource bank** (page 202)
Lesson 4 *Each case study is about 1½ to 2 hours.*	**Case study: Group Bon Appetit PLC** The management of a restaurant group decides to grow the business by making an acquisition. Ss analyse three target companies and make recommendations for which one to choose.	**Practice File** Writing (page 54)

For a fast route through the unit focussing mainly on speaking skills, just use the underlined sections.

For 1 to 1 situations, most parts of the unit lend themselves, with minimal adaptation, to use with individual students. Where this is not the case, alternative procedures are given.

Business brief

'Magnetic's board rejected TT's bid as "derisory, unsolicited, unwelcome and totally inadequate".' This is a familiar refrain from the board of a company that is the **target** of a **hostile bid**, one that it does not want, for example because it thinks that the **bidder** is **undervaluing** its shares: offering less for the shares than the target thinks they are worth in terms of its future profitability. A bid that a target company welcomes, on the other hand, may be described as **friendly**.

Bidders often already have a **minority stake** or **interest** in the target company: they already own some shares. The bid is to gain a **majority stake** so that they own more shares than any other shareholder and enough shares to be able to decide how it is run.

A company that often takes over or **acquires** others is said to be **acquisitive**. The companies it buys are **acquisitions**. It may be referred to, especially by journalists, as a **predator**, and the companies it buys, or would like to buy, as its **prey**.

When a company buys others over a period of time, a **group**, **conglomerate** or **combine** forms, containing a **parent company** with a number of **subsidiaries** and perhaps with many different types of business activity. A group like this is **diversified**. Related companies in a group can have **synergy**, sharing production and other costs, and benefiting from **cross-marketing** of each other's products. Synergy is sometimes expressed as the idea that two plus two equals five, the notion that companies offer more **shareholder value** together than they would separately.

But the current trend is for groups to **sell off**, **spin off** or **dispose of** their **non-core assets** and activities, in a process of **divestment** and **restructuring**, allowing them to **focus on** their **core activities**, the ones they are best at doing and make the most profit from. Compare an old-style conglomerate like GEC in the UK, with a wide variety of sometimes unrelated activities, and a group like Pearson, which has decided to concentrate on media, in broadcasting, publishing and now Internet ventures.

Companies may work together in a particular area by forming an **alliance** or **joint venture**, perhaps forming a new company in which they both have a stake. Two companies working together like this may later decide to go for a **merger**, combining as equals. But mergers (like takeovers) are fraught with difficulty and for a variety of reasons often fail, even where the merger involves two companies in the same country. One of the companies will always behave as the dominant partner.

Take the scenario where one company's base is used as the headquarters for the merged company. The other company's office closes, and many managers in both companies lose their jobs. Those remaining feel beleaguered and under threat of losing theirs later. They may dislike the way the managers from the other company work. In **cross-border mergers**, these difficulties are compounded by cross-cultural misunderstandings and tensions. Problems such as these explain why merged companies so often fail to live up to the promise of the day of the press conference when the two CEOs vaunted the merger's merits.

Read on

John Child, David Faulkner: *Strategies of Co-operation: Managing Alliances, Networks and Joint Ventures*, OUP, 1998

Timothy Galpin, Mark Herndon: *The Complete Guide to Mergers and Acquisitions*, Jossey Bass Wiley, 1999

Hazel Johnson: *Mergers and Acquisitions*, Financial Times Prentice Hall, 1999

J. Fred Weston: *Mergers and Acquisitions*, McGraw-Hill, 2000

Lesson notes

Special note

Teaching this unit will be much easier if you read it right through from beginning to end before the first lesson, as familiarity with later parts of the unit will be of great help in teaching the earlier parts.

Warmer

- Write TAKEOVERS AND MERGERS in big letters on the board. Ask the Ss to say what the difference is between a takeover and a merger.

A takeover is when one company buys more than 50% of the shares in another from its existing shareholders and thereby obtains a controlling interest. A merger is when two companies combine as equals, by mutual agreement. For more on this, see the Business brief on page 111.

Overview

- Ask the Ss to look at the Overview section at the beginning of the unit. Tell them a little about the things on the list, using the table on page 110 of this book as a guide. Tell them which points you will be covering in the current lesson and in later lessons.

Quotation

- Read out the quotation and ask the Ss to comment. What did Goldsmith mean exactly?

New owners may not fully understand how the company they're buying works, especially if they are unfamiliar with the industry it is in. You can buy the shares, but that doesn't change the 'culture' of the company.
New owners may damage the morale of previously motivated managers and employees, perhaps by putting their own senior managers in charge of the company, or by undervaluing the skills and experience of the existing staff.

Starting up

Ss talk about takeovers and mergers, the reasons for them and examples that they know of.

Ⓐ–Ⓒ

- Ask Ss to discuss these questions in pairs or threes. Circulate and assist. Ss' contributions to the Warmer and Quotation-related activities above will have shown if they have the knowledge and interest to do this independently. If you think they don't, discuss the points as a whole-class activity.

A

a) A takeover is when one company gets control of another company by buying over 50 per cent of its shares. This could be by mutual agreement or it could be a hostile takeover in which the company which is bought has no choice in the matter.

b) A merger is when two companies join together by mutual consent to form a larger company.

c) A joint venture is when two companies work together on a project, sharing the investment costs.

B

This list is not exhaustive and Ss may come up with other ideas.

- To reduce competition within the same market.
- To gain a foothold in another market where the other company has a strong presence.
- To expand its business, for example by obtaining new products to sell.
- To reduce overheads and increase profitability by combining departments and cutting staff.

C

Prepare to talk about recent takeovers and mergers by looking at publications such as the *Financial Times* or *The Economist*. They can be found on the Internet at www.ft.com and www.economist.com respectively. (Alternatively, if your Ss have access to the Internet, ask them to do some research and report back on it in the next session.)

Vocabulary: Describing takeovers and mergers

Ss study words and expressions related to different types of takeover and merger.

Ⓐ

- Tell your Ss they are going to look at the language of takeovers and mergers, and to work in pairs on matching the expressions with their meanings. Circulate and assist if necessary.
- With the whole class, ask for the answers and explain anything that is unclear.

1 e **2** d **3** b **4** f **5** c **6** a

Ⓑ

- Ask the Ss to choose one noun in each line which forms a word partnership with the verb at the beginning.

1 a stake
2 a bid
3 an alliance
4 a company
5 a joint venture
6 an acquisition

- Ask the Ss to complete the extracts in pairs and then elicit and discuss the answers with the whole class.

1 takeover bid
2 stake
3 merger
4 joint venture

Listening: Making acquisitions

Ss listen to a Financial Director talking about acquisitions and their results.

(A) 13.1

- Go through the questions with the class so they know what information they are listening for. You could ask them to predict what they think the speaker will say.
- Play recording 13.1 and ask the Ss to take notes.
- Check answers with the class.

1 Establish the goals of the acquisition. Establish the target of the acquisition. Put a valuation on the target company.
2 Make sure that the institutions who will fund the acquisition understand what you are trying to achieve and have confidence in your data.

(B) 13.1

- Play recording 13.1 again and ask the Ss to complete the goals.
- When you have checked answers, check the Ss' understanding of these goals. You may need to explain that in vertically integrated companies, different parts of the company produce a different product and the products combine to satisfy a common need. An example would be a steel company which owns not only the mills where the steel is manufactured but also the mines where the iron ore is extracted, the coal mines that supply the coal, the ships that transport the iron ore, etc.

1 share 2 benefits 3 integration 4 presence

(C) 13.2

- Go through the instructions with the class and emphasise that they should try to identify the two sides of success which the speaker mentions and find an example of each.
- Play recording 13.2
- Allow the Ss to work in pairs to formulate their answers. Then check with the class.

Hard success and soft success.
An example of hard success is achieving the strategic and financial goals of the acquisition in good time.
An example of soft success is successful communication of exactly what is going on.

(D) 13.2

- Play recording 13.2 again and ask the Ss to decide whether the speaker cites a), b) or c) as a sign that an acquisition has been successful.

c)

(E) 13.3

- Play recording 13.3 and ask the Ss to note down the example the speaker gives of a successful merger and the reasons she gives for its success.

The example is the merger of Coopers Lybrand and Deloitte, Haskins and Sells. She says it was a success because there was good communication with the employees and all the necessary changes were made very quickly. Everyone knew what was happening and how it affected them personally.

Reading: Making a corporate marriage work

Ss read an article on how to make a business merger successful.

(A)

- Explain that the language of betrothal and marriage is often used by journalists to talk about mergers.
- Have a brainstorming session to get ideas for the secrets of a successful marriage and of a successful merger. Put the two headings on the board and ask the Ss to call out ideas for you to write up under the relevant headings.
- Then ask the Ss to produce a list of similarities between a marriage and a business merger.

Your Ss may come up with a variety of ideas. Here are a few to give you a start.

1 **b)** love, mutual respect, patience, a willingness to persevere when things get difficult, a willingness to accept your partner's funny little habits, mutual support and loyalty, good communication ...
b) good preparation, good communication, making efforts to keep staff happy, consideration of the other company's culture, quick action to tackle any problems ...

2
- In both, two partners, previously operating independently, come together to form a single unit.
- The expectation is that the union will be permanent.
- It is expected that the union will bear fruit (children and profits).
- Good communication is needed to ensure the success of both.
- Neither should be entered into for the wrong reasons.
- Neither should be entered into hastily or without careful consideration.

(B)

- Ask the Ss to read the article carefully and underline all the dos and don'ts they can find.
- Put them in pairs to complete the chart.
- Check answers with the class, making sure you get a variety of dos and don'ts.

Dos

- Use a clean room where both sides can discuss plans in confidence.
- Ensure that there are rapid results which demonstrate that the merger is already producing added value.
- Give employees detailed information in the early stages about what is happening.
- Deal with the cultural issues, even though these are more subtle and challenging.
- Recognise cultural differences between the two companies.
- Take measures to avoid the worst consequences of mergers.
- Respond as the new situation demands.
- Learn about the history of the new partner.
- Give employees reasons why change is necessary.
- Find practical ways of communicating.
- Discuss employees' new working conditions and be visible on the shop floor.

Don'ts

- Assume that your company is better because it has taken over the other company.
- Take a dictatorial, top-down approach to management.
- Make great speeches in place of taking action.
- Get too preoccupied with practical administrative changes.
- Micro-manage the transition.

(C)

- Ask the students to find the names of the experts in the article and then match them to the opinions.

1 b **2** a **3** c

(D)

- Go round the class asking Ss to find the expressions and identify the most suitable answers.

1 a **2** c **3** b **4** a **5** b **6** c

(E)

- Ask the Ss to work in pairs to discuss these questions. Then ask them to report back to the class on their findings.

(F)

- Ask the Ss to work in different pairs for this exercise. When they have discussed the questions, ask them to join another pair to compare notes.
- Ask one representative of each group to present the group's findings to the class.

Language review: Headlines

Ss look at the particular features and vocabulary of newspaper headlines.

- Go through the points in the Language review box with the whole class. (If you have time before the class, find recent press headlines that have some of the same features, and show them to and discuss them with the Ss.)
- Say that, for the purposes of Exercise A, *several nouns* in point 1 means two or more nouns.

(A)–(B)

- Ask Ss to look at Exercises A and B together. Do the first headline with the whole class to give Ss the idea, then get them to do the rest in pairs. Circulate and assist. Discuss the answers with the whole group.

1	2	Renault is on the brink of two alliances.
2	1, 2	US law firms have agreed on a merger deal.
3	2, 3, 4	Austin Reed rejects an offer as unwelcome.
4	2, 3	Gazprom and Rosneft have agreed a merger.
5	1, 2, 4	Titan is in a £9.3bn bid for a US store group.
6	5	Chromogenex is to raise £2m.
7	2, 5	Sara Lee is to dispose of its 60 smallest units.
8	1, 2, 3	The AOL deal has called rivals' web plans into question.

(C)

- Explain why short words are used in headlines and do the exercise as a quick-fire activity with the whole class.

1 b **2** a **3** j **4** h **5** f **6** k **7** c
8 d **9** e **10** i **11** g
(Check Ss' pronunciation of *row* in this context.)

Skills: Summarising in presentations

Ss analyse different ways of summarising the points of a presentation, and put them into action.

(A)

- Explain the context of the presentation that the Ss are about to hear: a management consultant talking to a Board of Directors involved in a takeover.
- Tell them that some of the words he uses are quite difficult. This exercise covers some of them.
- Go through words 1–8 with the whole class, practising their pronunciation. (Practise *thorough* in b) on the right as well.) Point out that *sycophant* is pronounced *sicker-fant*, or, as they will hear in the recording, *sigh-co-fant*. (Some native speakers may not agree with the second pronunciation.)
- Ask Ss for the meanings of the words.

1 d	**2** b	**3** a	**4** g	**5** h	**6** e
7 f	**8** c				

(B) 13.4

- Play the recording once right through and ask Ss to put up their hands when they hear the words 1–8 in Exercise A above being used.
- Then tell the Ss they should listen out for the points Jeremy Keeley makes in his presentation, ready to summarise them, and name the pitfall listed here that he does not refer to.
- Play the recording again, explaining any remaining difficulties. Stop at the end of each of the main points he makes and ask Ss to summarise it. (Stop at *the basis of managing the change moving forward, so they can take it forward* and at the end of the recording.)
- Ask Ss for the point that was not mentioned: 'Pay attention to the cultural differences'.

(C) 13.4

- Ask Ss to look at the Useful language box and ask individual Ss to read out the utterances, with convincing stress and intonation. Explain what a rhetorical question is.
- Play the recording again and get the Ss to identify the utterances that they hear.

Referring back
So as you were saying a few minutes ago ...
Making points in threes
You really have to plan carefully, be rigorous in your analysis and be flexible ...
It's a long process. It's expensive. It can also be very profitable.
Asking rhetorical questions
But what are the sort of things that the experts forget generally?
Ordering
There are three things in my mind and the first thing is ...
Using emotive language
Beware of the sycophants in your organisation ...
Repetition
They're going to be saying Yes! Yes! Yes!
Exemplifying
... for example, caring as their primary task.
Asking for feedback
What's missing?

(D)

- Tell Ss that they will be discussing the advantages and the problems associated with takeovers and mergers. Ask them to think about some of the issues they have encountered so far. In the discussion, they will be able to talk about these and add some of their own.
- Divide the class into two groups, A and B. (If the class is large, you could have two Group As and two Group Bs.)
- Group A discusses the advantages and Group B the problems. Tell everyone to make notes of their discussion; these will be used as the basis for the pair work activity below.
- Circulate and monitor, but do not intervene unless necessary. If they are short of ideas, you could remind them of some of the points from the Starting up section at the beginning of this unit. Note language points for praise and correction.
- Call the class to order. Praise good language points from the discussion and work on three or four points that need improvement, getting individual Ss to say the correct forms.
- Then form pairs each with one student from Group A and one from Group B. The members of each pair summarise the discussion of the group they were in.
- Bring the class to order. Ask one of the pairs to repeat their presentations to each other for the whole class.
- Invite comments and encourage brief discussion.

Case study

Group Bon Appetit PLC

The management of a restaurant chain decides to grow the business by making an acquisition. Ss analyse three target companies and make recommendations for which one to choose.

Stage 1: Background

- Ask the Ss to read the background information about Group Bon Appetit. Meanwhile, write the points in the first column of the table on the board.
- With the whole class, elicit the information to complete the table.

Company name	Bon Appetit Plc
Activity	Restaurant chain
Present problem	No further opportunities for expansion
Proposed solution	Acquire an already established company in the food industry
Objectives of acquisition	◎ to boost profits ◎ to enhance the company's image ◎ to buy a company which will continue to grow and contribute to the group's success ◎ to buy a company which will not take up too much of the present management's time and energy
Target companies	◎ Coffee Ground ◎ Starlight ◎ Mario Ferrino

Stage 2: Analysing the information 13.5

- Ask the Ss to work in pairs and to look at the Key financial information section and the charts of past financial performance. Ask them to comment on the three companies' financial performance.
- Ask the Ss to read the reports about Coffee Ground and Starlight and note down the key points. They should also look at the graphs showing the share prices and the table showing the debt ratios.
- Play recording 13.5 and ask Ss to take notes of what they hear.

Stage 3: Task

- Divide the class into three groups, A, B and C. Tell them to discuss the information they have read and heard about all three target companies. Circulate, monitor and assist.
- Direct each group to the relevant role card. Each group should now concentrate only on the target company named on their role card and prepare a presentation based on the notes on the role card and the information discussed earlier. Explain that they don't have to be advocates for this company, they just have to give a presentation of the available information on it. Circulate, monitor and assist as the Ss prepare their presentations.
- When the Ss are ready, ask each group in turn to give its presentation. Remind the class that they need to listen carefully to the other group's presentations because they will need the information in the next stage of the task when they discuss which company to choose.
- Working in the same groups, the Ss consider the three target companies. They discuss which would be the most suitable acquisition for Bon Appetit and make their choice.
- Circulate and monitor, but do not intervene unless necessary. Note language points for later praise and correction.
- When the discussion has finished, praise good language use and work on three or four points that need improvement, getting individual Ss to say the correct forms.
- Ask one representative from each group to present the group's findings to the class and to say which company they favour and why. Invite comments and brief discussion, especially about the decisions that each group has made and the basis for these decisions, but do not pre-empt the final class discussion.
- Have a class discussion of which company to choose and try to reach a consensus.

1 to 1

This case study can be done 1 to 1, with your student analysing the information on the three target companies and then discussing which one would be best to choose. Don't forget to note language points for praise and correction afterwards. Highlight some of the language you chose to use as well.

Stage 4: Writing

- Ask the Ss to base their writing on the final decision made by the class on which company to recommend as an acquisition target. If no consensus was reached, they could base it on the decision made in their small groups.
- The writing can be done collaboratively in class or as homework.

Writing file pages 144–145.

UNIT 14

The future of business

At a glance

	Classwork – Course Book	Further work
Lesson 1 *Each lesson (excluding case studies) is about 45–60 minutes. This does not include administration and time spent going through homework.*	**Starting up** Ss comment on a range of social and technological predictions and the likelihood of them coming about. **Listening: The future of business** The Head of Knowledge Venturing at the Henley Centre talks about business opportunities in the future.	
Lesson 2	**Vocabulary: Describing the future** Ss study expressions used to talk about things from the past, present and future. They then look at the adjectives that can be used to talk about the future and use them in combination with particular adverbs. **Reading: New working model** Ss read about changing employment patterns and some predictions about the future.	**Practice File** Vocabulary (page 56) **Text bank** pages (184–187)
Lesson 3	**Language review: Prediction and probability** Ss look at verb tenses, such as *will*, *going to* and *may* and lexical phrases, such as *probable* and *not possible* used to talk about the future. They put them into action to make their own forecasts. **Skills: Getting the right information** Ss listen to situations where there are breakdowns of communication, look at language that can remedy these, and apply it to role play situations.	**Practice File** Language review (page 57) **ML Grammar and Usage** **Resource bank** (page 203)
Lesson 4 *Each case study is about 1½ to 2 hours.*	**Case study: Yedo Department Stores** A chain of Japanese department stores is in trouble, in the face of social changes and foreign competition. Ss suggest some solutions.	**Practice File** Writing (page 58)

For a fast route through the unit focussing mainly on speaking skills, just use the underlined sections.

For 1 to 1 situations, most parts of the unit lend themselves, with minimal adaptation, to use with individual students. Where this is not the case, alternative procedures are given.

Business brief

In the 1960s, we imagined a future of public transport based on elevated monorail systems, and private transport with personal helicopters, or even spacecraft, for everyone. Today, the future looks more like the past than we imagined it would. Development has been **continuous** in many ways. For example, the car has become a mundane object, but with technology far in advance of that available even 20 years ago. However, its future source of power, a **discontinuous** development that will replace petrol, is still uncertain.

Futurology, with its **futurologists** or **futurists**, is a haphazard activity, despite attempts to formalise it. There is the **Delphi method**, where experts make their forecasts about a subject independently, and a referee circulates each forecast to the other members of the group, who comment on each other's observations until they reach a consensus.

This can be one element of **strategy**, where companies make long-term plans about future activities. Here, they have to anticipate competitors' activities as well as trends in the general **economic environment**. Very large companies work on **scenario planning**, imagining different ways in which the current situation may evolve, and their place in it, including ways in which they may 'encourage' it to develop in their favour.

The main course unit makes a number of social and economic predictions. As the **Success** business brief mentions (see Unit 4), future successful products are notoriously hard to predict, as are the subtle combinations of social, cultural and technological circumstances that mean that something may succeed at one time but not another. The **E-commerce** business brief (Unit 7) looks at some of the trends in e-commerce and Internet use in this context.

One of the social predictions made 30 years ago was that people would work less and have more leisure time, but the opposite has occurred. No one foresaw how the computer would evolve away from the mainframe and facilitate a social development like working from home and while on the move, thanks to laptops and, in a parallel development, mobile phones. Similarly, the Internet may have social effects that we cannot envisage, let alone predict.

A powerful force 30 years ago was **protest** at the way society and the economy were organised, for example against 'faceless multinationals'. After a long period where youth shed its rebellious reputation, in this context at least, there are signs that **activism** outside traditional political parties is re-emerging as a social force, this time organised on a global level – witness the regular violent demonstrations against recent meetings of the International Monetary Fund and the World Trade Organization, with planning of protests co-ordinated over the Internet. This trend may intensify.

Another factor that will certainly affect the way the future of business develops is **global warming**, which is now, after years of debate over whether it is happening or not, an incontrovertible fact. Some possible consequences of the greenhouse effect have been predicted, but there will certainly be others we cannot even imagine.

Read on

Charles Grantham: *The Future of Work*, McGraw-Hill, 1999

Hamish McRae: *The World in 2020*, HarperCollins, 1995

Jonathan Margolis: *A Brief History of the Future*, Bloomsbury, 2000

Michael Zey: *Future Factor*, McGraw-Hill, 2000

Lesson notes

Warmer

- Write 'The future is ...' in big letters on the board. Add the word 'bright' and then ask your Ss to brainstorm other words that could follow the phrase and shout them out. (They do not all have to be adjectives.)

Possible answers
mobile
crowded
knowledge
healthy
efficient
our children
going to be more like the past than we think

- Invite comments and encourage discussion, but don't pre-empt the topics of the unit too much.

Overview

- Ask the Ss to look at the Overview section at the beginning of the unit. Tell them a little about the things on the list, using the table on page 118 of this book as a guide. Tell them which points you will be covering in the current lesson and in later lessons.

Quotation

- Ask Ss to look at the quotation and ask what they think it means. (Great advances are not made by asking people what they want because they can only envisage improvements on what they have.)

Starting up

Ss comment on a range of social and technological predictions and the likelihood of them coming about.

Ⓐ–Ⓑ

- Ask Ss to discuss the predictions in Exercise A in pairs, emphasising that they should concentrate on the next 50 years, and come up with other changes that are likely.
- With the whole class, get the pairs to report on their findings. Invite comments and encourage discussion.

Ⓒ

- Ask the Ss to discuss in pairs how they think their careers will develop in the future. Be tactful and allow them to make outrageous predictions if this is more acceptable than going into real details.

Ⓓ

- Again in pairs, ask Ss to comment on
  – the immediate future of business and the economy in their country
  – the longer-term prospects.
- Point out that the adjective is *optimistic*, the related noun is *optimism* and the person is *an optimist*. Do not allow Ss to say *I'm optimist* or *I'm pessimist*.
- With the whole class, ask the pairs for their findings, asking Ss to justify them. Where different Ss from the same country have different ideas about their country's future, encourage debate, but be tactful.

Listening: The future of business

The Head of Knowledge Venturing at the Henley Centre talks about business opportunities in the future.

Ⓐ 14.1

- Go through the charts with the class before you play the recording so the Ss know what information they are listening for.
- Play recording 14.1 once or twice and ask the Ss to complete the charts.
- Check answers with the class and answer any queries.

New business opportunities
1 services, luxuries
2 group, consumers, segment

Expanding business sectors
1 price competitive, discount supermarkets
2 charge, premium

Ⓑ 14.2

- Go through the questions with the class first.
- Play recording 14.2 several times, pausing at key points so that the Ss can take notes.
- Check answers with the class.

1 In some areas, such as manufacturing, technology has improved efficiency, but in others, such as e-mail and the use of computers to download and print documents, it has made us less efficient.
2 **a)** They cut costs by removing middle management within the company.
  b) They will need to look outside the company for ways of improving efficiency, such as squeezing suppliers or becoming more competitive by focussing more on the customer. Within the company they will aim to increase efficiency by keeping their staff happy.

Vocabulary: Describing the future

Ss study expressions used to talk about things from the past, present and future. They then look at the adjectives that can be used to talk about the future and use them in combination with particular adverbs.

Ⓐ

- Do as a quick-fire activity with the whole class.

1 up-to-date
2 a thing of the past
3 ahead of its time
4 old-fashioned
5 state-of-the-art
6 the way forward
7 out of date
8 up to the minute
9 at the cutting edge
10 behind the times

Ⓑ

- Go round the class for some quick-fire off-the-cuff predictions.

Ⓒ–Ⓓ

- Ask your Ss to work on these words in pairs and then use them to write down some predictions.

very bad	bad	good	very good
bleak dire dreadful terrible	depressing doubtful uncertain worrying	bright promising prosperous rosy	brilliant great magnificent marvellous

- With the whole class, go through the words and ask the pairs for their predictions.

Reading: New working model

Ss read about changing employment patterns and some predictions for the future.

Ⓐ

- Ask the Ss to work in pairs and to choose three or four of the items to make predictions about. Try to ensure that different pairs choose different items. If necessary, allocate the items yourself.
- Get the pairs to present their predictions to the class.

Ⓑ

- Go through the questions with the class and answer any queries. Ask the Ss to read the article and find the answers.

1 Countries such as India and China with huge populations are playing a fuller part in the world economy. Changes in technology are having an enormous impact on business.
2 The predictions are often wrong. For example, there were forecasts of large-scale unemployment in Europe and predictions that European workers would have more leisure time but these have not come true and French and German companies are trying to get their staff to work longer hours.
3 It has given countries like India and China opportunities to develop their people's skills. It has given companies around the world huge cost-saving opportunities and, at least in the short-term, the chance to gain a competitive advantage.
4 Capital is expensive and labour cheap in countries like India and China. It is the other way round in more developed countries.
5 An airline that found it uneconomic to chase debts of under $200 dollars now uses Indian accountants and can chase debts of even as little as $50.

Ⓒ

- You could divide the class in half and ask one group to find the key points on Germany, France, the UK and India and the other to find the key points on Japan, China and the US (make sure different groups do China and India as there is most information on these and it is the same for both). You might like to suggest that they look for the names of their countries in the text and underline them for ease of reference.
- Bring the class together to exchange information on the different countries.

Germany and France: They are still worried about large-scale unemployment, yet German and French companies are trying to find ways to get their staff to work more hours.

the UK: Employers and policy-makers are worried about a shortage of workers, not a shortage of work.

Japan: It once seemed poised to assume world economic leadership. It may face unforeseen problems in the future. It is an ageing society.

India: One of the countries that now seem poised to assume world economic leadership but may face unforeseen problems in the future. It has a very large population. It is already playing a fuller part in the world economy. It is benefiting from outsourcing by companies from more developed countries and is getting the opportunity to develop its people's skills. Capital is expensive and labour cheap there. It is also potentially a huge market. The most significant obstacle to becoming a world economic leader is the poor quality of its universities.

China: One of the countries that now seem poised to assume world economic leadership but may face unforeseen problems in the future. It has a very large population. It is already playing a fuller part in the world economy. It is benefiting from outsourcing by companies from more developed countries and is getting the opportunity to develop its people's skills. Capital is expensive and labour cheap there. It is also potentially a huge market. The most significant obstacle to becoming a world economic leader is the poor quality of its universities.

the US: People are worried about what local workers are going to do if companies outsource to India and China. Demographic changes mean that in future there will be fewer people in the US of working age; by 2015 there will be 5 per cent fewer than there are today.

Ⓓ

- Do this as a quick-fire exercise, eliciting the answers from around the class. Then ask the Ss to find and circle the expressions in the text so that they can see them used in context.

1 excessive labour market regulation (lines 16 to 17)
2 world economic leadership (lines 30 to 31)
3 in-house economic think-tank (lines 82 to 83)
4 potentially huge markets (lines 111 to 112)
5 lower vehicle development costs (lines 112 to 113)
6 new niche markets (lines 117 to 118)
7 world-class research centres (lines 182 to 183)

Ⓔ

- Again, do this as a quick-fire exercise. You could ask the Ss to try to use each one in a sentence.

1 increasingly difficult market conditions
2 exceptionally gifted university researchers
3 increasingly high unemployment rate
4 rapidly developing information technology

Ⓕ

- Ask the Ss to discuss in pairs. Circulate, monitor and assist, noting language points for praise and correction.
- Get pairs to report their responses to the whole class. Invite comments and encourage further discussion.
- Praise good language use from the discussion and work on three or four points that need improvement, getting individual Ss to say the correct forms.

Language review: Prediction and probability

Ss look at verb tenses such as *will*, *going to* and *may* and lexical phrases, such as *probable* and *not possible* used to talk about the future. They put them into action to make their own forecasts.

- Go through the points in the Language review box with the whole class.

- Go round the class, reading out the predictions and asking individual Ss to indicate the level of probability suggested by the lexical phrases.

1 impossible 2 certain 3 unlikely
4 probable (probable that they won't = unlikely that they will)
5 impossible 6 possible 7 possible
8 probable 9 probable 10 certain

Ⓑ

- Ask the Ss to discuss the predictions in pairs and report back to the class on their opinions.

Ⓒ

- Again, ask the Ss to work in pairs for this exercise. Circulate, monitor and assist, noting language points for praise and correction and encouraging use of the forms from the Language review box and Exercise A and those in the box.
- Get pairs to report their predictions to the whole class. Invite comments and encourage further discussion about the predictions made.
- Praise good language use from the discussion and work on three or four points that need improvement, getting individual Ss to say the correct forms.

Skills: Getting the right information

Ss listen to situations where there are breakdowns of communication, look at language that can remedy these, and apply it to role play situations.

Ⓐ 14.3

- Tell your Ss that they are going to hear a number of telephone conversations where people have trouble getting the right information.
- Play the first dialogue and, with the whole class, ask the Ss what the problem is.

1 Carla wants to get more information about a range of hairdryers sold by a company. She wants to speak to Li Wang, presumably in the sales department, but gets put through to Ken Tang in accounts, who transfers her back to the switchboard. The switchboard puts her through to Li Wang's extension but a colleague of his, Dan Chen, says that he is out of the office and asks if he can help.

- Play the other dialogues and ask Ss to give descriptions of the situations in order to answer the questions relating to each dialogue.

2 Michael Bishop is angry because some cash machines he ordered are now two weeks overdue. He gets through to someone who asks him to give details of the order, including the date, model number and order number. The supplier promises to look into the problem and call back as soon as possible.

3 A supplier and a customer are discussing an order. There is confusion over the reference number, but this is cleared up when the customer reads back the details to the supplier. There is also a mistake in the delivery date on record. The customer corrects this and the supplier confirms the new delivery date is feasible.

4 The customer is calling about an invoice that they have received for 50 CD players. The customer is surprised because they only inquired about prices and availability and did not actually place an order. The customer explains that they have obtained the CD players elsewhere and the supplier cancels the order. The customer apologises for any inconvenience caused and the supplier says they will tell the sales assistant to be careful in the future.

- Make sure that Ss use expressions such as *put someone through* and *transfer someone back* correctly.
- Go through the expressions in the Useful language box and ask individual Ss to read them with feeling.
- Play the dialogues again and ask your Ss to tick the expressions as they hear them.

The numbers refer to the dialogues on recording 14.3.

Making contact
Could you put me through to Mr Li Wang please? – 1
You seem to have got the wrong extension. – 1

Asking for information
Could you give me a few details? – 2

Asking for repetition
I'm sorry, I didn't catch that. – 3
What did you say the reference number was? – 3

Checking information
Fine. Shall I just read that back to you? – 3

Clarifying
I'm sorry, I don't follow you. – 4
Are you saying that ...? – 4

Confirming understanding
Fine – 3 / OK – 1, 2, 3, 4 / Right – 2 (and, as a question, 3)

Confirming action
I'll check it out right away. – 2
I'll call you back as soon as I can. – 2

- Check the answers with the whole class.

(B)

- Tell the Ss that they will now have a chance to use these expressions in role play situations.
- Divide the class into pairs. Some pairs can do role play 1 and others role play 2.
- Allocate the roles and get the Ss to absorb the information. Circulate and assist if necessary.
- When the Ss are ready they can do the role plays. If you have telephone equipment, you can use it. Otherwise, ask Ss in each pair to sit back to back.
- Circulate and monitor. Note language points for praise and correction, especially in relation to the expressions in the Useful language box.
- When Ss have finished, praise good language points from the discussion and work on three or four points that need improvement, getting individual Ss to say the correct forms.
- Ask one or two individual pairs to do a performance of their situation for the whole class.

1 to 1

These role plays can be done 1 to 1. Don't forget to note language points for praise and correction afterwards. Highlight some of the language you chose to use as well.

Case study

Yedo Department Stores

A chain of Japanese department stores is in trouble, in the face of social changes and foreign competition. Ss suggest some solutions.

Stage 1: Background

- Ask the Ss to read the background information about Yedo. Meanwhile, write the points in the first column of the table on the board.
- With the whole class, elicit the information to complete the table.

Activity of company	Department stores: six in Japan, one each in London and New York
Image	Prestigious, high quality
Strategy	Wide range of products, personalised service
Problems	Falling profits, similar situation elsewhere

Stage 2: Market research 14.4

- Divide the class into two groups, A and B.
- Each group will specialise in studying the information in one part of the market report commissioned by Yedo. Members of each group can work collaboratively in pairs or threes, but tell the Ss that one member of each group, chosen later at random, will give an overview of the information for the whole class.
- The two groups can start working separately. Go to each group and give them the specific instructions for that group.
- Ss in Group A work on the Yedo Department Stores fact file, commenting on its contents. Tell them that the person talking about it for the whole class will have to make a coherent presentation including comments, beginning something like this:

> Yedo was founded more than 100 years ago, in 1895. It employs about 3,200 people, mostly full-time, around the world and one of the first impressions that people get when they go into the stores is the number of assistants available to serve customers.
> Opening hours are 10 till 6, with late opening on Fridays till 7, allowing people to do some shopping after they leave work. Many of the stores are situated near main railway stations, which is very convenient for commuters, of whom of course there are large numbers, especially in Tokyo, New York and London.

- Ss in Group B look at Yedo's competition, as detailed in part 3 of the report. The person making the presentation will speak as if they are a member of TWCB, the marketing agency, talking to senior managers at Yedo. The speaker will expand on the notes in the market report, adding comments to back it up, like this:

> We've identified four potential sources of competition for Yedo. First, there are convenience stores. We used to think of these as being rather downmarket, for students and young people, but I'm sure you've all noticed how more and more different types of people are using stores like this. You can get a wide range of goods and services from them. (You can even pay your phone bill there!) What they offer changes very quickly in response to customer demand. And of course, they're open 24 hours a day, which is one of the reasons they're called convenience stores.

- Choose one person at random from each group to come to the front of the class and give their presentation.
- Invite comments and encourage brief discussion after each presentation, but don't pre-empt the issues that will be discussed during the discussion task below.
- Bring the class together to listen to recording 14.4 and ask the Ss to make notes on the five trends outlined by Susan Lam. Have a whole-class discussion on which of these will have the most influence on Yedo Department Stores.

> - The population is ageing, people are living longer and the over 50 segment of the market is getting bigger.
> - Japanese consumers put a high priority on value for money – they are looking for bargains.
> - Consumers traditionally favoured brand-name goods but they are now increasingly buying 'no-brand' goods.
> - Japanese society is changing from a luxury culture to a convenience culture.
> - Women are marrying later in life so the market segment of single women under 30 is increasing.

Stage 3: Discussion task

- Divide the class into groups of five or six. The Ss are TWCB agency personnel. They should concentrate on giving specific answers to the seven key questions posed by Yedo's CEO.
- Appoint a chair for the meeting. This person should control the meeting, using the seven questions as an agenda.
- Appoint one of the participants to be a notetaker who should take coherent and legible notes that can later form the basis for a writing task.
- Circulate and monitor, but do not intervene unless necessary. Note language points for later praise and correction.

- When the meeting(s) end(s), praise good language points from the discussion and work on three or four points that need improvement, getting individual Ss to say the correct forms.
- Discuss the meeting(s) with the whole class, getting each group to explain what happened.

1 to 1

This case study can be done 1 to 1, with the student analysing the information and then discussing recommendations. Don't forget to note language points for praise and correction afterwards. Highlight some of the language you chose to use as well.

Writing

- Ask the Ss to base their writing on the notes taken by the member of their team during the simulated meeting.
- The writing can be done collaboratively in class or as homework.
- If your Ss are doing the writing task for homework, you may want to photocopy the notes made by the notetaker in each group so that each student has a record of what was said and decided in their group.

Writing file pages 144–145

UNIT B Revision

This unit revises and reinforces some of the key language points from Units 8–14, and links with those units are clearly shown. You can point out these links to Ss if you think that would be useful.

This revision unit, like Revision Unit A, concentrates on reading and writing activities. Some of the exercise types are similar to those in the Reading and Writing section of levels 2 and 3 of the Business English Certificate examination organised by the University of Cambridge ESOL Examinations.

For more speaking practice, see the Resource bank section of this book beginning on page 196.

The exercises in this unit can be done in class individually or collaboratively, or for homework.

8 Team building

Negative prefixes

- This exercise revisits the negative prefixes studied in the Vocabulary section in page 69.

1 irresponsible
2 impractical
3 dishonestly
4 disloyal
5 uncommunicative
6 intolerant

Modal perfect

- The modal perfect, from the Language review section on page 72, is practised in this exercise.

Sample answers

1 have
2 replied
3 must
4 should
5 couldn't
6 have gone
7 would have
8 must have been

Writing

- The 'model' answer here is designed only to give an idea of what the Ss should produce, not the actual ideas, which should, of course, be their own.
- Refer the Ss back to the Case study on page 74 for further ideas on how things can go wrong with a sales team and what measures can be taken to remedy the problem.

Model answer

We are all aware that our team has not been working effectively for several months, and as a result several colleagues, the younger ones in particular, are rather demoralised.

My perception of the problem is that we are simply not helping each other. Instead, people compete with each other and are obsessed with meeting their sales targets and outdoing their colleagues.

When things go wrong, nobody will take responsibility for the problem. For example, there were a few complaints from customers earlier this month, and members of the team started arguing and blaming each other for the mistakes that had been made.

There is sometimes the feeling that we are always criticised for what we fail to do, and only occasionally praised for our results. So I think more 'positive reinforcement' might help. It would also help if criticism was not always collective and praise individual.

More importantly, our team's goals need to be clarified, and we all need to understand that we can't meet those goals individually, but that without our individual contribution, the team's goals will not be met.

It seems to me that individual sales targets are overemphasised. If group productivity was emphasised instead, I think we would be better able to understand that we are competing against rival companies, and not against each other.

Finally, we are all working under extreme pressure. I think one or two extra people on the team would take some of that pressure off, which would create a better working atmosphere.

9 Raising finance

Dependent prepositions

- Ask your Ss to look again at the Language review section on page 80 to remind themselves about the use of dependent prepositions.

1 on	**2** for	**3** on (*or* against)	**4** on	**5** for, with	**6** from, in
7 from	**8** to	**9** for	**10** in, for		

Negotiating phrases

- These exercises extend the ideas in the Skills section on page 80.

A
Open questions: 2 and 7
Closed questions: 6
Softening phrases: 3 and 5
Signalling phrases: 1 and 8
Summarising: 4

B
1 b **2** d **3** g **4** a **5** f **6** c **7** h **8** e

10 Customer service

Gerunds and infinitives

- This exercise revises some of the structures in the Language review section on page 88. This exercise can be quite tricky, so spend time explaining it to the Ss before asking them to do it.

1 were successful in
2 didn't expect to have
3 is no point in arguing
4 put off explaining
5 don't mind waiting
6 involve dealing
7 got used to working
8 you mind not interrupting
9 sometimes difficult to get
10 deny fiddling

Writing

◎ These exercises relate to the Case study on page 90.

A

Thank you for your February statement for £1,350, which we have just received. We would like to bring to your attention two accounting errors that have been made.

Firstly, you have charged us for a delivery of A3 photocopying paper, Invoice No. TG/507 for £120. We have checked our records and we are certain that we never ordered or received such paper.

Secondly, Invoice No. TG/573 for £75 has been debited twice.

We have deducted the sum of £195 from your statement and will send you a draft for £1,155 as soon as you confirm this amount.

B

Thank you for your letter of March 4 in which you inform us that two errors totalling £195 were made on our February statement.

We would like to apologise for these errors, which were due to an oversight. Meanwhile, we enclose another statement for February which shows the correct balance of £1,155.

Once again, please accept our apologies for any inconvenience caused.

We look forward to hearing from you again.

11 Crisis management

Linking ideas

◎ Ss look again at the language of contrast and addition, as in the Language review section on page 96.

1 Although they managed the crisis badly, their reputation was not damaged.
Despite/In spite of the fact that they managed the crisis badly, their reputation was not damaged.
They managed the crisis badly. However, their reputation was not damaged.

2 The airline was accused of incompetence although it reacted quickly to the crisis.
Despite reacting quickly to the crisis, the airline was accused of incompetence.
The airline reacted quickly to the crisis. However, it was accused of incompetence.

3 Although the rescue team showed efficiency and compassion, it was criticised by the media.
Despite showing efficiency and compassion, the rescue team was criticised by the media.
The rescue team showed efficiency and compassion. However, it was criticised by the media.

4 The passengers were not angry although the cruise was cancelled after just a few hours.
The cruise was cancelled after just a few hours. However, the passengers were not angry.
Despite/In spite of the fact that the cruise was cancelled after just a few hours, the passengers were not angry.

5 Although every service failure is different, some basic principles can assist in recovery.
Despite/In spite of the fact that every service failure is different, some basic principles can assist in recovery.
Every service failure is different. However, some basic principles can assist in recovery.

Reading

This exercise relates to the article *Keeping your client relationship afloat*, in the Reading section, on page 94.

1 d **2** b **3** d **4** c **5** a **6** a **7** b **8** c **9** a

12 Management styles

Opposites

These activities look again at the negative prefixes in the Vocabulary section on page 101.

A

1 Indeclslve
2 inefficient
3 uninspiring
4 illogical
5 disorganised
6 irrational

B

1 decisiveness
2 efficiency
3 inspiration
4 logic
5 organisation
6 rationality

C

1 irrational
2 uninspiring
3 logical
4 organised
5 indecisive
6 efficient

Text reference

Ss work further on the text reference ideas introduced in the Language review section, page 104.

Alex Magee, Chairman of Logonet, attended a meeting of the non-executive directors to discuss their draft interim results. After *that*, *he* went on to Brentford Business School to deliver a lecture on career management, which has been one of his passions since 2002.
It is in the summer of *that year* that he was asked to design and deliver a course on *that topic* at Mannheim College of International Management. He has been senior honorary visiting fellow at *the college* ever since.
In addition to those *European academic activities*, Brian has also delivered lectures on career management at Harvard.
All those lectures eventually led to 'Human Capital', published last week by Omega Books.

13 Takeovers and mergers

Reading

This exercise looks at the general theme of the unit.

1 a
2 c
3 a
4 b
5 d
6 b
7 c
8 d

Headlines

- Ask Ss to look again at the Language review section on page 112 before doing this activity.

1 deal	2 seek	3 unveil	4 split	5 backing	6 probe

14 The future of business

Vocabulary

- Ss look again at adjectives used to describe the future. Refer them to page 117.

1 bright	2 rosy	3 promising	4 brilliant	5 dire	6 dreadful
7 worrying	8 uncertain				

Telephoning

- Refer the Ss to the Skills section on page 121.

1 f	2 d	3 c	4 h	5 b	6 a	7 e	8 g

Text bank

Teacher's notes

Introduction

The text bank contains articles relating to the units in the *Market Leader Upper Intermediate New Edition* Course Book. These articles extend and develop the themes in those units. You can choose the articles that are of most interest to your students. They can be done in class or as homework. You have permission to make photocopies of these articles for your students.

Before you read

Before each article there is a discussion point, a warmer that allows students to focus on the subject of the article and prepares them for it. This can be done as a whole class discussion, or in pairs or small groups, with each group then reporting its ideas to the whole class.

Reading

If using the articles in class, it's a good idea to treat different sections in different ways, for example reading the first paragraph with the whole class, and then getting students to work in pairs on the following paragraphs.
The first comprehension question for each article is often designed to help Ss get an overview of the whole article. If you're short of time, get different pairs to read different sections of the article simultaneously. You can circulate, monitor and give help where necessary. Ss then report back to the whole group with a succinct summary and/or their answers to the questions for that section.
A full answer key follows the articles.

Discussion

In the Over to you sections following each article, there are discussion points. Again, these can be dealt with by the whole class, or the class can be divided, with different groups discussing different points. During discussion, circulate, monitor and give help where necessary. Ss then report back to the whole class. Praise good language production and work on areas for improvement in the usual way.

Writing

The discussion points can also form the basis for short pieces of written work. Ss will find this easier if they have already discussed the points in class, but you can ask Ss to read the article and write about the discussion points as homework.

UNIT 1 Communication

Communication with employees

Level of difficulty: ●●○

Before you read

In your organisation, what aspects of management do the employees have a right to know about? What aspects of management do the employees have a right to be consulted on?

Do you think it is an advantage for employees to be put in the picture? Why or why not?

Reading

Read the article from the *Financial Times* by Alicia Clegg and do the exercises that follow.

Why it pays to put the workers in the picture

Alicia Clegg

When workplace disputes flare up, the blame is often laid on a breakdown in communication. Talking may not always resolve disagreements, but withholding management plans until the last moment can certainly make a difficult situation worse. From 6th April 2005, UK employees gain the legal right to know about, and be consulted on, matters that affect them at work. This covers anything from the economic health of the business to decisions likely to cause redundancies or changes in how work is organised. The new rules, which implement a European Union directive, move the UK closer to other European states, most of which already require workplace consultation.

There are good reasons for businesses to forge ahead with such agreements voluntarily. First, there is the commonsense belief, backed by academic research, that companies do better when their employees are well informed and have a say in decisions that affect them. Second, by kick-starting negotiations the employer effectively takes charge. The regulations give organisations free reign to agree internally what consulting and informing employees amounts to in practice – what topics will be discussed, how often and by what means. In the UK – in contrast to most other EU states – once a framework for information and consultation has been agreed, there is no requirement to work through elected representatives. If the workforce approved, a business could rely solely on face-to-face and electronic communication.

The mobile operator 3 prefers the personal approach. Whenever possible, it uses video calls and e-mail to put its young workforce in contact with senior managers. At the other end of the spectrum is AstraZeneca, the Anglo-Swedish pharmaceuticals group, which has a history of consulting employees through elected forums and union representatives. Consulting through intermediaries can yield dividends, particularly during a change of ownership or under a redundancy programme. Another point in favour of a mediated approach, says Ross Hutchison, head of internal communications at KPMG, the accountancy firm, is that representatives can be taken into the confidence of management in a way that an entire workforce cannot.

But do the gains from indirect consultation outweigh the attractions of more direct approaches? Not everyone is persuaded that they do. Alison Gill, co-founder of Getfeedback, a talent management consultancy, argues that knowledge exchange and online polling, not elected assemblies, produce better performance. "The goal is to involve people directly and profit from their ideas." In spite of earlier opposition, a growing number of companies believe that putting employees in the picture is good for business. If the remainder do not follow suit, they may now find their workers give them little choice.

From the *Financial Times*

UNIT 1 Communication

1 Look through the whole article again and put these paragraph headings into the correct order.

a) Some advantages of consultation
b) European law encourages consultation
c) Some good reasons for acting now
d) The different approaches

2 Find expressions in paragraph 1 that mean the same as the phrases below.

a) people in a company getting angry because they disagree
b) saying who is responsible for something going wrong
c) not telling anyone about the directors' strategy
d) a law agreed in Brussels to be incorporated into the law of each member state of Europe

3 True or false (paragraph 2)?

a) It is a good idea for businesses to set up these consultation agreements before they are put under any legal pressure to do so.
b) Academic research shows that it is risky for companies to keep their employees informed and give them a say in decisions that affect them.
c) Employers are better able to be in control if they do not even start these negotiations about consultation.
d) Under the new regulations, bosses and employees can agree on the format of the information and consultation process.
e) There is, however, an obligation to use face-to-face and electronic communication.

4 Which of the information and consultation processes below were adopted by 3, AstraZeneca or KPMG? (lines 47–70)

a) sharing secrets with a small group of employees
b) addressing all employees by video
c) working with groups of employee and union representatives
d) sending e-mails to everyone

5 Find words or expressions from lines 71–89 that mean:

a) add up to more than
b) convinced
c) carrying out surveys by email or via the internet
d) do the same thing

Over to you 1

Work in two groups. Group 1 looks for all the arguments in the article in favour of direct information and consultation and group 2 looks for all the arguments in the article in favour of indirect consultation. Please add your own arguments and experience.
Then each group presents their arguments (and experience) to the other group.

Over to you 2

What would you like to know about the management of your company that would help you to do your job better? How would you like to be informed?

UNIT 1 Communication

The communication value of corporate websites

Level of difficulty: ●●●

Before you read

Who looks at company websites? Why do they do this?
What is the value of a website to a company?

Reading

Read this article by David Bowen from the *Financial Times* and do the exercises that follow.

Now, about this web thing

David Bowen

Your corporate website is an investment that is quite likely the biggest element in your communications budget; whose Return on Investment (ROI) you cannot measure; and whose benefits are difficult to describe. And now I would like to explain why you should be spending more on it.

It is easy to say why companies have websites. It is because they grew up for fun (it is fun building a website; you should try). But what purpose does the site serve and why have you just authorised another large cheque to keep it going and growing? Well, if you didn't sign that cheque and the site disappeared, what would happen? In the short term, unless your company actually sells things online, your revenue would not suffer, and your costs would fall; but here are the other effects I predict.

First, your company would see the flow of phone, fax or email enquiries from customers reduce sharply. They use your site, via Google, to find out your details – the most valuable role of any website is as a simple contact point.

Second, you would start getting worrying feedback from Human Resources that the staff were wondering what was going on. About one in ten visitors to your site are likely to be employees. They want to know what is happening in the company, too.

Third, your investor relations team would get irate phone calls from analysts looking for an elusive figure from the 1999 annual report. Analysts are used to finding historical data on company sites, and you don't want to upset them, do you?

Fourth, journalists would be phoning your press office to confirm such details as how the president of your Polish operation spelt his name, or whether you still owned that company in Indonesia. You may also get calls from careers officers in colleges, wondering if your company still existed and demanding extra copies of brochures for students. In due course, you would find the quality of recruits was falling, because people had come to rely on the web to get a feeling for a potential employer.

Disastrous though this may be, it does not explain why you should actually be increasing investment in your website. I said earlier that most websites grew up by mistake. As a result, most large organisations now have web presences that are grossly inefficient, racking up unnecessary 'hosting' costs on dozens or even hundreds of servers. Many large organisations are now looking at these costs, and thinking how much more sensible it would be to bring the sites together. Extra benefits would then tumble forth: further cost savings from sharing words, pictures and interactive tools, and greatly increased quality for the same reason.

But of course this is going to cost money in the short term. So when your corporate affairs director asks you to approve a project with no apparent ROI, please don't laugh in his face. Ask your fellow CEOs instead; I bet they are getting very similar requests.

From the *Financial Times*

UNIT 1 Communication

1 Here are the answers, complete the questions.

a) Why ....?
Because it is almost impossible to measure its return on investment and its benefits are difficult to describe.

b) Why ....?
Because customers use websites to find out company contact details.

c) Why ....?
Because employees also like to be informed about their company.

d) How ....?
They use company sites to find historical data, particularly in the form of annual reports.

e) Who ....?
Journalists, college careers officers and people looking for employment in your company.

f) Which costs ....?
The costs of the inefficiencies in their web presence, often including largely unnecessary hosting costs on many servers.

g) What ....?
They are being asked to invest more money in the corporate website.

2 Before looking at paragraphs 1 and 2 again, match the two halves of the expressions below.

a) authorise	(something) going
b) keep	online
c) measure	a cheque
d) sell	a purpose
e) serve	return on investment

Which one of them means:

1 to offer products and services over the internet?
2 to make sure something continues to operate?
3 to allow a payment to be made by a bank?
4 to do something for a reason?
5 to find out how quickly a project pays back the money you have put in it?

3 Now complete the sentences below with the expressions from Exercise 2, using the correct verb forms.

a) One way to find out how effective a project has been is to .... its ....

b) A manager will normally .... to be paid to a supplier.

c) Companies can often increase their sales by ....

d) Corporate websites .... even if this is sometimes difficult to describe.

e) A website can enable companies to .... their services .... 24 hours a day.

4 Find words or expressions in paragraphs 3, 4, 5 and 6 that mean:

a) important function
b) will probably be
c) in the habit of
d) after a while
e) gain an insight and understanding for

5 True or false (paragraphs 7 and 8)?

a) According to the article, most companies need to spend more money on their web presence in order to save money.

b) The more servers a corporation uses to host its website, the more money they have to pay for this service.

c) Many organisations believe that it would be more sensible to run their site from several different locations.

d) Reducing the number of servers would bring about many additional cost savings.

e) If all the websites of a large organisation operate together, many features can be shared across the whole site.

f) Mr Bowen proposes that it is a bad idea to support investment in the corporate website because there is no apparent ROI.

Over to you 1

What is the ROI of a corporate website in terms of communication value? What information do you expect to see on a company website? What do you think of companies that do not provide this information?

Over to you 2

In your class, draw up a list of communicative functions that you would like to see on all the websites you visit as a prospective customer. Now search the web for the companies that best meet your communicative criteria and present your findings to the rest of your class.

UNIT 2 International marketing

The fate of global brands

Level of difficulty: ●●○

Before you read

Coca-Cola, *McDonald's*, *Marlboro*, *Nike* and *Walt Disney* are examples of global brands. Can you think of some other examples?

The point of global brands is to produce products that dominate markets worldwide. So how successful are global brands in your area? Why are they successful or why are they not?

Reading

Read this article by Richard Tomkins from the *Financial Times* and do the exercises that follow.

Goodbye to the golden age of global brands

Richard Tomkins

In the Harvard Business School professor Theodore Levitt's seminal paper *The Globalisation of Markets*, written in 1983, he argued that, as new media and technology shrank the world, people's tastes would converge, creating a single global market that would be dominated by the world's most successful brands. So, when the Berlin Wall fell and the barriers to world trade came down, it seemed Prof Levitt would be proved right. Global brand owners poured into the newly opened markets and, facing little competition in countries unaccustomed to consumer culture, they thought they would clean up. Then, some awkward commercial realities started to close in.

Once local consumers had tried these new products, they found them far too expensive to buy on a regular basis, even if they liked them. And soon, local producers sprang up offering much better value for money with products of only slightly inferior quality at a vastly lower price. Usually, too, these products were better suited to local tastes and cultural preferences than those being foisted onto consumers by the global corporations. The global brand owners were left spreading their advertising and other fixed costs over tiny market shares and often faced extra costs, such as tariffs.

In many of these countries today, global brand owners command the super-premium end of the market in any given product category, while local brands command the rest. The global brand owners could try to move into the mass market by creating low-price products designed to suit local tastes, but that would throw them into head-on competition with local companies possessing better distribution channels and a far deeper understanding of the market. Increasingly, therefore, they have resorted to buying local brands and the companies that own them. And here, of course, lies the paradox. Whatever is the point of owning a global brand if it does not work in global markets?

Let us be optimistic and suppose the poor countries do become rich. But what do we see happening in rich countries? Ever-proliferating brand choices. There are more soft drink brands than there have been for years, more fast food chains, more packaged goods, more cars. Supermarkets are competing with brand owners by selling own-label products that are as good as the branded version but cost 20–30 per cent less.

Global brands, of course, are not about to disappear. But it must now be clear that Prof Levitt was mistaken in believing the world's tastes would converge on standardised products. Everything we have learned about consumerism over the decades shows that, as people become better off, they want more choices, not fewer. Global brands may be here to stay, but their golden age is over.

From the *Financial Times*

UNIT 2 International marketing

1 True or false?

a) When the Berlin Wall fell and the barriers to world trade came down, Professor Levitt was proved right.
b) Shortly after that time, local producers in countries with newly opened markets began supplying similar products to global brands at a much more attractive price.
c) Currently global brand products sell best as luxury products in many of these countries.
d) In rich countries there are fewer brand choices in supermarkets.
e) The more money consumers have, the more choices they want.

2 Complete the following definitions of expressions from paragraph 1 with the words in the box.

awkward	clean	consumer	converge
little	pour	seminal	

a) A .... academic paper is one that has a powerful influence on the way people think and act.
b) If people's tastes ...., more and more people prefer the same things.
c) When global companies .... into newly opened markets, an enormous number of them enter these markets at the same time.
d) Companies that are facing .... competition have very few competitors in their market.
e) Countries that are unaccustomed to .... culture are not yet familiar with the idea that buying and selling goods and services can be a central part of people's lives.
f) Companies that .... up in a particular market perform well and make big profits.
g) A company that has to face .... commercial realities has to work with business situations that make its life difficult.

3 Why has life been so difficult for global brand owners in these new markets? Which of the reasons listed below are **not mentioned** in paragraph 2?

a) These products did not reflect the local tastes and cultural preferences.
b) Many local consumers may have liked the new products, but they were too expensive for them to buy often.
c) The global brand owners had to pay a lot for local distribution and warehousing facilities.
d) After a while, the global brands were competing with local producers who were supplying similar products far more cheaply.
e) Although the global brand owners still have to pay fixed costs such as advertising, they do not really have enough market share to make this worth it.
f) It is not easy for global brand owners to set up offices locally and employ local sales forces.
g) Global brands also have a disadvantage compared with local products because they have to pay tariffs for importing their goods into these countries.

4 Before looking at paragraph 3 again, put a verb from the box into the following sentences in the correct form.

buy	command	create	design
own	possess	resort	throw

a) In many of these countries today, global brand owners .... the super-premium end of the market in any given product category.
b) The global brand owners could try to move into the mass market by .... low-price products .... to suit local tastes.
c) That would .... global brand owners into head-on competition with local companies .... better distribution channels and a far deeper understanding of the market.
d) Increasingly global brand owners have .... to .... local brands and the companies that own them.
e) Whatever is the point of .... a global brand if it does not work in global markets?

5 Find expressions in paragraphs 4 and 5 that mean:

a) a constantly-growing selection of products from particular manufacturers with particular names
b) products presented in special boxes or wrapping
c) goods that carry the brand of a particular supermarket
d) goods that have a particular, uniform identity and quality level
e) a period of time when something has great popularity

Over to you 1

Can you think of a global brand that has become particularly successful in your area? Why has it done so?
Can you think of a local product that is so successful that it could become a global brand? Why do you think it could do so?

Over to you 2

Choose a successful local product and give a presentation to your class about why it is successful and which countries it could expand into.

UNIT 2 International marketing

Moving your brand image upmarket

Level of difficulty: ●●●

Before you read

What products is Samsung, the South Korean electronics group, famous for? What can Samsung do to sell its products more effectively in Europe? What can Samsung do to appeal to people who buy more expensive products?

Reading

Read this article by Maija Pesola from the *Financial Times* and do the exercises that follow.

Samsung plays to the young generation

Maija Pesola

For hundreds of Europe's most fanatical computer gamers who took part in the first European championships this March there was glory up for grabs in best-selling games such as *Halo 2* and *Fifa Soccer 2005*, and €150,000 (£104,000) in prize money. For Samsung, the South Korean electronics group that sponsored the event, it was a chance to strut its brand in front of Europe's gaming community. It will be hoping that the seven-figure sum it spent on the championships at Hanover's CeBIT computer industry exhibition will help it win over an audience that has been difficult for advertisers and marketers to reach. The games at the Samsung Euro Championships were all displayed on the company's 19-inch liquid crystal display flat panel screens, the mobile phone event of the games was played on Samsung's D500 handsets and the company created a special game for the event called *Babe Rally*. "The games are a platform for us to communicate with the youth sector and early adopters," says Hadrian Baumann, Samsung's general manager for European marketing.

Over the past five or six years, Samsung has fought to move its brand image more upmarket to compete with premium names, such as Sony. As a result, much of its marketing strategy has focused on what it calls the "high-life seeker" segment of the market – people who adopt technology early and are willing to pay a high price for it. Interbrand, the brand consultancy, recently ranked the company as the world's 21st most valuable brand, up from 42nd in 2001.

But pressure has mounted on Samsung to keep up its efforts. The company recently slipped back into third place behind Motorola in mobile handset sales. At the same time, Samsung is suffering from falling prices for its LCD screens, due to a glut in the market. Stimulating demand for the screens among gaming fans could be one way to help ramp up sales.

Although Samsung scores well in overall brand surveys and is strong in Asia, studies indicate that in Europe it struggles to compete with strong local manufacturers, such as Nokia and Philips. Over the past three years, the company's internal research has shown a 25 per cent increase in positive attitudes towards Samsung in the 18 to 29-year-old age group. Positive attitudes among older consumers, however, have grown more slowly.

In order to enhance its hip, youth image, Samsung has also signed a number of partnerships, including one with Quiksilver, the sportswear label, and Xbox, Microsoft's games console for which it makes DVD drives. Being associated with brands such as these, says Mr Baumann, helps to give Samsung credibility in the youth market: "It is clear that young people have a huge impact over their parents and older people when it comes to choosing technology. We are using younger people as spokespeople for our products."

From the *Financial Times*

UNIT 2 International marketing

1 Replace the words *in italics* in the sentences below with the expressions from the article in the box.

early adopters enhance its hip, youth glory was up for grabs keep up its efforts move its brand image more upmarket seven-figure sum win over an audience

a) In the first European championships this March, *participants could win the admiration of many people* in best-selling games such as 'Halo 2' and 'Fifa Soccer 2005', and €150,000 in prize money.
b) It will be hoping that the *more than €999,999.00* it spent on the championships at Hanover's CeBIT computer industry exhibition will help it *get a section of the public on their side* that has been difficult for advertisers and marketers to reach.
c) The games are a platform for us to communicate with the youth sector and *people who quickly like to use new technology*.
d) Over the past five or six years, Samsung has fought to *make its brand appeal to people who buy more expensive products*.
e) But pressure has mounted on Samsung to *continue to work very hard*.
f) In order to *improve its fashionable, young* image, Samsung has also signed a number of partnership contracts with other famous brands.

2 Look through the whole article and answer these questions.

a) Which different items was Samsung promoting at their Samsung Euro Championships event at the CeBIT exhibition in Hanover?
b) What is Samsung trying to do with its brand and is it successful?
c) What are the problems Samsung is having?
d) Which part of the market is it most difficult for Samsung to penetrate?
e) So how does that affect Samsung's overall strategy?

3 Find words or expressions in paragraph 1 that mean:

a) participated
b) paid for in exchange for advertising and public attention
c) to present in a confident way
d) to make contact with
e) part of the market

4 True or false (paragraph 2)?

a) Samsung wants to compete in the same market as Sony.
b) 'High-life seekers' want to be the first to buy products with state-of-the-art technology.
c) A 'valuable brand' is one that is well-known and respected for the quality of its products.

5 Which words in paragraph 3 tell us that:

a) not long ago, Samsung had sold more phones than Motorola?
b) there are currently too many LCD screens on sale?
c) it may be a good idea to generate a demand for LCD screens among people who enjoy playing computer games?

6 True or false (paragraph 4)?

a) The Samsung brand is currently more successful in Europe than in Asia.
b) Nokia and Philips are not competing effectively with Samsung in Europe.
c) Samsung has hired the services of a European research institute to find out how people feel about their products.

7 Before looking at paragraph 5 again, complete the sentences below with a correct form of one of the verbs in the box.

associate	come	give	make	sign

a) Samsung has .... a number of partnership agreements.
b) Samsung .... DVD drives for the Microsoft Xbox.
c) Samsung is .... with brands such as Xbox and Quiksilver.
d) Being thought of together with these brands .... Samsung credibility.
e) Young people have a huge impact over their parents when it .... to choosing technology.

Over to you

Think of five international brands that are successful in your country. Why is this?
Now think of five more local brands. What could they do to expand into other markets?
In groups or pairs, choose a local brand and prepare a presentation of what they could do to expand into an English-speaking market (maybe into your teacher's country or a business associate's country).

Text bank

UNIT 3 Building relationships

Partnering among consultancies

Level of difficulty: ●●●

Before you read

If a company has a difficult project to manage, is it best served by a single global consultancy or a consortium of specialist consultancies? Why?

Reading

Read the following article by Stefan Stern from the *Financial Times* and do the exercises that follow.

Teams seek strength in affiliations

By Stefan Stern

The global consultancies share some characteristics of the largest branches of Tesco. Vast out-of-town supermarkets may offer everything you need to keep the home well stocked, but do they really give you the quality that could be yours by spending a couple of hours in boutiques, delicatessens and food halls? Perhaps the one-stop shop can meet all your basic and immediate needs. But some management challenges require a pooling of expertise and talent from a team of consultancies working together.

"On paper the biggest firms have all the capabilities you might want," says Andrew Crowley, vice-president of consulting and systems integration for CSC, the international information technology consultancy. "But there is a risk element to that. A consortium gives you a slightly different view on life, and probably better value as well." That view is echoed by Bernard Brown, senior vice-president for consulting in the UK, Americas and Asia-Pacific for Atos Origin, the IT consultancy. "You won't necessarily have all the skills to meet the 'end-to-end' requirements of a large client," he says. "But we have to partner. It is an essential part of our work."

For Mr Brown, there are several core elements to a successful collaboration. "First, what are the rules of engagement?" he asks. "How will we work together, how will we measure progress? Then we look for seamless teamwork – can we keep the same team throughout a project lasting between six and 18 months? Then there is personal integrity: do our strategies and approaches fit? Personal relationships matter enormously too. Business hasn't changed that much, in spite of all the new ways of communicating. Then there is the commitment of all involved, and the question of cultural fit and values: if your values are not shared at the outset you will find out later to your cost. Finally, there is the question of joint marketing: how do we protect each other's brand?"

Mr Crowley does not underestimate the difficulty of making consortia work for both client and consultant. "You need explicit work-share agreements up front," he says. "Otherwise you will find yourself arguing over what percentage of the work goes to one partner or another. You need that commercial relationship in place, with agreed milestones for the project. Partnerships are dynamic. They evolve, and like a marriage there will be ups and downs. The interpersonal relationships are vital, and greed will destroy it. You need the same ethics, the same values, so you can combine your skills and not fight over revenues."

Last year Atos Origin replaced IBM as the International Olympic Committee's IT partner for the next three Olympic games. In Athens last summer Atos was managing more than 2,300 different suppliers, often without written contracts in place. "Without our experience of partnering, we would never have been able to pull that off," Mr Brown says.

From the *Financial Times*

UNIT 3 Building relationships

1 Match the following expressions from the article with their correct definitions.

a) A *one-stop shop* is ...
b) A *pooling of expertise* is ...
c) The *end-to-end requirements* of a large client are ...
d) In this article, to *partner* means ...
e) The *rules of engagement* are ...
f) If you have *personal integrity* ...
g) Clearly-stated agreements *up front* ...
h) To *pull* something *off* ...

1 ... to work in close cooperation with other companies.
2 ... the combination and cooperation of people with different knowledge and experience.
3 ... the principles under which a team of people working together from different companies agree to operate.
4 ... are those made before the team starts working together.
5 ... every detail of carrying out a project from its beginning to its final operation.
6 ... is to manage it successfully.
7 ... a store where you can buy everything you need for a particular purpose, or a company that can plan, implement and manage every aspect of a particular project for another company.
8 ... you do what you say you are going to do according to a particular set of beliefs and principles.

2 Choose the best heading for each paragraph of the article.

a) The value of experience
b) Why consultancies need to partner
c) Some issues that need to be handled
d) Global consultancies as one-stop shops?
e) The essential ingredients of a successful collaboration

3 Before looking at paragraph 1 again, complete the expressions below with the correct preposition.

a) Global consultancies share some of the characteristics .... the largest branches of Tesco.
b) Big supermarkets offer everything you need .... keep the home well stocked.
c) But do they give you the quality that could be yours .... spending a couple of hours in boutiques, delicatessens and food halls?
d) Some management challenges require talent .... a team of consultancies working together.

4 Find words and expressions in paragraph 2 that mean the following:

a) experience and expertise
b) a factor that could cause harm or damage
c) broadly agreed with
d) fundamental

5 In paragraphs 3 and 4, which of the following are *core elements of a successful collaboration* i) according to Bernard Brown? ii) according to Andrew Crowley?

a) rules for how the cooperation will function
b) systems for assessing its effectiveness
c) maintaining the same team throughout the project
d) acting in accordance with a set of principles and beliefs that are adopted by each member of the consortium
e) everyone getting on well together on a personal level
f) each member of the consortium feeling equally dedicated to the project
g) making sure that the values and assumptions of each member of the consortium are shared by the whole consortium right from the very beginning – even though it is made up of people with different national, professional and company cultures
h) making a distinction between the way each member of the consortium is perceived by the market
i) clear agreements right from the very beginning about who is going to do what – and what proportion of the project as a whole each task represents

6 Before looking at paragraph 5 again, put the correct verb into the following phrases in its correct form.

a) Last year Atos Origin .... IBM as the International Olympic Committee's IT partner.
b) In Athens last year Atos was .... more than 2,300 different suppliers.
c) Without our experience of partnering we would never have .... to pull that off.

Over to you 1

Has your company, or a company you know, had any experience with working on a project in a consortium with other companies? How did it work? Why do you think it worked that way?

Over to you 2

Working in small groups, decide on a project you can do together and draft a set of 'rules of engagement for successful cooperation' for your project.

Text bank

UNIT 3 Building relationships

Blogging as a relationship tool

Level of difficulty: ●●○

Before you read

What do you know about blogs or web logs? Are they a good way for corporations to build relationships with their employees or customers? How do you think this might work?

Reading

Read this article by Scott Morrison from the *Financial Times* and do the exercises that follow.

The rise of the corporate blogger

By Scott Morrison

Bob Lutz, the vice chairman of General Motors, does it. So does Jonathan Schwartz, chief operating officer of computer maker Sun Microsystems. A handful of executives at Hewlett-Packard and Boeing are also getting in on the act.

Welcome to the blogosphere – home to those informal, frequently updated online journals that people create to share their thoughts and opinions. Web logs, or blogs, have for the most part remained the domain of millions of independent bloggers who want to talk politics, trade tech ideas, share their daily lives – or criticise corporations. Now those same corporations are trying to figure out how they can take advantage of this new medium to attract attention, cultivate customer relationships, respond to criticism – and perhaps sell a few more computers, cars or aircraft along the way.

One way for a company to enter the blogosphere is to establish a system on the corporate intranet, where web logs can be used as an internal communications tool. IBM, for example, says thousands of its employees blog on the company's internal network, where they trade idle gossip and discuss corporate business strategy.

Much more visible are web logs targeting customers and the general public, such as GM's FastLane and Boeing's blog written by Randy Baseler, the group's vice-president for commercial aircraft marketing.

There are a few key rules that a successful corporate blogger must follow: they must write in a chatty informal tone, tell the truth, update their blogs on a regular basis and be willing to accept any criticism. The blogosphere is regarded as a source of unpredictable and often irreverent commentary and any dry, dull blog that smacks of corporate PR and legalese will quickly draw criticism from readers.

Blogging can pose legal risks however – so there are often company guidelines stipulating what can and cannot be posted on a corporate blog. Yahoo, for example, says that employees are not allowed to mention anything that has not been made public and bloggers are also asked to notify the corporate PR department if they receive queries from journalists.

Given the potential damage that a disgruntled or careless employee could cause, why would a company allow its workers to spout off in cyberspace? With so much downside, what is the upside?

Well, blogging is transforming the way companies communicate and, for a customer, direct contact with an employee is so much more preferable than dealing with a huge faceless corporation. Robert Scoble, a Microsoft marketing executive specifically hired to blog about the company, has emerged as one of the blogosphere's most popular citizens because he pulls no punches when it comes to his employer. He argues that Microsoft's tolerance of employee blogs has helped shift perceptions of the software giant from strongly negative to surprisingly positive. And if blogging can help Microsoft soften its image, imagine what it could do for any other company.

From the *Financial Times*

UNIT 3 Building relationships

1 At the time of printing, the following words were relatively new.

a blog	blogs	blog	blogger
the blogosphere		blogging	

Can you guess the meaning of each word from the context? Which of them means:

a) an informal, frequently updated online journal where people can share their thoughts and opinions?
b) the activity of writing such an online journal?
c) the world of online journals?
d) a person who writes such an online journal?
e) more than one online journal?
f) write or manage an online journal?

2 Answer these questions.

a) What do Bob Lutz, Jonathan Schwartz and a handful of executives at Hewlett-Packard and Boeing all do?
b) Why are several large corporations trying to take advantage of this medium?
c) What do many IBM employees do on the company's internal network?
d) Why are web logs that target customers and the general public much more visible?
e) What happens to blogs that 'smack of corporate PR and legalese'?
f) How does Yahoo avoid any legal risks from its blogging activities?
g) Why is Robert Scoble one of the blogosphere's most popular citizens?

3 In paragraphs 1 and 2 find words or expressions that mean:

a) becoming involved in an activity with the purpose of gaining an advantage
b) area of activity and knowledge
c) exchange
d) develop
e) at the same time

4 Before looking at paragraphs 3 and 4 again, complete the following sentences with a correct form of the verbs in the box.

blog	discuss	enter	establish
target	trade	write	

a) One way for a company to .... the blogosphere is to .... a system on the corporate intranet.
b) IBM, for example, says thousands of its employees .... on the company's internal network.
c) This is where they .... idle gossip and .... corporate business strategy.
d) Much more visible are web logs .... customers and the general public.
e) Examples of these are GM's FastLane and Boeing's blog .... by Randy Baseler, the group's vice-president for commercial aircraft marketing.

5 Which of the following statements express the 'key rules that a successful corporate blogger must follow' according to paragraph 5 in the article?

The writer should:

a) be strong enough for people to write bad things and good things about them.
b) be honest.
c) express themselves carefully and along the same lines as their company press department.
d) have a friendly, talkative manner.
e) never write unfavourable comments on their own company.
f) use the same formal language as lawyers do.
g) frequently add things to their blog.

6 Before looking at paragraphs 6 and 7, match the two halves of the expressions below.

a) pose	public
b) post	off
c) make	the PR department
d) notify	on a blog
e) receive	damage
f) cause	queries
g) spout	risks

Which one of them means:

1 make something happen that has a negative effect on something?
2 tell everybody (usually through the media)?
3 inform the company press office?
4 speak freely without thinking?
5 get requests for information?
6 display in an online journal?
7 present possible dangers?

7 True or false (paragraph 8)?

a) Customers prefer to deal directly with an employee who works for a very large, powerful organisation rather than writing to or telephoning the organisation itself.
b) Robert Scoble was employed by Microsoft to say good things about his company on the internet.
c) He believes that Microsoft should be more tolerant about its employees' blogs.
d) Mr Scoble is happy with the way that blogging has changed the way people think about his company.

Over to you

Does the public need to think differently about your company, or a company that you know? Why? Why not?
How could blogging help the image of your company? How could it create a better relationship between the management and the employees? How could it create a better relationship between the company and its customers?

Text bank

UNIT 4 Success

A company strategy for a successful product

Level of difficulty: ●●●

Before you read

What products can you think of that have become truly successful over the past five years? What do you think their manufacturers did to make these products so successful?

Reading

Read this article by Bernard Simon from the *Financial Times* and do the exercises that follow.

Message machine creates a buzz

By Bernard Simon

Like Google in search engines and Hoover in vacuum cleaners, Research In Motion (RIM) has achieved the distinction of having its product turned into a verb. Almost 3m people around the world now "BlackBerry" their friends and colleagues with messages using the Canadian company's distinctive hand-held device.

The BlackBerry has transformed RIM over the past six years from an obscure supplier of two-way pagers into the maker of one of the world's hottest products. RIM reported earlier this week that it had signed up 470,000 new subscribers in the quarter to February 29; it expects to add more than 500,000 more over the next three months. RIM shares have rocketed from less than $10 in autumn 2002 to $73 this week. The company now has a market value of $14bn, (£7.5bn), overtaking Nortel Networks as Canada's technology superstar. Not surprisingly, RIM's success is attracting attention from some of the giants of the communications and software industries, and observers are wondering how long the company can sustain its phenomenal record.

The BlackBerry – whose name comes from the supposed resemblance of the miniature keyboard on its original device to the beads of the fruit – "remains the pre-eminent mobile messaging solution in the market today," says Jason Tsai, analyst at ThinkEquity Partners, an investment bank.

RIM has so far kept the competition at bay with a canny, three-pronged strategy: expanding its target market, co-opting potential rivals as partners and customers and constantly adding fresh features to the BlackBerry device and its supporting software. The BlackBerry began life as a gadget for Wall Street investment bankers, Washington politicians and corporate executives. More recently, RIM has turned its attention to the professional consumer retail market, which now makes up about one-fifth of its subscriber base.

RIM has vastly broadened its market by licensing almost 100 distributors, including Vodafone, Verizon Wireless, Cingular Wireless and T-Mobile. RIM expects to sign up China Mobile Communications later this year. To make the devices more affordable, many carriers offer BlackBerry contracts similar to those for mobile phones. According to Mr Tsai, "the carriers love BlackBerry not only for the higher average revenue per unit it generates, but for the strong margins, since it consumes very little bandwidth."

Unlike some other companies, RIM has not jealously guarded its technology, seeking out alliances with friend and potential foe alike, including Microsoft. "If you partner well and thoughtfully, you get pulled along by the current," says Jim Balsillie, RIM's joint chief executive.

The question is whether RIM's success will ultimately jeopardise its independence. Mr Balsillie and RIM's founders Mike Lazaridis and Doug Fregin own only about 16 per cent of the company stock in total. Brant Thompson, analyst at Goldman Sachs, singles out Nokia and Motorola as possible predators. Alex Slawsby, an analyst at International Data Corporation, the research group, says that "there are many different companies with designs on being an alternative to RIM". In his view, the BlackBerry's biggest advantage is an intangible one. For the time being, he says, none of its rivals possesses "that buzz-creating element that the public loves".

From the *Financial Times*

UNIT 4 Success

1 Put the two halves of these sentences together so that they have the same sense as the article.

a) If the name of your product gets turned into a verb ...
b) If more customers subscribe to the BlackBerry messaging service ...
c) You could have been one of the first BlackBerry customers ...
d) If you sign a contract with Vodaphone or T-Mobile ...
e) If you make alliances carefully ...
f) The RIM management may lose its independence ...

1 ... RIM will earn more money.
2 ... it is a sign that it is successful.
3 ... you may be able to get a BlackBerry device.
4 ... if Nokia or Motorola buy large quantities of the company shares.
5 ... your company benefits from the success of the other companies you do business with.
6 ... if you were a Washington politician, a Wall Street banker or an American corporate executive.

2 Find words or expressions in paragraphs 1 and 2 that mean:

a) easy to recognise
b) not very well known
c) small radio devices that tell the wearer that they have received a message
d) people who pay for a service over a period of time
e) increased dramatically
f) continue to keep up

3 True or false (paragraphs 3 and 4)?

a) According to Jason Tsai, the BlackBerry mobile messaging solution is better than anyone else's in today's market.
b) RIM has been using three different approaches to prevent its competitors from entering its market.
c) RIM has been co-opting potential rivals to develop the supporting software for its device.
d) RIM has been expanding its target market to include the needs of the professional consumer.

4 Answer these questions according to the information in paragraphs 5 and 6.

a) How else has RIM broadened its market?
b) Why is BlackBerry so attractive to mobile phone network carriers?
c) How is the RIM approach different from that of other companies?

5 Before looking at paragraph 7 again, put the correct verbs into the following sentences.

a) The question is whether RIM's success will ultimately .... its independence.
b) Brant Thompson .... out Nokia and Motorola as possible predators.
c) There are many different companies with designs on .... an alternative to RIM.
d) For the time being, none of the BlackBerry's rivals .... 'that buzz-creating element that the public loves'.

Over to you

The RIM three-pronged strategy for holding back its competition consisted of:
– expanding its target market;
– co-opting potential rivals as partners and customers;
– constantly adding fresh features to its product.
How well would these strategies work in your own company (or in a company that you know well)? Which ones would work straight away? Which ones would have to be changed? What changes would you have to make?

Text bank

UNIT 4 Success

A record year for a supermarket chain

Level of difficulty: ●●●

Before you read

It is now the end of another successful year for Tesco, the British supermarket chain.
Why do you think its sales staff are happy? Why do you think its shareholders are happy? Why is Tesco an attractive business for potential investors?

Reading

Read this article about Tesco, written by Lucy Killgren in the *Financial Times*, and do the exercises that follow.

Tesco breaches £2bn profit mark for first time

Tesco yet again confirmed its dominance in the UK retail sector, shrugging off fears of a spending slowdown and reporting underlying annual profits breaching £2bn ($3.78bn). The UK's biggest supermarket, which has a 29.5 per cent share of the domestic grocery market, said it would accelerate expansion, with plans to open 207 new stores in the current year, compared with 98 openings last year. Well over half of these will be in Asia.

The retailer's performance flies in the face of fears in the retail sector that consumers are reining in sales. Like-for-like sales in the final seven weeks of the financial year grew 9.3 per cent in the UK, with UK clothing sales growing by 28 per cent overall. Tesco said: "The broader picture is unclear, but as far as Tesco is concerned, consumers are still spending."

Underlying annual profit before gains on disposals, integration costs and goodwill amortisation rose 18.8 per cent to £2.02bn. Pre-tax profits rose 22.6 per cent to £1.96bn, on sales which rose 10.5 per cent to £37.07bn for the 52 weeks to February 26. Sales in the core UK business, which accounts for 80 per cent of total sales, were up 9 per cent on a like-for-like basis. Overall sales grew by 11.9 per cent to £29.5bn over the same period. Tesco.com sales grew 24.1 per cent to £719m, with profit increasing by 51.8 per cent to £36m. During the second half of the financial year, like-for-like sales increased 9.5 per cent including petrol and by 7.4 per cent excluding petrol.

Terry Leahy, chief executive, said: "These results demonstrate the broad appeal of the Tesco brand. They show that our new growth businesses in international, in non-food and in services, have contributed as much profit as the entire business was making in 1997."

International sales grew 13.1 per cent to £7.6bn. Like-for-like sales grew 5.5 per cent in the first quarter of 2005. International sales contributed £370m to underlying operating profit, up 20.9 per cent on last year. In non-food, which includes clothing and home entertainment, sales grew by nearly 18 per cent to £6bn. Personal finance reported a profit of £202m, with Tesco's share reaching £101m, up 26.5 per cent. The telecoms arm, which Tesco said was still in its start-up phase and which has been operating one year, made an operating loss of £4m.

Tesco said that the adoption of International Financial Reporting Standards (IFRS) was expected to have a small adverse impact on statutory declared profit after tax of up to £30m for 2004/5 and no impact on group pre-tax cash flow. Tesco said it intended to issue 2004/5 financial information, restated for IFRS, towards the end of next month. Operating profit increased 12.3 per cent to £1.94bn. Earnings per share were up 17.7 per cent at 17.73p. The board has proposed a final dividend of 5.27p a share, an increase of 10.5 per cent, bringing the full year dividend to 7.56p, up 10.5 per cent.

From the *Financial Times*

UNIT 4 Success

1 Match the financial terms a–e with their definitions 1–5.

a) goodwill
b) gross profit
c) annual profit
d) underlying annual profit
e) operating profit

1 The profit that a company makes each year
2 Profit after deducting operating costs from gross profit
3 The price a buyer pays for successful aspects of a business such as a large number of customers, loyal staff or a good reputation
4 Profit calculated to exclude confusing factors such as one-off investments, income from disposals, integration costs and goodwill
5 The difference between the money a company earns and the cost of making a product or providing a service, before overheads, salaries and wages, and interest payments are deducted

2 Complete the sentences below with the words and expressions in the box.

disposals goodwill amortisation integration costs like-for-like sales operating loss

a) .... are the costs of merging two businesses.
b) Any losses after deducting operating costs from gross profit are the ....
c) The cost of a goodwill payment spread over several years is called ....
d) .... are the selling off of assets such as shops, buildings or equipment.
e) Sales figures that compare the business last year with the same business this year, excluding income from new business, are ....

3 Match the two halves of these expressions from paragraphs 1 and 2.

a) to confirm	in the face of (something)
b) to shrug off	(your) dominance
c) to report	expansion
d) to accelerate	annual profits
e) to fly	fears
f) to rein in	sales

Which one of them means:

1 to publicly declare income figures?
2 to actively reduce the amount of buying?
3 to show once more that you are the market leader?
4 not pay attention to worries about possible danger?
5 to do something different to what people expect?
6 to speed up investment in increasing business operations?

4 Before looking at paragraph 3 again, put the correct prepositions into these phrases.

a) Underlying annual profit before gains .... disposals, integration costs and goodwill amortisation rose 18.8 per cent .... £2.02bn.
b) Sales .... the core UK business, which accounts .... 80 per cent of total sales, were up 9 per cent .... a like-for-like basis.
c) Overall sales grew .... 11.9 per cent to £29.5bn .... the same period.

5 Complete the two-word expressions from paragraphs 4 and 5 in the sentences below.

a) A brand that has *broad* .... is one that is attractive to many people.
b) A company's *growth* .... make more profit every year.
c) The *international* .... of a British company come from its retail business outside the UK.
d) Sales of televisions, DVD players, CDs, DVDs and computer games generate income in a *home* .... business.
e) Loans, mortgages (loans for buying a house or flat) and other banking services are part of the Tesco *personal* .... programme.
f) The *telecoms* .... of a business could deal with the sales of mobile phones and the provision of a mobile network service.
g) The *start-up* .... of a business is the period when its profits may not cover the capital investments.

6 Find words or expressions from paragraph 6 that mean:

a) choosing to follow a course of action
b) a negative effect
c) the income and payments of a company in a given period of time
d) publish and distribute
e) the last bonus payment in a financial year paid to shareholders

Over to you

Look at the annual report of your own company or a company you know.

- **What are the underlying annual profits (or losses)?**
- **How is the company expanding (or consolidating) its business?**
- **Has the company gained any money on disposals?**
- **Has the company spent any money on integration costs and goodwill amortisation? Which other companies were involved?**
- **Does the company have any growth businesses?**
- **Is the company making any operating losses? Why?**
- **Is the company adopting IFRS or any other new reporting standards? What impact is this having on the company's figures?**

Now give a presentation of this information to the rest of your class.

Text bank

UNIT 5 Job satisfaction

Managing flexible working practices

Level of difficulty: ●●○

Before you read

Why do companies adopt flexible working practices? Who benefits the most from these – the company or the employees? Why?

Reading

Read the article below by Philip Manchester from the *Financial Times* and do the exercises that follow.

More about results than time

Philip Manchester

On the surface, flexible working might seem to be about people being able to choose their working hours and, perhaps, spend some time working away from the office. But it is also a fundamental change in the way people work – and, more importantly, the way they are managed. Flexible working is a shift from "time-based" to "results-based" working practices and could herald the biggest change in the workplace since the start of the industrial revolution.

New employee legislation is one of the main motivations for employers to introduce flexible working practices – but not the only one. In Europe, for example, employers are obliged to offer parents with young or disabled children the right to request flexible working. While legislation is a major catalyst to introducing flexible working, there are other reasons. In the US, for example, the fall in the price of mass market computer and communications technologies is encouraging organisations to allow more home working.

Flexible working is also likely to appeal to a wider skill pool and help with staff retention. Mary Sue Rogers, human capital management leader at IBM Global Services, says that IBM has embraced flexible working to help with recruitment. "In Europe, companies have to provide flexible working because of legislation – but it is also a way to recruit from a broader skill pool, including women and older people. With an ageing workforce we have to find ways to retain older staff. It also gives greater scope to male employees who increasingly want flexible working to create a better work/life balance. A recent survey of UK graduates found that work/life balance was third on their list of career priorities." She adds that 55 per cent of IBM's employees work flexibly and 90 per cent are "enabled" to do so. "To us, it is foremost a business imperative. It is about staff retention, increased productivity and cost reduction," she notes.

A survey of 300 UK human resource professionals in small to medium-sized enterprises (SMEs), commissioned by Arizona-based telecommunications company Inter-Tel, found that 40 per cent found it difficult to attract the right skills from their local market and 30 per cent thought they could attract staff if they were offered flexible working. But they also had significant reservations – with 93 per cent concerned that staff were more likely to bend the rules if they work from home. Doug Neal, research fellow at the US Computer Sciences Corporation, identifies this attitude as being at the heart of the cultural shift prompted by flexible working: "The problem is not all with the worker – it is also with the boss. Management has to find a way to measure 'results' rather than time. We have to find new ways to evaluate workers – and their bosses."

He adds that organisations must find ways to build trust between employer and employee: "How do I evaluate people when I can't see them? In formal terms, trust is the outcome of a series of beneficial transactions. You have to build a culture of trust from working together."

Although new legislation is forcing organisations to adopt flexible working practices, there are sound business reasons to give employees more flexibility. Organisations which have embraced flexible working have found that it can cut costs and improve productivity. More importantly, it enables them to recruit staff from a much broader skill pool and retain staff. But it does mean a fundamental change in the relationship between staff and management. Both must learn to trust each other and focus on results rather than time spent in the office.

From the *Financial Times*

UNIT 5 Job satisfaction

1 Look through the whole article and answer these questions.

a) What are the main motivations for employers to introduce flexible working practices?
b) What kind of employees are attracted to companies that embrace flexible working?
c) What changes are necessary for flexible working to be effective?

2 Find words or expressions in paragraphs 1 and 2 that mean the following:

a) when you first look at it
b) an important alteration
c) a change in approach
d) announce
e) the law
f) ask for
g) an important factor in

3 True or false (paragraph 3)?

a) IBM introduced flexible working practices in order to attract a broader range of staff with different abilities.
b) It is difficult for older people to work flexibly.
c) It is important for many people who have a university degree that they have enough time for themselves outside work.
d) At IBM, flexible working is good for business.

4 Before looking at paragraph 4 again, put a correct form of the verbs in the box into the sentences below.

evaluate	measure	attract	prompt
find	bend	commission	

a) A survey was .... by the Inter-Tel telecommunications company.
b) The survey .... that 40 per cent found it difficult to attract the right skills.
c) 30 per cent thought they could .... staff if they offered flexible working.
d) But 93 per cent thought that staff would .... the rules if they work from home.
e) This is at the heart of the cultural shift .... by flexible working.
f) Management has to find a way to .... 'results' rather than time.
g) We have to find new ways to .... workers – and their bosses.

5 Write down the three questions from the survey commissioned by Inter-Tel referred to in paragraph 4.

6 Choose the best definitions for these expressions from paragraphs 5 and 6.

a) in formal terms
i) for polite deals
ii) correctly expressed
iii) on official documents

b) beneficial transactions
i) productive communicative activities
ii) financial arrangements
iii) secret talks

c) sound business reasons
i) viable, but unacceptable excuses
ii) words that are good to hear
iii) good, solid commercial arguments

Over to you 1

Design a questionnaire about flexible working practices for the Human Resources Department of a company that you know. What ten questions would you like to include in it?

Over to you 2

How far have the companies in your country embraced flexible working practices? Why is this? Is the situation likely to change in the future?

UNIT 5 Job satisfaction

Satisfying employees and customers

Level of difficulty: ●●○

Before you read

What can companies do to have satisfied employees? What can companies do to have satisfied customers? Is there a link between satisfied staff and satisfied customers?

Reading

Read this article by Michael Skapinker from the *Financial Times* and do the exercises that follow.

How to engage your employees

Michael Skapinker

Ade Sodeinde, a 17-year-old Nigerian, became famous last week for making some of Britain's trains run on time. Ms Sodeinde, in her year working for Central Trains before going to university, solved the puzzle of why trains leaving the depot ran late. She found that the tracks in the depot needed upgrading and were slowing the trains' journeys to their starting platforms. Drivers and conductors also had to wait before boarding because of the time taken for safety inspections and cleaning. By refurbishing the tracks and reorganising inspection and cleaning, Central was able to eliminate the problem, potentially saving itself £750,000 ($1.37m) a year in fines for late running – and vastly reducing passenger frustration and delay.

Ms Sodeinde will no doubt be in great demand when she graduates. But just how large, established companies persuade employees to put in that extra effort is one of management's great puzzles. Staff know where the problems and opportunities lie and there will always be employees with ideas for new products or better service. All it requires is for them to speak up and for someone to listen.

Most companies say they listen to their people – but as managers are often unhappy to have their current strategies disrupted and new ideas get trapped in corporate bureaucracy, would-be innovators become jaded, and cynical.

Yet there is a link between engaged employees, satisfied customers and corporate profitability, according to a recent study by the Forum for People Performance Management & Measurement at Northwestern University. The Forum studied 100 US companies to find out how engaged their staff were and whether this had any effect on corporate profitability. The Northwestern researchers wanted to look at employees, such as Ms Sodeinde, who did not deal directly with customers. What impact did their attitudes have on the company's success? Well, the results were clear. The companies with the happiest and most engaged employees had the most satisfied, highest-spending customers.

So how do you make employees more engaged and content? Roger Martin, dean of the Rotman School of Management at the University of Toronto, argues that people are happiest not only when they are respected members of a team they admire but when the team and the company are respected by the world outside.

Being part of a trusted, honest group is an indispensable component of employee happiness and engagement. So is establishing ties with colleagues you respect. When groups appear to be performing, companies should hesitate before disrupting them. The vogue for forming new teams for each task may work in companies small enough for everyone to know each other. When people constantly have to establish new links of trust, customers will probably suffer. Companies should think hard, too, before they outsource the work of a functioning team. The company you outsource to may be a happy, engaged bunch, but I would not count on it.

From the *Financial Times*

UNIT 5 Job satisfaction

1 Look through the whole article and answer these questions.

a) What were the problems with the trains leaving the depot?
b) Why is it important for companies to persuade staff to put in that extra effort?
c) What are the problems for people with good ideas?
d) What was special about the Northwestern University research?
e) Who needs to respect whom, for employees to be happiest?
f) What is the danger of large companies forming new teams for each task?

2 Before looking at paragraph 1 again, put the correct verbs into the sentences below.

a) Ade Sodeinde .... famous last week for making some of Britain's trains .... on time.
b) Ms Sodeinde solved the puzzle of why trains .... the depot ran late.
c) Central was able to .... the problem by refurbishing the tracks and reorganising inspection and cleaning.
d) Central is potentially .... itself £750,000 a year in fines for late running – and vastly .... passenger frustration and delay.

3 Before looking at paragraphs 2 and 3 again, put the expressions in the box into the sentences below.

trapped in corporate bureaucracy where the problems lie in great demand that extra effort their current strategy disrupted

a) Many people want to employ a person who is ....
b) Many managers would love to know how to make their staff put in ....
c) People who are familiar with an area of work know ....
d) When managers have ...., they let someone else change the way they do things.
e) Innovative ideas that get .... are only realised very slowly, if at all.

4 Find words or expressions in paragraph 4 and 5 that mean:

a) people who are committed to their work and their company
b) the earning power of a whole company or group
c) influence (two possible answers here)
d) opinions and feelings
e) happy and satisfied
f) respect and approve of

5 True or false (paragraphs 4 and 5)?

a) The Forum for People Performance Management & Measurement at Northwestern University wanted to find out whether the degree of staff commitment in a company has an influence on their profitability.
b) They only interviewed employees who dealt directly with customers.
c) They found that customers were more satisfied and spent more money with companies who had the most committed staff.
d) According to Roger Martin, the happiest employees are part of a team that respects and admires its customers and the world outside.

6 Match the two halves of the following sentences to summarise paragraph 6. One of the first halves of the sentences a) to e) can be used twice.

a) If companies want their employees to be happy and engaged, ...
b) If a team is performing well, ...
c) If a company is so small that everyone can know each other, ...
d) The quality of customer service can go down ...
e) You cannot always be sure that companies that you subcontract work to ...

1 ... will be happy and committed people.
2 ... if new teams are always made up of people who do not know each other.
3 ... the fashion for creating new teams for each task could work.
4 ... their tasks should not be given to another company to do.
5 ... it is not always a good idea to break it up.
6 ... the employees should be able to work regularly with the colleagues they respect and belong to a team that is trusted and respected.

Over to you

What can companies do in your part of the world to make their employees (even more) happy and engaged? What can they do to retain happy, engaged employees? How can you measure the effect this has on the contentedness and spending power of your customers?

UNIT 6 Risk

The priority of safety

Level of difficulty: ●●●

Before you read

In your opinion, how great is the risk that the astronauts will not return safely to Earth on US manned space missions? Who do you think carries the responsibility for safety standards in space projects?

Reading

Read this article by Victoria Griffith from the *Financial Times* about the Nasa risk management programme and do the exercises that follow.

Nasa's exercise in managing risk

By Victoria Griffith

The US space agency grounded its three remaining space shuttles after *Columbia* disintegrated upon re-entry to Earth's atmosphere in February 2003, killing the seven crew members. Yet even today, scientists are still divided over whether the management culture at Nasa has changed enough to ensure the shuttle's safety. Behavioural Science Technology, the California-based consulting group that works with other industries such as railways on safety issues, was hired 18 months ago to help change the management culture at the agency.

Nasa set out to improve employees' relationships with supervisors to encourage dissent, emphasise teamwork and raise management credibility. Although they are still under pressure from budgets and deadlines, Nasa managers say they now take the time to listen to concerns of engineers and others on issues that may compromise safety. BST measured attitudes to safety and the work environment in February 2004, then again six months later, and says the culture at Nasa has changed. But although 40 per cent of the managers surveyed said they saw changes for the better, only 8 per cent of workers said the same.

James Wetherbee, a former shuttle commander, has in recent months questioned whether the culture at Nasa has changed enough to make safety a priority. And a report released last month from George Washington University says the pressures of getting the shuttles back into space leads the space agency to make questionable safety decisions. The study places the current chances of a catastrophic failure on the shuttle at about one in 55 for every mission. Despite Nasa spending nearly $2bn over the past two years making safety improvements to the shuttle, the risk remains high enough to make any astronaut's heart dance at take-off and re-entry. In fact, the George Washington researchers argue that more money and effort should be spent to come up with an alternative to the space shuttles.

In the wake of the *Columbia* disaster, an independent panel, the Columbia Accident Investigation Board, was formed to investigate the accident. Some of the findings of the CAIB report were embarrassing for Nasa. Engineers had expressed concern about the falling debris, but their fears were dismissed. The CAIB severely criticised a lax safety culture at Nasa as contributing to the disaster, and issued a check-list of 15 points to get the shuttles back up and running.

Some critics believe Nasa should be doing more to reduce the number of manned missions. Much of the cargo for the shuttle, they argue, could be transported robotically. Others have called for the space agency to adopt a more aggressive schedule in developing a replacement for the shuttle. But those are issues for the medium term. In the coming weeks, getting the shuttle safely into space and back to Earth will be the priority, and the world will be waiting with bated breath to see if *Discovery* can get off its launch pad without mishap.*

From the *Financial Times*

* In fact, the launch of *Discovery* was successful.

UNIT 6 Risk

1 True or false?

a) Behavioural Science Technology was hired because many scientists believe that the management culture at Nasa has not changed enough to ensure a safe space shuttle programme.
b) There is evidence that the new safety culture at Nasa has not filtered down from the management level.
c) The report from George Washington University indicates that pressure to get the shuttles back into space is taking priority over safety at Nasa.
d) The Columbia Accident Investigation Board was made up of Nasa engineers.
e) The replacement for the shuttle will transport cargo robotically.

2 Find words in paragraph 1 that mean:

a) did not allow an aircraft to fly
b) fell apart
c) not in agreement
d) guarantee

3 Read paragraph 2 and answer these questions.

a) What has Nasa tried to do to improve its safety culture?
b) How are Nasa managers changing?
c) Has the culture at Nasa changed?
d) Has it changed enough?

4 Before you read paragraph 3 again, match the two halves of these sentences.

a) James Wetherbee, a former shuttle commander, has questioned ...
b) The pressures of getting the shuttles back ...
c) The study places the current chances of a catastrophic failure on the shuttle ...
d) The risk remains high enough ...
e) The George Washington researchers argue that more money and effort should be spent to come ...

1 ... up with an alternative to the space shuttles.
2 ... to make any astronaut's heart dance at take-off and re-entry.
3 ... into space leads the space agency to make questionable safety decisions.
4 ... whether the culture at Nasa has changed enough to make safety a priority.
5 ... at about one in 55 for every mission.

5 Replace the words in *italics* in the sentences below with words or expressions from paragraph 4.

a) *Directly after* the 'Columbia' disaster ...
b) ... an independent panel was formed to *examine* the accident.
c) Engineers had *mentioned* their concern about the falling debris, ...
d) ... but their fears were *not considered to be important*.
e) The CAIB severely criticised *an inadequate* safety culture at Nasa ...
f) ... as *being partly responsible for* the disaster ...
g) ... and issued a check-list of 15 points to get the shuttles *back in operation*.

6 Before looking at paragraph 5 again, put the correct verbs into the following sentences.

a) Some critics believe Nasa should be .... more to reduce the number of manned missions.
b) Much of the cargo for the shuttle, they argue, could be .... robotically.
c) Others have .... for the space agency to adopt a more aggressive schedule in .... a replacement for the shuttle.
d) In the coming weeks, ... the shuttle safely into space and back to Earth will be the priority ...
e) ... and the world will be .... with bated breath to see if *Discovery* can get off its launch pad without mishap.

Over to you

How important is safety in your company, or a company you know? Should it be the main priority? Why or why not? Should safety be the main priority in every company, regardless of what its business is? Why do you think this?

UNIT 6 Risk

The risk of loss of brand value and reputation

Level of difficulty: ●●○

Before you read

What effect can strikes and industrial action have on the reputation of a company? If a company has a well-known brand, what are the risks to its brand value?

Reading

Read this article by Richard Gillis from the FT.com site and do the exercises that follow.

One strike and you're down

By Richard Gillis

"Companies forget that staff have the power to wreck the brand." This warning comes from Martin Langford, a corporate reputation specialist. But brand owners that probably don't need reminding of this include British Airways, Royal Mail and Jaguar, because of the high profile which staff industrial action, or threats of industrial action, has assumed at all three.

Management at large organisations do not embark on widespread and risky company restructurings unless they believe their businesses are in straitened financial circumstances. And the potential long-term damage to company branding that can be done if staff and managers clash publicly over plans will almost always take a back seat to other priorities, such as getting the business back into profit.

Nevertheless, brands are a key part of the intangible assets that are playing an increasingly important role on company balance sheets. This means that it can be a serious issue for any business if its brands emerge as tainted in the long term by strikes and other industrial conflicts. If this is the risk, how can corporations or other branded organisations reduce this danger?

Langford estimates that about a third of his clients' problems with respect to this risk are caused by the behaviour of their staff; with industrial action and disaffected workers being the most common examples.

John Williamson, board director of brand consultants Wolff Olins, says: "Poor industrial relations do not come about in isolation. They reflect on the business as a whole and the way in which it is being managed. If the management thinks the brand is something done by the marketing communications department, this makes for very poor brand strategy."

The danger here for service companies is that the impression of the brand given to the customer is often dictated by the behaviour of staff at the bottom of the organisation hierarchy. And, in the maelstrom of media activity that goes with major industrial action, the senior management can develop the habit of briefing journalists before their own staff. This has a direct impact on the quality of the service.

"Brands represent the value of the organisation's relationship with its customer. It's the one thing a competitor cannot copy," says Brenda Banks of insurers Aon, which works with clients on the issue of brand risk. Companies are not able to insure against declines in brand value, but often compound the problem by not managing the risk to their most valuable asset. "Reputation risk only comes home to roost when things go wrong."

From the *Financial Times*

UNIT 6 Risk

1 Choose the heading that best summarises each paragraph of the article.

a) It is important to tell the staff first.
b) Brands are unique – and an important part of a company's reputation.
c) Effective brand strategy means effective industrial relations.
d) Brands are also reflected in the company accounts.
e) Getting the company back on its feet usually has to take priority.
f) Employees who are dissatisfied with their management are often the biggest problem.
g) Brand owners such as British Airways, Royal Mail and Jaguar know how their employees have the power to wreck their brand.

2 True or false (paragraphs 1 and 2)?

a) Brand owners don't need reminding that their staff have the power to wreck their brand.
b) British Airways, Royal Mail and Jaguar have all had a lot of bad publicity in the media concerning staff industrial action or threats of industrial action.
c) The management of large organisations only carry out difficult company restructurings if the business is losing a lot of money.
d) Settling disagreements between staff and managers will almost always have priority over other business concerns.

3 Before looking at paragraphs 3 and 4 again, match the two halves of the expressions below.

a) intangible	organisations
b) balance	brands
c) tainted	assets
d) branded	action
e) industrial	sheets

Which one of them means:

1 things that employees of companies or institutions do as a protest?
2 part of the value of a company but without any physical form?
3 companies or institutions that have a particular identity and character with the public?
4 statements of what a company owns, how much money a company owes and the amount of money it has at a particular point in time?
5 things that identify a company or product with the public, associated here with poor industrial relations and the resulting unreliability?

4 Now use the two-word expressions from Exercises 3 to complete these sentences.

a) Companies will suffer from .... in the long term if they have a lot of strikes and industrial action.
b) Even threats of .... can affect the value of a company's brand.
c) It is important for .... to manage the risks to their most valuable asset.
d) Successful, and unsuccessful, brand management is reflected in a company's ....
e) The value of a company's brand is one of its most important ....

5 Find words or expressions in paragraph 5 that mean:

a) bad management of the way staff and managers work together
b) are not something that happens without relation to other people or things
c) give an insight into
d) results in
e) long-term planning

6 Before looking at paragraph 6 again, choose the correct forms of the verbs from the box to complete the sentences below.

brief	have	develop
dictate	give	go

a) The danger is that the impression of the brand .... to the customer is often .... by the behaviour of staff at the bottom of the organisation hierarchy.
b) There is a maelstrom of media activity that .... with major industrial action.
c) Senior management can .... the habit of .... journalists before their own staff.
d) This .... a direct impact on the quality of the service.

7 Answer these questions according to the information in paragraph 7.

a) What, according to Brenda Banks, is at risk for companies with a well-known brand?
b) Why does she believe it is important for companies to manage the risk to their brand?

Over to you

Choose a company with a well-known brand in your area and find out about them. What good qualities do people associate with their brand? How well are their industrial relations managed? What is at risk for the company if their brand becomes tainted?
Report your findings to the rest of your class.

UNIT 7 e-commerce

Internet shopping – ten years on

Level of difficulty: ●●○

Before you read

What does the word *retail* mean? What large retail businesses can you think of? Can you buy products from these businesses online? How important is online shopping where you live?

Reading

Now read the article by Elizabeth Rigby from the *Financial Times* and do the exercises that follow.

Online shopping expected to grow by 35% this year

Elizabeth Rigby

Consumers are expected to spend 35 per cent more buying a host of items from clothes to CDs online this year, taking total spending for 2005 to an estimated £19.6bn, according to the Interactive Media Retail Group. In its first annual report, published today, IMRG said it expected 4m more Britons to shop online this year, taking the total shoppers to 24m, more than half the UK's adult population. The latest figures underline the sharp growth of internet shopping in the decade since 1994. While internet shopping accounted for just £300m of retail sales in 1999, by 2004 consumers were spending £14.5bn online, according to IMRG.

Online shopping is also counteracting sluggish consumer spending on the high street. Household expenditure grew by only 0.2 per cent in the fourth quarter of 2004. "For a sector to have grown from scratch in ten years with very little investment suggests that the internet's time has come," said James Roper, IMRG chief executive.

The larger retailing groups – Kingfisher, Argos, Dixons, Tesco and Boots – are spending money on developing their internet offering, but many retail chains are not investing in online shopping, which in turn is allowing entrants such as figleaves.com, which sells underwear, and asos.com, the clothing e-shop, to gain a foothold in the market.

In 2004, the IMRG estimated that the top 100 retailers in the UK spent just £100m on their internet presence – and most of this came from a handful of stores. But in spite of the neglect from big retailers, the growing popularity of online shopping looks set to continue as more people gain access to the internet.

Figures out from 2004 from Ofcom, the communications regulator, showed that more than 56 per cent of homes had internet access, with a third of those having a broadband connection. The emergence of mobile commerce technology could also mean that people will be able to shop online from their mobile phones.

IMRG said electrical and clothing goods were experiencing strong growth online, with more than £2bn of electrical goods sold over the internet in 2004. Dixons, the high street electrical retailer, expects its online sales – currently at £170m – to hit £1bn in the next five years. Meanwhile, clothing is another big expansion area, with sales growing 37 per cent to £644m in 2004.

From the *Financial Times*

UNIT 7 e-commerce

1 Complete the following sentences with a correct form of the word *retail* (this could be *retail*, *retailer*, *retailers*, *retails*, *retailing*, *retailed*).

a) .... is the selling of goods, often individually or in small quantities, to the end consumer.
b) Internet shopping in the UK accounted for just £300m of .... sales in 1999.
c) The larger .... groups are spending money on developing their internet offering.
d) Many .... chains are not investing in online shopping.
e) Last year, the top 100 .... in the UK spent just £100m on their internet presence.
f) Dixons, the high street electrical ...., expects its online sales to hit £1bn in the next five years.

2 True or false?

a) In 2000, people in the UK were spending almost five times more online than they were in 1999.
b) People are spending more money, but they are spending less money in the shops.
c) Because many retail chains are not investing in an internet presence, this is opening up a market for online-only businesses.
d) All of the top 100 retailers in the UK are spending a lot of money on online shopping facilities.
e) Ofcom is a business information service like the IMRG.
f) People prefer to buy their electrical goods in the shops.

3 Find words or expressions in paragraph 1 that mean:

a) a large number
b) raising the amount to
c) emphasise
d) ten-year period
e) was the reason for

4 Before looking at paragraph 2 again, put the correct verbs into the following sentences.

a) Online shopping is also .... very slow consumer spending on the high street.
b) Household expenditure .... by only 0.2 per cent in the fourth quarter of 2004.
c) For a sector to have .... from scratch in ten years with very little investment .... that the internet's time has come.

5 Find words in paragraphs 3 and 4 that mean **the opposite** of:

a) saving
b) preventing
c) lose
d) care
e) stop

6 Before looking at paragraphs 5 and 6 again, match the two parts of the phrases *in italics*.

a) Ofcom is a *communications*	*area*
b) 56 per cent of homes have *internet*	*sales*
c) A third of them have a *broadband*	*regulator*
d) There is a new technology for *mobile*	*connection*
e) Dixons expects to hit £1bn in *online*	*access*
f) Clothing is another big *expansion*	*commerce*

Over to you

In groups or pairs, look at the websites of some big high street retailers and discuss how their online shopping facilities are improving their business.

Now find out which well-known companies in your area do not yet have an internet shopping presence.

Write a letter to one of these companies explaining why it is such a good idea for them to offer their products online – and compare your letter with a colleague.

UNIT 7 e-commerce

User-friendliness

Level of difficulty: 

Before you read

When you look at company websites, which of them would you say are user-friendly? Why? What is it important for a company website to have in order to promote its business?

Reading

Read this article by David Bowen from the FT.com site and do the exercises that follow.

Webhiker's guide to galaxies

By David Bowen

One of the frustrations of people who run large websites is that their efforts are often judged on superficial criteria. It is always nice to win an award, but the sad truth is that judges rarely have time to go into sites in enough depth. So, what is never analysed is whether the site really functions properly and does what it is meant to do. This is not the fault of the judges; it is because large online presences are complex beasts. You really have to get stuck into them to see whether they are coherent.

Few big organisations have just one site – typically they have one at the centre and a galaxy of others covering countries, subsidiaries, brands and other specialities. This means we have to look both at the way the central site works, and at the way the galaxy spins around it (or fails to).

There are always reasons why a web presence has the structure it does, but they are rarely simple – usually a mix of historical accident, lack of budget, decentralised organisation, internal politics, the whimsy of bosses, and any number of other factors.

So here are three questions to ask yourself to see just how coherent your own presence is. First, is your central site one coherent beast, or is it made up of a group of vaguely co-ordinated offerings? The US State Department site, for example, looks neat – with nice bold links across the top, which are the same wherever you are in the site. But it soon becomes clear that it is a federation of sites that have little in common. Some areas have no links back to the main site, and are not covered by the same search engine.

Second and third, can visitors easily get to your country, business and other sites, and can they get back? Many people will find a corporate site by writing in the name of the company and adding '.com', or by putting its name into Google. Now you need to get them to the information they need. A well-classified directory can do the trick, but check out ICI (*www.ici.com*), with its neat expandable 'pilot' mechanism. Or UBS (*www.ubs.com*), with its logical service finder. Or look at Thyssen Krupp's Base (*base.thyssenkrupp.com*), a highly sophisticated search engine that lets visitors find the relevant site or information by product, customer sector, location, subsidiary name, or other criteria. The basic journey back from an outlying site should be more straightforward – a link to your home page.

But can, say, a visitor to your French site get direct to the central investor area? If not, why not? Can a jobseeker in Singapore look for positions across your entire organisation? Is a journalist in Brazil getting the right mix of local and global news? Thought not. These are the subtleties that may not win you an award – but they will make your site work better. That is good for your organisation, its customers and other stakeholders. And of course, for your job.

From the *Financial Times*

UNIT 7 e-commerce

1 Choose the best heading for each paragraph of the article.

a) Getting there – and getting back again
b) Why websites are the way they are
c) Features of a site that make users happy
d) Examining the sites of big organisations
e) Linking and coordination problems
f) Criteria for evaluating websites

2 Find words or expressions in paragraph 1 that mean:

a) hard work is
b) not deep or detailed
c) an official prize or reward
d) websites or combinations of websites
e) things
f) to examine carefully and in detail

3 True or false (paragraphs 2 and 3)?

a) Most big organisations have only one website.
b) To assess the coherence of online presences, we need to look at the way central websites interact with the other sites they are connected to.
c) The reasons why most web presences have the structures they do are many and varied.
d) The reasons why many company websites are complicated are often due to poor organisation and internal politics.

4 Before reading paragraph 4 again, put the correct verbs into the following sentences.

a) Here are three questions to ask yourself to .... just how coherent your own presence is.
b) First, is your central site one coherent beast, or is it .... up of a group of vaguely .... offerings?
c) The US State Department site, for example, looks neat, but it soon .... clear that it is a federation of sites that have little in common.
d) Some areas are not .... by the same search engine.

5 Before reading paragraph 5 again, put the correct prepositions into the following sentences.

a) Can visitors easily get .... your country, business and other sites, and can they get back?
b) Many people will find a corporate site .... writing in the name .... the company and adding '.com'.
c) Now you need .... get them .... the information they need.
d) A well-classified directory can do the trick, but check .... ICI.
e) It is a search engine that lets visitors find the relevant information .... product, customer sector, location, subsidiary name, or other criteria.
f) The basic journey back .... an outlying site should be more straightforward – a link to your home page.

6 Find words or phrases from paragraph 6 to replace the words *in italics* in the sentences below.

a) The *pages for shareholders and potential investors* can be accessed from our home page.
b) You can find *jobs* in a range of different countries by looking at our website.
c) As a journalist, I need the right *combination* of national and international news when I look at a company website.
d) Our website has many *clever features* that make it efficient and user-friendly.
e) *People who have an interest in an organisation*, such as suppliers, employees, investors and service providers, like to have access to a clearly coordinated website.

Over to you 1

What features of company websites have impressed you? Why? What aspects of company websites have really annoyed you? Why?

Over to you 2

Look at the website of a company you know well. Apply Mr Bowen's three questions to find out how coherent it is. If it is a coherent website, compose an email to the company management congratulating them on the quality of their website and explaining why it is so effective and satisfying to use. If it is an incoherent website, compose an email to the company management explaining why their site is so bad for their business, with your proposals for improving it.

UNIT 8 Team building

Managing teams across different countries and cultures

Level of difficulty: ●●○

Before you read

The members of a virtual team can be located anywhere in the world. Of course, they will have different backgrounds and speak different languages – and they will communicate regularly and electronically. So how can they work effectively together? What problems do you think they may have?

Reading

Read this article by Sarah Murray from the *Financial Times* and do the exercises that follow.

Virtual teams: Global harmony is their dream

Sarah Murray

If managing diversity in the workplace is a tough task for business leaders, the challenges of keeping executives from different backgrounds working together efficiently in various parts of the world is even more difficult. "One of the things you should take into account is whether your team includes members who don't speak English well," says Joanne Yates, a professor of management at MIT Sloan, who has studied the use of communication and information systems in companies. "Any good virtual team has a communication plan that includes weekly conference calls or e-mail check-ins, but with a virtual team where not everyone speaks English well, the regular report-ins should be in written mode rather than by phone or conference call."

The other advantage of e-mail communications is that, for those working in different time zones, group messages can be responded to when it is convenient, reducing the need for early morning or late night calls. At the same time, using e-mail can remove much of the hierarchy of professional communications, since many executives find it far less intimidating to send an e-mail to someone in a senior position than to telephone them.

However, cultural or behavioural differences that can manifest themselves in face-to-face working situations can be exacerbated in virtual team working, particularly when the group has members from different backgrounds. One reason for this is that, when one is physically immersed in a new culture, it takes less time to adapt to the social norms and become aware of cultural sensitivities. So those trying to do this at a distance may find it tougher to fit in, increasing the potential for misunderstandings between team members. "You don't build the relationships in the same way as you do working face-to-face," says Martin Galpin, managing psychologist at Pearn Kandola, a UK-based research business and consultancy of occupational psychologists.

Prof Yates points out that, when people in professional groups come from different backgrounds or cultures, it is often useful to appoint someone in the team who knows both cultures as the person responsible for setting the norms of working behaviour during a project that is being carried out from different locations.

And virtual working certainly does not eradicate the sort of cultural misunderstandings that can arise in a face-to-face situation. Prof Yates cites an online mini-conference she recently observed that took place between a group of US and Japanese executives working in the research and development unit of a Japanese company. "A Japanese executive was putting text into a window for instant messaging when one of the Americans started asking questions in the middle of the presentation," she explains. "That was not culturally familiar and required an instant response, which caused real problems."

From the *Financial Times*

UNIT 8 Team building

1 Here are the answers, complete the questions.

a) What ....?
A communication plan that includes weekly conference calls or e-mail check-ins.

b) Why ....?
Because many executives find it far less intimidating to send an e-mail to someone in a senior position than to telephone them.

c) How ....?
By being physically immersed in it.

d) Who ....?
Someone who knows both cultures.

e) Why ....?
Because it was not culturally familiar and required an instant response.

2 Before looking at paragraph 1 again, complete the sentences below with correct forms of the verbs from the box.

be	include	keep
speak (x2)	study	work

a) The challenges of .... executives from different backgrounds .... together efficiently in various parts of the world are difficult.

b) You should check whether your team .... members who don't .... English well.

c) Professor Joanne Yates has .... the use of communication and information systems in companies.

d) With a virtual team where not everyone .... English well, the regular report-ins should .... in written mode rather than by phone or conference call.

3 Now find words or expressions in paragraph 1 that mean:

a) a range of differences
b) tasks or situations that test people's abilities
c) consider
d) in preference to

4 Before looking at paragraph 2 again, put the correct preposition from the box into the following expressions.

for (x2)	in	of	to (x2)

a) the advantage .... e-mail communications
b) for people working .... different time zones
c) respond .... messages
d) reduce the need .... late night calls
e) using e-mail .... work exchanges
f) find it intimidating .... telephone a senior manager

5 True or false (paragraph 3)?

a) Problems with cultural or behavioural differences in a local team can be much worse in a virtual team.

b) People trying to adapt to the social norms and cultural sensitivities of a virtual team can increase the misunderstandings between team members.

c) According to Martin Galpin, people build relationships differently when they see each other.

6 Before looking at paragraph 4 again, replace the words or expressions *in italics* in the text below with the words or expressions from the box.

as	appoint	carried out
knows	points out	responsible for

Prof Yates (a) *argues* that, when people in professional groups come from different backgrounds or cultures, it is often useful to (b) *choose* someone in the team who (c) *is familiar with* both cultures (d) *to be* the person (e) *in charge of* setting the norms of working behaviour during a project that is being (f) *performed* from different locations.

7 Match the two halves of the sentences below, which summarise paragraph 5.

a) You definitely cannot eliminate the kind of cultural misunderstandings that happen when a team meets in the same room ...

b) Prof Yates gives us a short online conference between a group of US and Japanese R & D executives ...

c) A Japanese executive was interrupted with questions from an American colleague ...

d) The fact that this was culturally unfamiliar and demanded an instant response ...

1 ... as an example of this.
2 ... caused real problems.
3 ... by having virtual teams.
4 ... in the middle of his instant messaging presentation.

Over to you

How many people do you do business with over the phone or by e-mail, whom you have not met in person? Which of these do you think you could work with in a team? Why would you choose them? Is it an advantage or a disadvantage for you not to have met them in person? Why?

Text bank

UNIT 8 Team building

Team-building exercises

Level of difficulty: ●●○

Before you read

What can you do to build a good team? Are there any team-building activities that you have done in your work or your life? Were they effective? Why or why not?

Reading

Read this article by Sathnam Sanghera from the *Financial Times* and do the exercises that follow.

Team-building for charity brings tears to my eyes

By Sathnam Sanghera

58 British managers from John Lewis, the privately run retailer have released a music album for charity. The worthwhile cause is Whizz-Kidz, a charity dedicated to helping "non-mobile children". And the record in question is entitled *New Shop On the Block*.

These managers were given the task of composing, arranging, producing and recording the LP as part of a team-building exercise, the aim of which was to bond them in a "powerful collective experience". As he gave me the CD, the man from the training company that organised this "Face the Music" exercise for John Lewis remarked that the task had "created one of the most highly bonded teams" he had ever come across. It was also "very deep" in terms of the changes it made in them. "The managing director involved in the project was crying by the end," he explained.

A couple of hours later, when I played the CD for the first time, I understood exactly what he meant. The record made me want to weep too. And it wasn't just the awfulness of the music that upset me. It was also the fact that "Face the Music" marked a worrying trend in team-building exercises.

Once upon a time, people just came to work and bonded by "working and getting along with each other". Sometimes they would "go for a drink after work", "play football on Saturday" or "go for dinner at the weekend". But, generally speaking, team-building was a casual, natural, informal thing.

Then, in the 1980s, the business world decided that the only way of establishing a rapport between colleagues was by getting them to do group activities together – preferably on weekends, preferably outdoors and preferably in the rain. The idea was that workers would become immersed in an activity, learn new skills together and become closer-knit as a result. A search through the cuttings shows that, over time, businesses have asked employees to participate in every group activity under the sun in the name of team-building: paintballing, mountain climbing, Porsche racing, sailing, horse whispering, clowning, treasure hunting, potholing, go-karting, cookery, international folk dancing, wine blending – and, my own favourite, motorised toilet-bowl racing.

While such exercises are generally useless, as most take place behind closed doors or in the middle of nowhere, they are also mostly harmless. However, exercises such as "Face the Music" represent something new and ominous. Unlike paintballing and motorised toilet-bowl racing, these "multi-sensory experiences" require an audience.

And if there is one thing more excruciating than being involved in a team-building exercise, it is watching or enduring someone else's team-building exercise. I speak from experience, having listened to *New Shop On the Block* three times. John Lewis may defend the release of its atrocious album by saying it will raise money for a good cause. And the charity element is certainly a mitigating factor. But I suspect that the people who have heard it would give even more generously if their donations meant they would never have to listen to *New Shop on the Block* ever again.

From the *Financial Times*

UNIT 8 Team building

1 Choose the best heading for each paragraph of the article.

a) Bonding at work in the days before team-building exercises
b) Department store managers make a record for charity
c) The project is a team-building exercise
d) The range of team-building activities
e) But someone has to watch or listen
f) How could the album generate bigger donations?
g) And the music?

2 Answer these questions according to the information in paragraph 1.

a) What is the name of the charity and what does it do?
b) What is the name of the album – and why does it have that name?

3 Complete these sentences about paragraph 2 with correct forms of the verbs in the box.

bond	come across	cry	give
involve	organise	remark	

a) These managers were .... the task of composing, arranging, producing and recording an LP.
b) The aim of the team-building exercise was to .... the managers in a "powerful collective experience".
c) The man from the training company that .... this "Face the Music" exercise for John Lewis .... that the task had "created one of the most highly bonded teams" he had ever ....
d) The managing director .... in the project was .... by the end of the activity.

4 Before looking at paragraphs 3 and 4 again, match the two halves of the expressions below.

a) to understand	a trend
b) to upset	for a drink
c) to face	with someone
d) to mark	what someone means
e) to get along	someone
f) to go	the music

Which one of them means:

1 to make a person unhappy?
2 to indicate the start of a new fashion?
3 to see the significance in a person's words?
4 to go out to a pub or bar with friends or colleagues?
5 to live or work with a person successfully and in a friendly way?
6 to have to deal with the unpleasant consequences of your own actions?

5 Before looking at paragraph 5 again, match the two halves of the sentences below.

a) In the 1980s, the business world decided that there was only one way ...
b) This was by getting them ...
c) The idea was that workers would become immersed ...
d) They would learn new skills together and become closer-knit ...
e) Mr Sanghera, the author of this article, has made a search ...
f) This shows that, over time, businesses have asked employees ...

1 ... to participate in every group activity under the sun in the name of team-building.
2 ... through his collection of old articles from newspapers.
3 ... of establishing a rapport between colleagues.
4 ... to do group activities together.
5 ... in an activity.
6 ... as a result.

6 Answer these questions according to the information in paragraph 6.

a) How does Mr Sanghera rate team-building exercises?
b) What does he find ominous?

7 Here are the answers, complete the questions.

a) What ....?
Watching or enduring someone else's team-building exercise.
b) How ....?
Three times.
c) How ....?
By saying it will raise money for a good cause.
d) What ....?
The charity element.
e) What ....?
Guaranteeing that they would never have to listen to the CD again!

Over to you 1

Do you agree with the author when he writes that team-building exercises are generally useless? Why or why not? What would you do to help the members of your company, or a company that you know, work more effectively together as a team?

Over to you 2

If you could choose a team-building exercise from this article for your class to do, which one would it be? Why? Present your arguments to the rest of your class.

Text bank

UNIT 9 Raising finance

Options for start-up companies

Level of difficulty: ●●●

Before you read

How can start-up companies raise capital? What can they do if they need further investment in their companies after several years of successful operation?

Reading

Read this article by John Gapper from the *Financial Times* and do the exercises that follow.

Silicon Valley's lesson in patience

By John Gapper

From the point of view of investors in technology shares, last week was a painful one. Rising inventories at semiconductor manufacturers and disappointing earnings announcements led to a fall in share prices. The Nasdaq index surged last year on expectations of a sharp recovery but has since drifted slowly downwards.

Seen from Silicon Valley, however, the decline in share prices is a good thing. A mini-bubble threatened to develop this spring, as investment banks lined up to take Google public, and the number of initial public offerings (IPOs) surged. That bubble is now deflating, forcing venture capitalists to focus on their task: long-term investment in innovation.

A healthy stock market helps innovation, of course. When valuations of technology companies are strong, it encourages new enterprises to come to market through IPOs. A successful IPO is the ultimate prize for entrepreneurs who must pass through several rounds of venture capital funding to make their companies worth buying.

But the formula only works when venture capital firms select a few of these companies and filter them through four or five stages of funding. Most start-ups must develop their business for up to ten years before they are mature enough to be acquired by other companies, or come to market.

But the decline in technology shares since spring this year is making the IPO market more testing – and the Silicon Valley consensus is that the decline will continue. Asked which of them thought the Nasdaq was still overvalued, all four members of a panel of venture capitalists and bankers raised their hands. Indeed, a member of the panel predicted either a sharp fall in the Nasdaq or five flat years before earnings catch up. That may not be good news for the bankers, but venture capitalists can be thankful. They are now making profits again, and institutions are eager to put money into new funds that will invest in technology start-ups – as, aside from the bubble years, venture capital has been a far more profitable way to invest in technology than putting money into IPOs of venture-funded companies.

As long as markets overestimate the growth prospects and earnings quality of technology stocks, venture capitalists will be tempted to rush immature start-ups towards IPOs before they are strong enough. In contrast, markets that are stable, or falling towards true value, encourage them to stick to cultivating enterprises with long-term potential. So, in the face of a deflating market, everyone will have to learn, or relearn, the virtue of patience: today's early-stage investments may not mature for a decade.

It sounds unfortunate, but venture capital investors should realise the danger of trying to force independence on too many companies too fast. For shareholders of publicly quoted technology companies, the state of the stock market is depressing. For Silicon Valley, it could be just the ticket.

From the *Financial Times*

UNIT 9 Raising finance

1 Match the expressions on the left with the words on the right to make three correct definitions.

a) Investors in technology shares **b)** Venture capital investors **c)** Investment banks	1 invest their money in start-up businesses in return for a share in the company. 2 lend money to businesses in return for interest. 3 invest their money in shares of publicly quoted companies.

2 Answer these questions.

a) What can make life painful for investors in technology shares?
b) What sort of businesses are there in Silicon Valley?
c) Why is a technology market that is not performing well good news for businesses there?
d) What is an initial public offering and why is this the ultimate prize for entrepreneurs?
e) What is the danger if markets overestimate the growth prospects and earnings quality of technology stocks?

3 Before looking at paragraphs 1 and 2 again, choose a word or word group from column A and a word or word group from column B to complete each of the sentences below.

A	B
long-term	earnings announcements
a sharp	inventories
venture	recovery
rising	capitalists
disappointing	investment

a) A company that is not managing to sell the goods it produces has ....
b) Such a company will also have to make ....
c) Share performance indices, such as Dow Jones, Nasdaq or Dax, can make a .... if many people invest in shares again.
d) Groups of investors that finance innovative start-up companies are called ....
e) Giving technology companies financial support until they are ready to make an initial public offering is often a ....

4 True or false (paragraphs 3 and 4)?

a) When investors are willing to pay high prices for technology shares, this is a good incentive for new technology companies to begin selling shares of their company on a stock market.
b) If a company can sell its shares on a stock market, it no-longer requires venture capital funding.
c) It is important for venture capital firms to bring all their companies to market.

5 Before looking at paragraph 5 again, replace the words *in italics* in the following sentences with the words in the box.

catch up	eager	profitable
testing	consensus	predicted

a) But the decline in technology shares since spring this year is making the IPO market more *difficult* – and the Silicon Valley *opinion* is that the decline will continue.
b) A member of the panel *forecasted* either a sharp fall in the Nasdaq or five flat years before earnings *recover*.
c) Institutions are *happy* to put money into new funds that will invest in technology start-ups.
d) Venture capital has been a far more *financially rewarding* way to invest in technology than putting money into IPOs.

6 Match the two halves of the sentences below to summarise paragraphs 6 and 7.

a) Whenever stock markets overestimate the degree of potential growth and earnings of technology stocks ...
b) Yet venture capitalists are encouraged to do their more traditional job of supporting companies with long-term potential ...
c) This means that, at the moment, with a deflating market ...
d) Venture capital investors should be aware that too many IPOs for too many companies at the same time ...
e) So, although the value of shares of publicly quoted technology companies may be falling, or not going up, at the moment ...

1 ... when markets are stable or falling towards their true value.
2 ... everyone involved will have to adjust to being patient once more.
3 ... venture capitalists feel tempted to rush start-up companies towards IPOs before they are mature enough for this.
4 ... this may be just the right thing for start-up companies with innovative ideas.
5 ... is potentially dangerous for the whole market.

Over to you 1

How does your company, or a company that you know, finance its projects? What do they do if they need some additional capital? What are the choices open to them for raising capital?

Over to you 2

Choose a company in your region and find out how it is being financed by looking on the web. See also if you can find out about this company's investors (shareholders, investment banks, venture capitalists, etc.). If you have problems with vocabulary, a good place to look is *http://en.wikipedia.org/wiki/investment_banks* Report your findings back to your class.

UNIT 9 Raising finance

An alternative to the banks

Level of difficulty: ●●○

Before you read

How do people who are self-employed or working freelance normally raise money for their businesses or for special business projects? How well do banks understand these people?

Reading

Read this article by Paul J Davies from the *Financial Times* and do the exercises that follow.

Lending exchange that bypasses high street banks attracts interest

Paul J Davies

An online service designed to allow borrowers and lenders to bypass the big high street banks has garnered strong interest in its first four months of operation. From a 300-member beginning, Zopa – short for zone of possible agreement – now has more than 26,000 members, according to James Alexander, a co-founder and chief financial officer. About 35 per cent are lenders, who between them have £3m of capital waiting to be handed out. Mr Alexander will not say how much has been lent, but average loans have been between £2,000 and £5,000; Zopa is hoping that will creep more towards £8,000 in coming months.

The idea for the business, which describes itself as a "lending and borrowing exchange", came from market research that came up with the notion that there was a market of "freeformers" to be tapped. They might be self-employed or do work that is project-based or freelance, Mr Alexander says. "They're people who are not understood by banks, which value stability in people's lives and income over everything else."

Most importantly, he adds, while their incomes and lifestyles may be irregular, they can still be assessed as creditworthy. The exchange matches people who want to borrow with people who want to lend, although each lender's money is parcelled out between at least 50 borrowers. Zopa earns its money by charging borrowers 1 per cent of their loan as a fee, and from commission on any repayment protection insurance.

Lenders are so far seeing average returns of 7.6 per cent, Mr Alexander says. There have yet to be any defaults, however. Borrowers who fail to pay will be pursued through the usual channels and get a black mark against their credit histories. But for the lender, their investment is not protected by any compensation scheme, unless they have been defrauded. Borrowers, meanwhile, can find rates as low as 5.9 per cent.

Zopa says it has 20 countries where people want to set up franchises. The most important though is the US, where Zopa has had a team working on finding a route through the regulatory hurdles since late last year. Banks do not generally see Zopa as a threat to their high street business. One analyst called it "one of these things that could catch on but probably won't".

The challenge for Zopa, which has been relying mainly on word of mouth and online marketing, is to make people aware of its services and to attract credit-worthy borrowers. And in a climate of high indebtedness and slowing consumer spending, that may be the biggest challenge of all.

From the *Financial Times*

UNIT 9 Raising finance

1 Choose the best heading for each paragraph of the article.

a) How it all works
b) A new loan market
c) But what are the risks?
d) The marketing challenge
e) Expanding into other countries
f) A new facility for borrowers and lenders

2 Find words or expressions in paragraph 1 that mean:

a) avoid using
b) the traditional location for shops, banks and businesses in a town or district
c) gathered or collected
d) as stated by
e) sums of money lent
f) move very slowly but firmly

3 At the time of printing, the word 'freeformer', in paragraph 2, had not yet appeared in any dictionary. Here is an extract from the Zopa website that uses this word again:

"Certainly, the statistics appear to confirm the rise of the Freeformer. One in five working people in the UK is planning to start a business in 2005, according to one report, while almost half have gone as far as writing a business plan and having it reviewed by a professional adviser."

So is a 'freeformer'

a) a person who cannot pay their bills?
b) a type of person who is becoming more important?
c) a person who is starting their own business project?

4 Match the verbs on the left with the nouns on the right to make expressions from paragraphs 2 and 3.

a) come up with	creditworthy
b) tap	money
c) value	a fee
d) assess as	commission
e) parcel out	a market
f) charge	stability
g) earn	a notion

Which of these expressions means:

1 take advantage of a particular group of people as a source of income
2 receive a percentage of the price of something as payment
3 judge someone as a reliable person to lend money to
4 divide and distribute capital in portions
5 consider permanence to be important
6 demand as a price for a service
7 generate an idea

5 True or false (paragraph 4)?

a) The average interest lenders receive is 7.6 per cent.
b) So far, all the borrowers have been making their payments on time.
c) If borrowers don't pay their debts, the company lenders have clever new ways to get their money back.
d) Borrowers who are bad payers will be rated as less creditworthy with the credit assessment agencies.
e) Lenders are covered by insurance so, even if the borrowers don't pay, they will always get some of their money back.
f) If the borrowers have got their loan illegally by lying to Zopa, lenders will have lost their money.
g) It is possible to borrow money from Zopa without paying a lot of interest.

6 Before looking at paragraph 5 again, put the right forms of the verbs in the box into the following sentences.

catch on	find	see
set up	work	

a) People want to .... franchises in 20 countries.
b) In the US, a team is .... on .... a route through the complex regulations there.
c) Banks do not generally .... Zopa as a threat to their high street business.
d) Zopa is one of these things that could ....

7 Here are the answers, complete the questions.

a) How ....?
Mainly by word of mouth and online activity.
b) What ....?
To make people aware of its services and attract creditworthy borrowers.
c) Why ....?
Because currently many people owe a lot of money and, at the same time, people are not buying so many things.

Over to you

If you could borrow between £2,000 and £5,000 from Zopa for a business project, how would you invest the money?
Write down your business idea, how much you would like to borrow and how and over what period you would be able to pay the money back. Then present your idea to the rest of your class.

UNIT 10 Customer service

Using technology to handle customers

Level of difficulty: ●●●

Before you read

What can medium-sized and small companies do if they only have a few people to answer their phones? What technology is available to improve their service? How does this work?

Reading

Read this article by Keith Rodgers from the FT.com website and do the exercises that follow.

Balance between cost control and service

By Keith Rodgers

One of the problems in dealing with customer service calls is that you can never be sure whether they're going to end up as a net cost or generate additional revenue. The more people you employ to handle incoming calls, the greater your overheads, yet the better you're able to satisfy a customer, the greater your chances of selling them something else. To achieve a balance between cost control and quality of service, many leading telecoms and software suppliers are now applying the lessons they have learnt in larger businesses to the small-to-medium-sized enterprise (SME) market.

Relatively simple telephony techniques can make a big difference to the way you cater for fluctuating call volumes, route customers to the best person, or avoid answering the phone altogether. Likewise, customer support software designed for SME businesses allows you to streamline your support processes, let customers find their own answers on your website, and even use your service teams as part-time credit control agents.

With telephony, much can be done using technologies such as interactive voice response (IVR), the self-service facility that helps companies filter customers by prompting them to select from a menu of options when they first call in.

With application software, the core techniques available to SMEs are similar to those provided for larger call centres. A good customer service application will help you track an inquiry from its creation through to its resolution, escalating it to the appropriate levels if it can't be solved on first contact. The application will also create customer histories, which pop up in front of agents as they answer a call. If you know what products the caller owns and all the previous service issues they've had, you're halfway to resolving their problems.

You can of course reduce the overall volume by encouraging customers to seek answers on the web. This can be as simple as posting answers to frequently-asked questions (FAQs) on your website. There are also tools for small businesses to build self-learning knowledge bases – if customer queries aren't resolved online, an agent steps in, and the resulting exchange is fed back into the knowledge base for future reference.

Ultimately, much of the value from such customer service applications will depend on how well they're integrated with other systems. It is important to be able to pool customer information from both the sales and service departments, so both teams have an up-to-date customer history. By linking credit control or warranty systems to the customer service application for example, you can automatically warn agents that the customer they're speaking to is past due payment. That's a powerful weapon for cash-conscious businesses – when a caller needs help, there's no better time to encourage them to settle their bills.

From the *Financial Times*

UNIT 10 Customer service

1 Choose the best summary for each paragraph of the article.

a) Technologies for sorting incoming phone calls.
b) Tracking enquiries and creating customer histories.
c) The value of integrating systems and pooling information.
d) The value of telephone technology and customer support software.
e) Inviting customers to go online and maintaining an up-to-date knowledge base.
f) Technology to help smaller businesses provide customer satisfaction over the phone.

2 Match the two halves of the sentences below so that they best define the expressions *in italics* from paragraph 1.

a) The *overheads* of a business ...
b) Customer service calls that *generate additional revenue* ...
c) Employees who *handle incoming calls* well ...
d) Customer service calls that *end up as a net cost* ...
e) Achieving *a balance between cost control and quality of service* ...
f) People who *apply the lessons they have learnt* ...

1 ... means you provide a good service at an affordable price.
2 ... use their knowledge and experience to solve problems.
3 ... are the money it costs to run the business.
4 ... answer the phone with a friendly, helpful telephone manner.
5 ... earn more money for the company.
6 ... eventually lose money for the company.

3 Look at paragraph 2 again and put the following business benefits into the correct part of the table below.

a) your customers can help themselves to the information they need on your website.
b) you can make sure that each customer speaks to the most suitable employee.
c) your agents can check whether your customer has paid their bills or not.
d) you can use all your customer service resources more efficiently.
e) you can handle any number of calls at the same time.
f) you sometimes don't have to answer the phone at all.

With the right telephony techniques ...	With good customer support software ...
....	....

4 Look at paragraphs 3 and 4 again and complete the questions for these answers.

a) How ....?
It helps companies filter customers by prompting them to select from a menu of options when they first call in.
b) What ....?
It will help you track an inquiry from its creation through to its resolution.
c) When ....?
They pop up on the screen in front of agents as they answer a call.
d) What ....?
They will provide a list of products the caller owns and all the previous services the caller has had.

5 Here is paragraph 5 again. Fill in the gaps with the correct forms of the verbs in the box.

build	encourage	feed	post
reduce	resolve	seek	

You can of course **(a)** .... the overall volume by **(b)** .... customers to **(c)** .... answers on the web. This can be as simple as **(d)** .... answers to frequently-asked questions (FAQs) on your website. There are also tools for small businesses to **(e)** .... self-learning knowledge bases – if customer queries aren't **(f)** .... online, an agent steps in, and the resulting exchange is **(g)** .... back into the knowledge base for future reference.

6 Find words or expressions in paragraph 6 that mean:

a) in the end
b) connected to and functioning as part of
c) bring together in one place
d) monitoring of payments received
e) an agreement to ensure that a product works over a period of time
f) has not yet paid their bill
g) companies who keep a careful eye on their money

Over to you

When you telephone companies, do you always manage to speak to a person? If you get the service you require, does it matter that you don't speak to a person? What kind of service would you like from the companies you telephone? Is this the same kind of service provided by your own company or a company you know? Why or why not?

Text bank

UNIT 10 Customer service

Customer satisfaction surveys

Level of difficulty: ●●○

Before you read

How useful are customer satisfaction surveys? When are they important and when are they unnecessary? Why are some companies not very good at providing customer service?

Reading

Read this article by Richard Tomkins from the *Financial Times* and do the exercises that follow.

Can't get no ...

Richard Tomkins

I cannot be the only person to have noticed that customer satisfaction surveys have become a modern-day plague. Market researchers phone us, write to us, e-mail us or stop us in the street to ask us about products or services we have used. When we are online, questionnaires pop up asking us about the usefulness and effectiveness of websites we are visiting. There is no escape even within the workplace where we are quizzed about our satisfaction with the staff canteen, the IT department help desk and our working conditions generally.

One good thing about customer satisfaction surveys is that they make us feel important, giving us the opportunity not just to hand out plaudits or brickbats but, seemingly, to have them brought to the attention of the right people. This is a refreshing change from the experience with which most of us are familiar.

But why are most companies hopeless at providing good customer service? Patrick Barwise of London Business School says one reason is that it goes against human nature. Placing someone else's needs above your own just does not make sense unless it helps perpetuate your genes. From this, we may deduce that employees are rarely predisposed to give any customers good service unless they fancy them. Another big reason, says Prof Barwise, is that everyone lies to their boss (at least a bit, even in good companies), but bosses always underestimate the extent of the deceit; so when problems emerge, they tend to be hidden instead of being reported and solved. Look at it this way: if you are responsible for dealing with customers every day, and your customers are intensely dissatisfied, are you going to risk getting the blame by telling the management?

This, I surmise, explains the mania for customer satisfaction surveys; instead of asking your employees to report customer dissatisfaction, you ask the customers themselves. But identifying problems is not the same as solving them. And I am not sure that customer surveys are even very good at identification.

Above all, though, my criticism of these surveys is that they are a sign of failure. Good companies with good products or services do not need to pester people with questionnaires; their measure of customer satisfaction is rapidly rising revenues and profits. Do Amazon or Starbucks assail their customers with questionnaires? I doubt it. Interestingly, they do not advertise much, either. So many companies spend colossal sums on advertising and branding, yet destroy the value potentially created by delivering poor quality products or services. The intelligent response, perhaps, would be to demote the marketing director and create a customer satisfaction director instead.

From the *Financial Times*

UNIT 10 Customer service

1 Complete the title of the article: 'Can't get no ...' what? Now choose the headings that best summarise each paragraph.

a) Why they shouldn't be necessary.
b) But why is customer service so bad?
c) But there is something good about them.
d) Why customer satisfaction surveys are necessary.
e) There is no escape from customer satisfaction surveys.

2 Before looking at paragraph 1 again, put the correct verbs into the following sentences.

a) I cannot be the only person to have .... that customer satisfaction surveys have .... a modern-day plague.
b) When we are online, questionnaires .... asking us about the usefulness and effectiveness of websites we are ....
c) Even within the workplace we are .... about our satisfaction with the staff canteen.

3 Find words or expressions in paragraph 2 that mean:

a) chance
b) praise
c) critical remarks or comments
d) apparently
e) awareness
f) something different that is pleasantly new and interesting

4 True or false (paragraph 3)?

a) One reason why most companies are hopeless at providing good customer service is that most human beings place the needs of other people above their own.
b) The logical consequence of Prof Barwise's theory is that most employees won't give their customers good service unless they are sexually attracted to them.
c) Prof Barwise believes that people never tell their bosses the truth.
d) He also thinks that bosses tend to believe their employees a little bit too much.
e) Employees prefer to hide problems rather than telling their bosses about them.
f) Hidden problems don't get solved.
g) People who deal with customers every day always tell the management if their customers are angry with them.

5 Answer these questions according to the information in paragraph 4.

a) Why are customer satisfaction surveys so popular?
b) How effective are they?

6 Look at paragraph 5 again and complete the questions for the following answers.

a) What ....?
That they are a sign of failure.
b) How ....?
Through growth in their revenues and profits.
c) How ....?
By delivering poor quality products or services.
d) What ....?
Perhaps it would be to demote the marketing director and create a customer satisfaction director instead.

Over to you 1

Why do you think the author describes customer satisfaction surveys as 'a modern-day plague'? Are there any products or services for which customer satisfaction surveys are useful or even important? What kind of products or services are these?

Over to you 2

Think of a situation when you were not satisfied with the service you received from a company. Describe the situation to your class. In groups, develop a set of proposals for that company so that they can improve their customer service (but remember Prof Barwise's observations that good customer service is against human nature and that most people lie to their bosses). Present your proposals to your class.

UNIT 11 Crisis management

Managing crises effectively

Level of difficulty: ●●○

Before you read

What kind of crises do companies face? How can they be anticipated? How can they be managed?

Reading

Read the following article by Morgen Witzel from the FT Summer School published in the *Financial Times* and do the exercises that follow.

FT SUMMER SCHOOL: Expect the unexpected

By Morgen Witzel

Crises are an inevitable part of management and the larger the business grows the bigger the crises seem to become. However robust a business seems, it is still fallible – as has been shown by the recent histories of Arthur Andersen and Marconi.

An understanding of risk is essential in crisis management. Sophisticated modelling techniques and expert consultants can help managers appreciate risks better, especially those stemming from global issues such as terrorism and climate change. Closer to home, risks such as changing customer preferences or takeover threats may be best analysed within the company itself. The constant monitoring of what is going on in the larger world is an essential activity. Once a range of possible future crises has been established, contingency plans can be put in place.

However, not every crisis can be foreseen. The chances of an airliner crashing, for example, are extremely small, but every airline must still live with the possibility. When an Air France Concorde crashed on take-off from Paris – the first accident involving a Concorde – Air France was prepared to deal with the issue. Managers moved quickly to withdraw Concorde from service, announce an investigation into the accident and reassure the travelling public that it was still safe to fly Air France. The following day the airline's share price did decline, but not by much and not for very long.

Intel, the world's leading maker of semiconductors, suffered a huge and unforeseen crisis when it emerged that a small proportion of its Pentium microprocessors were faulty. Quickly assessing the options, the company took the brave step of recalling and replacing the entire production run of the series. The move cost more than $1bn (£550m) and probably saved the company. Intel showed that it was committed to its product, whatever the short-term cost, and customers responded positively.

Looking back on the incident, Andy Grove, Intel's chairman and then chief executive, compared managing in a severe crisis to an illness. Strong, healthy companies will survive, although at a cost to themselves. Weak companies will be carried off by the disease and will die. In Mr Grove's view, the key to successful crisis management is preparedness. Forward thinking and planning are essential; understanding the nature of the crisis that might occur can help managers be better prepared, as the Air France example shows.

Yet even while managers are planning how to deal with seismic events such as terrorist attacks or natural disasters, they may be missing more subtle threats such as the development of new technologies that could undermine their business. Good crisis management requires the ability to react to events swiftly and positively, whether or not they have been foreseen.

From the *Financial Times*

Text bank

UNIT 11 Crisis management

1 Choose the best heading for each paragraph of the article.

a) The Intel story
b) The Air France story
c) Ready to act, come what may
d) A measure of company health
e) Global issues and market issues
f) The bigger the company the greater the danger

2 Before looking at paragraphs 1 and 2 again, replace the words *in italics* in the sentences below with words from the box.

appreciate	customer preferences	essential
established	fallible	inevitable
put in place	robust	

a) Crises are an *unavoidable* part of management.
b) However *sound* a business seems, it is still *able to make mistakes*.
c) An understanding of risk is *of fundamental importance* in crisis management.
d) Sophisticated modelling techniques and expert consultants can help managers *get a better understanding of the implications of* risks.
e) Closer to home, risks such as changing *market demands* or takeover threats may be best analysed within the company itself.
f) Once a range of possible future crises has been *agreed on*, contingency plans can be *set up*.

3 True or false (paragraphs 1 and 2)?

a) Arthur Anderson and Marconi are examples of robust companies that have suffered very large crises.
b) Risks from global issues such as terrorism and climate change can be assessed with the help of sophisticated modelling techniques and expert consultants.
c) An assessment of the risks in the areas around customers' homes can best be analysed within the company itself.
d) The author of the article believes that it is always important to follow what is going on in the world to manage risk properly.

4 Answer these questions according to the information in paragraph 3.

a) How did the Air France managers deal with the issue of the Concorde crash?
b) What happened to the airline's share price?

5 Here are the answers, complete the questions (paragraph 4).

a) Why ....?
Because it was discovered that a small proportion of its Pentium microprocessors were faulty.
b) What ....?
They recalled and replaced the entire production run of the series.
c) How ....?
More than $1bn (£550m), but it probably saved the company.
d) Why ....?
Because Intel showed that it was committed to its product, whatever the short-term cost.

6 Match the two halves of the sentences below so that they summarise paragraphs 5 and 6.

a) In the same way as in an illness, strong, healthy companies will survive, ...
b) Andy Grove believes that managers who think and plan ahead ...
c) But managers who plan how to deal with seismic events such as terrorist attacks or natural disasters ...
d) It doesn't matter whether the events have been foreseen or not, ...

1 ... may well miss more subtle threats to their business.
2 ... although at a cost to themselves, and weak companies will die.
3 ... good crisis management requires the ability to react swiftly and positively.
4 ... understand the nature of the risks that might occur and are better prepared to deal with crises.

7 Find words or expressions in paragraph 5 that mean:

a) event
b) illness
c) thing that helps us to understand

Find words or expressions in paragraph 6 that mean:

d) earth-shaking
e) clever and indirect
f) slowly weaken
g) rapidly

Over to you 1

What developments in the market could threaten your company, or a company you know? What could the company do about this to keep its customers happy?

Over to you 2

In groups, choose a well-known company in your area and discuss what kind of events could become a crisis for that company. Present the events, and your proposed reactions from the management, to the rest of your class.

Text bank

UNIT 11 Crisis management

Carrying out a rescue plan

Level of difficulty: ●●●

Before you read

In a crisis – when a business is losing money and orders – what can a company do to survive? What are the consequences if the rescue plan is successful? And what are the consequences if it is not successful?

Reading

Read this article by John Gapper about Marconi from the *Financial Times* (the first sentences of paragraphs 1–3 are missing) and do the exercises that follow.

Desperate days, drastic measures

By John Gapper

(1) The telecommunications equipment company was losing cash and the flow of orders had dried up. George Simpson, its chief executive, and Sir Roger Hurn, its chairman, both resigned that day. The new management team appointed by Derek Bonham was not brought in from outside. They were insiders who were eager to fix the mess in which they were implicated. They were given the chance partly because of their links with customers and partly because there was no time to seek an alternative.

(2) In that period, it defaulted on its debts, sold many businesses and trimmed others, cut £1bn of costs from its operations and supply chain, and made 20,000 people redundant. Yet it has survived. Its original shareholders lost virtually everything, but those who invested in the company when it relisted in May 2003 have done very well.

(3) Michael Tory of Morgan Stanley, which advised Marconi, says that their achievement was extraordinary: "They retained their customers' confidence, rebuilt morale and kept the company operating in the cruellest environment the industry has ever seen." This is how Marconi put their rescue plan into practice.

(a)
A small group of senior executives worked closely together on a plan to revive the company. They had detailed ideas for how to cut staff and other costs, restructure the company's finances, focus the company on a few key products and maintain customers' confidence.

(b)
Each task was carefully planned and targets were set for what had to be achieved over a set period. The work was divided among managers with individual responsibilities who were answerable to the wider group.

(c)
The company's senior managers explained to investors, staff and key customers exactly what they intended to do, the difficulties they faced, and the milestones they intended to hit. They reported on progress regularly.

(d)
Marconi eventually made 20,000 people redundant across global operations in Italy, Germany, the UK and the US. They had clear procedures, offered retraining and counselling, and convinced unions not to stand in the way.

(e)
They enlisted the help of their biggest customers to decide which products they needed to invest in, and which should be dropped.

(f)
The company continued to invest heavily in research and development to find products that it believed customers would eventually start to buy again.

(g)
The managers worked with Marconi's suppliers and its engineers to raise operating margins. This involved not just cutting costs, but finding ways to innovate while keeping product costs steady. It encouraged suppliers to move production facilities to countries in Asia and eastern Europe.

From the *Financial Times*

Note: In October 2005 (after this article appeared), Marconi was purchased by Ericsson for €1.2bn.

Text bank

UNIT 11 Crisis management

1 Here are the first lines from the first three paragraphs. Match them to the correct paragraph.

a) So too have the 50 managers who pulled off the feat.
b) On September 4 2001, Marconi announced that it was in deep trouble.
c) Three years on, Marconi is a sadder, wiser, smaller company.

2 Here are the headings for each item of the Marconi rescue plan. Put them into the correct position in the plan.

i) Communication
ii) Process analysis
iii) Preserving the core
iv) Teamwork
v) Customer focus
vi) Laying off staff
vii) Project management

3 Before reading paragraph 1 again, put the verbs from the box into the following sentences in their correct forms.

implicate	seek	bring
fix	dry	give

a) The flow of orders had .... up.
b) The new management team was not .... in from outside.
c) They were insiders who were eager to .... the mess in which they were ....
d) They were .... the chance partly because there was no time to .... an alternative.

4 Find words or expressions in paragraphs 2 and 3 that mean:

a) failed to pay
b) sums of money owed to someone that have not yet been paid
c) made a little smaller
d) All the companies involved in getting and selling materials and goods to a company – from raw materials to final product.
e) laid off
f) made its shares available on a stock exchange once more
g) didn't lose
h) trust

5 True or false (Marconi rescue plan)?

a) A small group of senior executives decided that the company should concentrate on a small number of important products.
b) The managers who were responsible for each task had to answer questions in front of a large group of people.
c) The senior managers of the company kept investors, personnel and important customers up to date on their progress.
d) The Marconi management enlisted the support of the unions.
e) Their biggest customers helped the Marconi management choose which products to put money into.
f) Marconi continued to make heavy losses in their research and development programme.
g) The Marconi managers worked with their suppliers and engineers to make their products less expensive to manufacture.

6 Find words or expressions in the Marconi rescue plan that mean:

a) bring back to life
b) a fixed amount of time
c) had to handle
d) planned to meet
e) finally
f) official ways of doing things
g) professional help and advice to resolve personal, social or psychological problems
h) discontinued
i) not changing the amount of money you have to spend to make a product

Over to you

Imagine that your company's most important competitor (or the most important competitor of a company that you know) is in the same situation as Marconi at the beginning of this article, and that you are the management team who has to rescue them.

Look carefully at the Marconi rescue plan again. Then, in pairs or groups, decide who you will need to speak to. Write a list of these people, then make notes about:

- **What you will need to tell each of them.**
- **What help and advice you will need to get from each of them.**

Now present your findings to the rest of the class, choose which ideas you will adopt and write out a detailed rescue plan for that company.

UNIT 12 Management styles

Leadership qualities

Level of difficulty: ●●●

Before you read

What are the differences between a manager and a leader? How can companies find good people for their management/leader positions?

Reading

Read this article from the *Financial Times* by Gill Plimmer (several sentences are missing) and do the exercises that follow.

A field marshall's baton in every soldier's knapsack?

By Gill Plimmer

The legendary Jack Welch, former chief executive of General Electric, said, "call people managers, and they are going to start managing things, getting in the way". But *leaders* "inspire people with a vision of how things can be done better". (1) Much like military commanders, they need to determine a strategy, then inspire the workforce to follow it.

As a result, most companies operate on the premise that successful succession planning involves both nature (picking the right people) and nurture (providing training and work experience to develop them). Lucy Hatt, a managing consultant at a leading recruitment and management consultancy said that most FTSE 100 companies have leadership training programmes, but this is lacking in many smaller companies. "Smaller companies often don't feel they have the resources to invest in training although ironically they're the ones more likely to have problems," she says. (2) But over the long term you'll find that the ones who invest in their staff are the ones who are most successful".

She says one problem is that employers are looking for candidates with exactly the experience they require, whereas prospective employees are looking to stretch themselves to the next level. (3)

The job of nurturing leaders can involve everything from a company wide assessment to identify rising stars, to seconding staff to particular roles or holding short courses or individual coaching for executives.

(4) He says the biggest mistake most companies make is failing to acknowledge that different attributes are required in different jobs. "When organisations look for talent they tend to look at everyone in the same way; they tend to think about what makes a 'top chap'. In fact, what makes a great first line manager – someone who is able to take an instruction and turn it into action – doesn't necessarily make a great executive."

The consultancy helps run short leadership training courses and advises companies on how to develop stars. (5) "So, if someone is not particularly good socially, we'd encourage the company to put them into roles where they're forced to work with people until they get better at it and so on."

Whether leaders are born or made may prove as elusive as the secret of happiness. But that, it seems, will not stop companies or their employees trying to find it. (6)

From the *Financial Times*

UNIT 12 Management styles

1 The following sentences have been removed from the article. Put them back into positions 1 to 6.

a) The result is too important.
b) A lot of organisations are happy firefighting.
c) Mr Newton likens the process to strengthening muscles.
d) But with staff tending to move jobs more often, picking the right employees in whom to invest is important.
e) So when companies are grappling with globalisation, consolidation and technology, corporate leaders are required to bring direction and vision.
f) Clive Newton is managing director of leadership development solutions at Korn Ferry, the recruitment and management consultancy that works with companies to identify and nurture talent.

2 Find words or expressions in paragraph 1 that mean:

a) talked about and admired by many people
b) stopping somebody from doing something
c) to give people the wish, the confidence and the enthusiasm to do well
d) decide on

3 Before looking at paragraph 2 again, use a word from column A and a word from column B to make the two-word expressions that complete the sentences below.

A	B
long management nature operate succession	consultancy nurture premise planning term

a) Companies that .... on a .... function according to a belief.
b) Effective .... involves picking the right people to become future managers and providing the right training and work experience for them to develop.
c) .... and .... are the qualities you are born with and the qualities you learn, respectively.
d) A .... can help companies to manage aspects of their work.
e) Companies who measure things over the .... look at what happens over a period of several years.

4 True or false (paragraphs 3 and 4)?

a) Companies want to give jobs to those people who have done exactly the same kind of work in other companies.
b) Most people are looking for a new job which will give them more skills and responsibilities.
c) There are many different ways of giving people the skills and abilities they need to become leaders.
d) One way is to give potential leaders a special job with special responsibilities for a short period of time.
e) Another way is to hold regular personal discussions with senior managers about how they organise and handle their work.

5 Before looking at paragraph 5 again, choose verbs from the box and put them into the sentences below in their correct form.

able	make	acknowledge	turn
require	look	tend	

a) The biggest mistake most companies .... is failing to .... that different attributes are .... in different jobs.
b) When organisations .... for talent they .... to look at everyone in the same way.
c) A great first line manager is someone who is .... to take an instruction and .... it into action.

6 Before looking at paragraphs 6 and 7 again, match the two halves of the sentences below so that they express the meaning of the text in different words.

a) In courses that are designed to help companies to produce their own leaders, companies ...
b) So a manager who does not get on well with people ...
c) We still cannot say definitely whether leadership ...
d) Leadership may be a difficult, secret recipe, ...

1 ... is given a function where they have to deal with many people until they can do this more effectively.
2 ... but many companies believe that it is too important to ignore.
3 ... are advised to give prospective leaders jobs that practise and give them experience of the things they are currently not good at.
4 ... is a personal quality or one that can be trained.

Over to you 1

In the article Clive Newton, of the Korn Ferry consultancy, says 'the biggest mistake most companies make is failing to acknowledge that different attributes are required in different jobs'.
What personal qualities, special talents and abilities does a prospective employee need to do *your* job? And what personal qualities, special talents and abilities does a person need to do your boss's job?

Over to you 2

The article has discussed the leadership qualities of *people*. But how do we know whether a *company* has managers or leaders?
Agree on a set of parameters that show evidence of *companies* with leadership qualities with the rest of your class. Then search the web to find companies that show leadership qualities and present your findings to your class.

UNIT 12 Management styles

The advantages of diplomats

Level of difficulty: ●●●

Before you read

What are the important characteristics of a General Manager or Chief Executive Officer? Why are these characteristics so important?

Reading

Read this article by John Gapper from the *Financial Times* and do the exercises that follow.

When companies need diplomats

By John Gapper

You may recall a song released 23 years ago, by Fun Boy Three and Bananarama, called "T'aint What You Do, It's The Way That You Do It". Translated into a corporate motto, this means: it matters more to be able to engage and inspire those around you than to be a master strategist. Or, as Lou Gerstner famously declared at the start of his tenure at the then-troubled IBM: "The last thing that IBM needs right now is a vision."

Lately, big companies seem to be heeding this dictum in their choice of chief executives. Instead of hard-driving alpha males (and females) who come to their jobs like whirlwinds, vowing to shake everything and everybody up, boards are turning to diplomats. The latest is Sir Howard Stringer, who was named chairman and chief executive of Sony on Monday. For a long time, Sir Howard's uncertain role in his early days at Sony in the US and willingness to chat genially not only to Japanese executives but also to analysts, journalists and even passers-by led to him being written off as powerless. It turns out he was talking to the right people.

His rise follows the elevation of Dick Parsons, whose previous role as vice-chairman included being an amiable front-man for Gerald Levin, at Time Warner, and the ascent of Chuck Prince, a sagely reassuring lawyer, at Citigroup. So these are good days for diplomats. But if a glad-hander wants to get the top job, he ought to work for a company with two traits: big and in trouble. When conglomerates such as Time Warner and Citigroup get into trouble, they need alternative medicine. Time Warner was in turmoil following its takeover by America Online, and was riven by infighting, when Mr Parsons was promoted. Citigroup was doing better financially but had to convince the office of the New York State Attorney General and its regulators that it could behave itself as well. Mr Prince is still working on that.

In the MIT Sloan Management Review last year, Jay Conger and David Nadler drew a distinction between "content" and "context" corporate leaders. Content leaders are people who believe in strategy, the power of the right answer and "direction by declaration". Context leaders emphasise values, culture, relationships and teamwork.

Nobuyuki Idei, former CEO of Sony, faced a choice between the two types in considering Sir Howard and Ken Kutaragi, the head of its PlayStation division, who has been openly critical of failures in other parts of the company. If he had been brave, he might have taken a bet on Mr Kutaragi. But it is hard to argue with Mr Idei's instinct that Sony first needed a rejuvenating leader.

Of course, the choice between a context and a content leader can be cyclical. If the first type is most effective in troubled organisations, the second may outperform when things are better. One reason for Mr Kutaragi to accept demotion from the board this week with good grace was that, if 63-year-old Sir Howard does a good job, his moment could come.

But there will always be a place for a corporate diplomat when things have gone awry. Companies are comprised of human beings, not just ideas and strategies, and it helps when the person in charge knows it. As Fun Boy Three and Bananarama put it, that's what gets results.

From the *Financial Times*

UNIT 12 Management styles

1 Who were the following people at the time the article was written? Match the names to the ends of the sentences in the table below.

a) Lou Gerstner **b)** Sir Howard Stringer **c)** Dick Parsons **d)** Chuck Prince **e)** Nobuyuki Idei **f)** Ken Kutaragi **g)** Jay Conger and David Nadler	1 was CEO of Sony before Sir Howard Stringer. 2 is head of the Sony PlayStation division. 3 became CEO of IBM at a time when the company was in trouble. 4 are authors of articles on business management. 5 is currently CEO of Sony. 6 is CEO of Time Warner. 7 is CEO of Citigroup.

2 Answer these questions.

a) In your own words, what is the difference between 'content' and 'context' corporate leaders?

b) Which companies are best suited to 'context' corporate leaders?

3 Find words or expressions in paragraph 1 that mean:

a) it is not

b) get people interested

c) give people enthusiasm to do things

d) period of time when a person has an important job

4 Before looking at paragraph 2, complete the sentences below with the words or expressions in the box.

turn	chat genially	an alpha male
write	heed	shake

a) Companies who .... a dictum are paying attention to a particular principle.

b) The man (or male animal) in a particular group who has the most power is ....

c) Hard-driving managers who .... everything and everybody up like to change the people, structures and systems of whole companies.

d) Managers who .... to their staff talk to them in a kind and friendly way.

e) People who .... a person off decide that they will not succeed and do not pay attention to them any more.

f) Things that .... out have a particular result.

5 True or false (paragraph 2)?

a) Company management boards currently prefer to appoint managers who are diplomats rather than managers who approach their jobs with too much fire and thunder.

b) The new CEO wants to shake up the whole Sony group.

c) When Sir Howard began working for Sony in the US, it was not clear what his responsibilities were.

d) Sir Howard has been able to develop a useful network of business acquaintances.

6 In paragraph 3 there are five different expressions to describe someone moving upwards in a company to the most important and responsible job. What are they?

7 Find words or expressions in paragraphs 4 and 5 that mean:

a) defined an important difference

b) pay special attention to

c) weighing up the strengths and weaknesses of

d) shown courage

e) able to make (a company) feel younger

8 Before looking at paragraphs 6 and 7 again, choose words or expressions from the box to replace the words *in italics* in the sentences below.

awry	with good grace	most effective	be cyclical

a) The choice between a context and a content leader can *change from one to the other over time.*

b) If the first type is *much more likely to produce the intended results* in troubled organisations, the second may outperform when things are better.

c) One reason for Mr Kutaragi to accept demotion from the board this week *in a pleasant, friendly way* was that his moment could still come.

d) There will always be a place for a corporate diplomat when things have gone *wrong.*

Over to you 1

What are the characteristics of the boss of your company or a company that you know? What kind of managers are preferred in your business or the area where you live? Why is this?

Over to you 2

In groups, find out about three large companies in your region. What kind of CEOs do they now have? What kind of CEOs will they need in the future? Why?

UNIT 13 Takeovers and mergers

A year after a merger

Level of difficulty: ●●○

Before you read

If two large companies merge, how can they save costs? How else can they benefit?
The article below is about the merger between KLM and Air France. What savings do you think they have been making?

Reading

Read this article by Kevin Done from the *Financial Times* and do the exercises that follow.

Air France-KLM ahead on savings

By Kevin Done in Paris

Air France-KLM, Europe's largest airline, said on Monday it was achieving cost benefits from the coordination of its international sales and station organisations abroad faster than forecast. Patrick Alexandre, executive vice-president of international commercial affairs and operations at Air France, said the savings in international markets for the combined group in its sales and foreign stations were forecast to total €92m ($119m) within four years. This would account for more than 15 per cent of the total €580m synergy benefits forecast for the whole group from the merger.

The takeover of KLM, the Dutch flag carrier, by Air France in 2004 was a pioneering step in the consolidation of the fragmented European airline sector, and has been followed by the announcement of Lufthansa's planned acquisition of Swiss International Air Lines.

The combined Air France-KLM has 225 international destinations, 107 long-haul and 198 short-haul, with the international operations accounting for 58 per cent of total passenger revenues. While merging at shareholder level and consolidating financial reporting, Air France-KLM has continued to pursue a strategy of "one group, two airlines" by maintaining separate brands and fleet operations.

A large part of the synergy benefits is planned to come from increased revenues generated by the combination of the two groups' global networks, centred on its twin hubs at Paris Charles de Gaulle and Amsterdam Schiphol airports. Around the world it is seeking to save costs by coordinating sales strategies on international routes and by rationalising its presence at international destinations. Mr Alexandre said the biggest savings had come from the joint procurement of services, such as passenger and baggage handling and catering. Wherever possible the two airlines are seeking to rent offices and ticket offices jointly and to renegotiate station-handling services.

Synergy benefits in the first year to March 31 2005 in international commercial affairs had totalled €8.3m, up from the €7m originally forecast, while the forecast for cumulative annual savings after four years had been raised from €78m to €92m, said Mr Alexandre.

From the *Financial Times*

Text bank

UNIT 13 Takeovers and mergers

1 Match the questions with the answers.

a) I know what a station is for a railway service, but what is a station for an airline?
b) Which airline took over which other airline in 2004?
c) What parts of the airline have been joined together and what parts have been kept apart?
d) What does the group intend to do with its presence at international destinations?
e) What will this rationalisation involve?
f) How do we know that the group has had a successful first year?

1 The financial reporting system is being consolidated and Air France-KLM is a single company as far as shareholders are concerned – but the airline has two hubs close to different cities, two brands and two fleets to look after.
2 Contracting services, such as passenger and baggage handling and catering, together; renting offices and ticket offices jointly; and renegotiating existing station-handling service contracts.
3 Well, they have had €1.3m more synergy benefits than forecast in their first year – and that looks good.
4 It is the offices and other facilities managed by an airline at international destination airports.
5 The group wants to rationalise its stations at international airports.
6 Air France took over KLM.

2 Read through the whole article again and choose the best title for each paragraph.

a) Size and strategy
b) The bottom line
c) Swift savings for Air France-KLM
d) How it's all going to work
e) The start of a trend?

3 Before reading paragraph 1 again, put the correct forms of the verbs in the box into the sentences below.

account	achieve	forecast (x2)	say

a) Air France-KLM said it was .... cost benefits faster than ....
b) Patrick Alexandre .... the savings were .... to total €92m within four years.
c) This would .... for more than 15 per cent of the total benefits from the merger.

4 Find words or expressions in paragraphs 2 and 3 that mean:

a) the most important airline
b) a first action towards something
c) made up of several separate parts
d) intended takeover

5 True or false (paragraph 4)?

a) 42 per cent of the Air France-KLM business comes from domestic flights.
b) It is the policy of the group to keep a clear distinction between its two brands.

6 Before looking at paragraphs 5 and 6 again, match the two halves of the following sentences.

a) A large part of the synergy benefits is planned ...
b) These networks are centred ...
c) Wherever possible the two airlines are seeking ...
d) Synergy benefits in international commercial affairs in the first year to March 31 2005 had totalled €8.3m, up ...

1 ... from the €7m originally forecast.
2 ... to rent offices and ticket offices jointly.
3 ... to come from increased revenues generated by combining of the two groups' global networks.
4 ... on its twin hubs at Paris Charles de Gaulle and Amsterdam Schiphol airports.

Over to you

Where could the savings be made, and greater purchasing power gained, if your company, or a company you know well, merged with an important competitor?
Which sorts of businesses do you think are benefiting, and which businesses do you think are losing out from a merger strategy? Why is this?

UNIT 13 Takeovers and mergers

How to manage takeovers and mergers

Level of difficulty: ●●●

Before you read

When a company acquires or merges with another company, what changes happen? Is it better for a company to expand by acquisition or by internal growth? What do you think?

Reading

Read the article below by Nancy Hubbard from the FT.com website and do the exercises that follow.

Caveat emptor: a rule for the new deal

By Nancy Hubbard

Enough time has passed since the great merger wave of the late 1990s for us to reflect on its lessons. But we do not have long to contemplate them, for acquisition momentum is growing again.

Yet success still eludes most mega-acquirers. Evidence suggests that the majority of acquisitions do not benefit shareholders in the long term. Valuations tend to be excessively high and targets impossible to achieve. Add to that the vast amounts of management time required by acquisitions and it is clear most acquirers would have been better off channelling their efforts into growth from within.

Imagine bringing together two organisations that ostensibly mirror each other in size and function: two finance, marketing and research and development departments, two sets of manufacturing or retail sites, differing information technology and international operations. Add to that the extra complexity of different countries, cultures, time zones and languages, and it becomes easier to see why most acquisitions fail.

Yet some succeed. Corporate acquirers can achieve their cost saving and synergy objectives even across different countries and cultures. In the earlier wave, most successful mega-acquirers used external consultants to assist with implementation. But now, increasingly, acquirers are bringing the implementation process in-house, hiring former consultants, among others, and building their own expertise in acquisition.

But why create a significant internal resource for something that happens only occasionally? In the long term, it may cost less than hiring consultants, who can charge up to £15m a month. It also offers companies greater control over the process. Over time, a company's internal merger and acquisition (M & A) skills may become so well honed that they become much more likely to make future deals succeed.

Less expensively, managers can develop an in-house acquisition methodology. Such a methodology is a set of guidelines and documented processes created by managers, representing the company's collective knowledge and experience about mergers and acquisitions. An in-house methodology can also aid pre-acquisition processes by setting out guidelines for planning, checklists and a database of key individuals with specialist acquisition expertise. Such guidelines can also help when selecting and managing consultants, and ensures they operate within the company parameters without duplicating work.

Some might argue that creating this kind of in-house methodology for acquisitions is more expensive and time-consuming than it sounds. Yet the cost of getting deals wrong is growing ever higher. As M & A returns to the corporate agenda, it is high time companies took control of the processes that determine their future success or failure.

From the *Financial Times*

UNIT 13 Takeovers and mergers

1 Complete the following table, based on the article.

a) working with people in different languages
b) using specialist external consultants
c) there is a long-term benefit for shareholders
d) the integration of different information technologies and international operations
e) the process does not take up too much management time
f) working with people from different cultures
g) the cost of the company to be acquired is not overvalued
h) the combination of two finance, marketing and research and development departments
i) coordinating work in different time zones
j) the reorganisation of two sets of manufacturing or retail sites
k) developing an in-house acquisition methodology
l) cost-saving targets can be achieved fairly quickly
m) creating an in-house acquisition implementation department

In a successful merger or acquisition ...	**Most mergers and acquisitions involve ...**
Mergers across different countries often involve ...	**Implementing successful mergers and acquisitions can be achieved by ...**

2 True or false (paragraphs 1 and 2)?

a) Growing acquisition momentum comes at the beginning of a merger wave.
b) In spite of lessons learnt from the late 1990s, large mergers and acquisitions are not often successful.
c) There are good reasons to believe that most acquisitions benefit shareholders.
d) Acquisitions require a lot of management time.
e) Most acquirers think that it is better to concentrate on developing their companies internally.

3 Find words or expressions in paragraphs 3 and 4 that mean:

a) look as if they
b) additional complication
c) do not succeed
d) the added value gained by people working together
e) help
f) body of knowledge and experience

4 Look at paragraph 5 again. What are the advantages of developing an in-house resource for managing acquisitions?

5 Before looking at paragraph 6 again, match the two halves of the expressions below. (One of the words on the right can be used twice.)

a) an in-house	of guidelines
b) a set	processes
c) documented	knowledge
d) collective	individuals
e) pre-acquisition	parameters
f) key	expertise
g) specialist	methodology
h) company	

Which one of them means:

1 what everyone knows?
2 the limits and boundaries within a given company?
3 people who are very useful for a particular purpose?
4 knowledge and experience that not many people have?
5 a system for doing a particular task, developed within a particular company?
6 a collection of information that advises people how to do something?
7 sequences of things to do before starting a merger?
8 a series of actions designed to produce a particular result, which has been written down in detail?

6 Put the expressions from Exercise 5 into these sentences.

a) When considering acquiring, or merging with, another company, you need to access your company's .... and experience about mergers and acquisitions.
b) Before carrying out a merger or acquisition, it is useful for a company to have a .... and .... based on past experience.
c) Managers can develop an .... for managing acquisitions to help the company carry out all the necessary .... before the beginning of the operation.
d) During merger processes, it is important that external consultants operate within the ....
e) There are often several .... within a company who have the .... necessary to manage acquisition processes.

7 Find words or expressions in paragraph 7 that mean:

a) point out
b) not doing business successfully
c) is being considered by large companies once more
d) (something that) should have been done sooner
e) to control or influence

Over to you

Do you know a company that has acquired, been acquired by or merged with another company? What happened?
What difficulties would a national competitor have merging with your company, or a company you know? What difficulties would an international or foreign company have in integrating with your company, or a company you know?

Text bank

UNIT 14 The future of business

Solving impossible problems

Level of difficulty: ●●●

Before you read

Are the people who manage large corporations and groups of companies ever confronted with problems that are too complex or too difficult? What kind of problems could these be?

William Pulleyblank, the mathematician behind IBM's Blue Gene, the fastest computer in the world, is looking for just these types of challenges for his company's Centre for Business Optimisation.

Reading

Read this article by Alan Cane from the *Financial Times* and do the exercises that follow.

Super-fast Blue Gene looks for answers

By Alan Cane

William Pulleyblank, the mathematician behind IBM's world supercomputing record, has a new mission: to find ways to help chief executives make better decisions faster and to tackle problems that they have put in the "too difficult" box. Mr Pulleyblank, working with a team hand-picked from the company's brightest and best, is taking a fresh look at some of the most complex problems facing businesses and governments around the world.

His credentials for the job as head of IBM's Centre for Business Optimisation, which was established in 2004, are impeccable. He led the team that built Blue Gene, the supercomputer that last November took the world supercomputing record by a huge margin, processing information at an extraordinary speed. With Blue Gene, Mr Pulleyblank has huge computational resources at his command. He and his team can help chief executives manage highly diverse types of data and, by doing so, help them to understand and improve the performance of their business.

The Centre for Business Optimisation, located in upstate New York, is an in-house think-tank, drawing on expertise across IBM. The aim is to find practical solutions to practical problems. "If we provide an airline with new schedules that save 20 per cent of the cost of current schedules, that is pretty compelling," says Mr Pulleyblank. "If we can raise customer satisfaction with an airline by 10 per cent, that is also persuasive."

This practical advice is becoming a new and potentially lucrative strategic direction for IBM. It is part of a category of services worth, according to Sam Palmisano, IBM's chief executive, about $500bn (£263bn) globally – that is in addition to the $1,200bn business spends on information technology every year.

So far IBM's centre has tackled a series of practical business problems. These include:

- The flow of passengers through airports. The "Paxflow" simulator combines flight reservation data from Amadeus, the airlines' computer system, with IBM's algorithms. It predicts how many passengers will be arriving or departing at any particular time up to a week in advance.
- The diagnosis and treatment of illness. IBM is collaborating with the well-known Mayo Clinic to improve the way that it diagnoses and treats illness. In particular, it is helping in the development of new ways to analyse the patient data that the clinic has built up over the years.
- Firefighting. The research centre is working with the US Federal government to plan for forest fires. Mathematical models are being created to predict how a fire will behave and how to allocate resources to tackle it.

Of course, some problems may be impossible to solve and even the world's largest IT company cannot afford to have its top people working for months on end without profitable results. But Mr Pulleyblank insists that the tougher the challenge, the more likely IBM will be ready to take it on. "Sometimes, we like to say that if there is not a significant chance of failure, then it may not be worth doing."

From the *Financial Times*

UNIT 14 The future of business

1 Choose the best heading for each paragraph of the article.

a) A selection of projects
b) Persuasive practical solutions
c) Harnessing the power of Blue Gene
d) An important prospective source of income
e) Weighing up the chances of success or failure
f) The challenge of problems that are "too difficult"

2 Before reading paragraph 1 again, put the correct forms of the verbs in the box into the sentences below.

face	find	make	put
tackle	take	work	

a) William Pulleyblank's new mission is to .... ways to help chief executives .... better decisions faster and to .... problems that they have .... in the "too difficult" box.
b) Mr Pulleyblank, ... with a team hand-picked from the company's brightest and best, is .... a fresh look at some of the most complex problems .... businesses and governments around the world.

3 Before looking at paragraph 2 again, match the two halves of the expressions below.

a) impeccable	speed
b) huge	margin
c) extraordinary	performance
d) computational	executives
e) chief	resources
f) business	credentials

Which one of them means:

1 amazing quickness?
2 information technology equipment?
3 people who manage large companies?
4 degree of success of company activities?
5 the highest standard of achievements and experience?
6 a very large distance between the leader and the next competitor?

4 True or false (paragraph 3)?

a) You can find the IBM Centre for Business Optimisation in New York City.
b) The Centre for Business Optimisation is made up of the best people from the computer industry.
c) They specialise in saving airlines costs by providing them with new schedules.
d) Raising customer satisfaction with an airline would be a good result for the Centre for Business Optimisation.

5 Look at paragraph 4 again. Why is this kind of advice such a potentially lucrative direction for IBM?

6 Look at paragraph 5 again, including its subsections. Match the IBM solutions to practical business problems to these descriptions of their advantages.

a) This means that we can send the right number of vehicles and personnel to the scene and move any people who may be in danger away to a safe place.
b) Now we know when our restaurant will be busy and we can make sure we have more personnel at these times.
c) Under the new system we are in much less danger of giving a patient the wrong medicine.

7 Find words or expressions in paragraph 6 that mean:

a) should not risk having
b) without stopping
c) the greater the probability that
d) a definite possibility that you won't succeed
e) to accept responsibility for doing a particular job

Over to you

What are the big management problems facing local, regional and national governments and companies in your area? In groups, choose one of these problems and define it more clearly. Then present your problem as a project for Blue Gene and the IBM Centre for Business Optimisation to the rest of your class.

UNIT 14 The future of business

Keeping up with technology

Level of difficulty: ●●○

Before you read

Which newspapers do you know that have a good online presence? What is so good about it? How could it be improved?

Reading

Read this article by Aline van Duyn from the *Financial Times* and do the exercises that follow.

Papers must embrace the internet, Murdoch tells editors

By Aline van Duyn in New York

Rupert Murdoch, one of the world's biggest newspaper proprietors, yesterday told American editors that they had all been "remarkably complacent" about the effects of growing internet use on the newsprint industry. "I didn't do as much as I should have after all the excitement of the late 1990s," Mr Murdoch admitted. "I suspect many of you in this room did the same, quietly hoping that this thing called the digital revolution would just limp along. Well it hasn't ... it won't ... and it's a fast-developing reality we should grasp."

Mr Murdoch is chairman of News Corporation, the global media company, and is mapping out an internet strategy for the group. His willingness to discuss ways for News Corp to embrace the internet follows years of shunning the subject after News Corp lost considerable sums when the internet bubble burst. However, the recent growth in advertising spending on the internet and declining newspaper circulation has pushed the issue to the forefront again.

"The threat of losing print advertising dollars to online media is very real," Mr Murdoch told the American Society of Newspaper Editors in Washington. He said his newspapers, which include the *New York Post* in the US and *The Times* and *The Sun* in the UK, had to find a way of bringing news to young people, who access news in an entirely different way. "They don't want to rely on a God-like figure from above to tell them what's important," Mr Murdoch said. Not making these changes would mean the newspaper industry would "be relegated to the status of also-rans".

He said that, although most newspapers had websites, most of these were "a bland repurposing" of print content. Instead, they had to become destinations, much as internet portals and search groups such as Yahoo and Google were today. As well as finding ways to incorporate blogs into news coverage, Mr Murdoch said it was important to link text with video. "We've spent billions of dollars developing unique sports, news and general entertainment programming," Mr Murdoch said. "Our job now is to bring this content profitably into the broadband world ... and to garner our fair share – hopefully more than our fair share – of the advertising dollars that will come from successfully converging these media."

From the *Financial Times*

Text bank

UNIT 14 The future of business

1 Answer these questions

a) Who is Rupert Murdoch?
b) What do we learn about his company's current strategy from this article?
c) Why did he give this particular speech to the American Society of Newspaper Editors at that time (mid-April 2005)?

2 Find words or expressions in paragraph 1 that mean:

a) owners
b) people who are responsible for the content of newspapers and magazines
c) uncritically pleased with themselves and what they have done
d) consequences
e) great enthusiasm
f) confessed
g) move forward slowly and with difficulty
h) take advantage of

3 True or false (paragraph 2)?

a) Mr Murdoch is developing a long-term plan for deploying the internet within his company.
b) People at News Corp have been discussing how to use the internet since the internet bubble burst.
c) The company invested in some unsuccessful internet projects in the late 1990s.
d) Income for newspapers from advertising has been growing recently.
e) The issue of embracing the internet has become important again as fewer people buy newspapers.

4 Before looking at paragraph 3 again, complete the sentences below with a correct form of the verbs in the box.

access	include	lose	make
relegate	rely	tell	

a) The threat of .... print advertising dollars to online media is very real.
b) The News Corp newspapers .... the *New York Post* in the US and *The Times* and *The Sun* in the UK.
c) Young people .... news in an entirely different way.
d) They don't want to .... on a God-like figure from above to .... them what's important.
e) Not .... these changes would mean the newspaper industry would be .... to the status of also-rans.

5 Before reading paragraph 4 again, match the two halves of the expressions below.

a) a bland	dollars
b) print	portals
c) internet	content
d) news	repurposing
e) advertising	coverage

Which one of them means:

1 material that appears on the pages of a newspaper?
2 the way the media manages information about recent events?
3 income from displaying information that sells products or services?
4 locations on the world wide web where you can access a range of information?
5 a not-very-interesting adaptation of something so that it functions in a different medium from that which it was designed for?

6 True or false (paragraph 4)?

a) Mr Murdoch is not impressed with the internet presences of most newspapers.
b) He believes that the websites of newspapers should have links to Yahoo and Google.
c) He would like parts of websites to function like journals or diaries and be constantly updated with new information.
d) He believes that, as his company has invested heavily in television programming, he can provide written news coverage with moving pictures on the net.
e) He would like to earn money from the advertising income from many separate forms of media.

Over to you

Is your company, or a company that you know well, making the best use of the internet? Why or why not? Is it keeping up with, and taking advantage of, the latest communication technology? What benefits could this bring to the company? Present your arguments to the rest of your class.

Text bank answer key

Unit 1

Communication with employees

1 b, c, d, a
2 **a)** workplace disputes **b)** the blame is laid on **c)** withholding management plans **d)** a European Union directive
3 **a)** true **b)** false (academic research backs the belief that companies do better when their employees are well informed) **c)** false (you kick-start a motor to make it start and by kick-starting these negotiations employers can take control) **d)** true **e)** false (face-to-face and electronic communication is just one possible solution)
4 **a)** KPMG **b)** 3 **c)** AstraZeneca and KPMG **d)** 3
5 **a)** outweigh **b)** persuaded **c)** online polling **d)** follow suit

The communication value of corporate websites

1 **(Model answers)**
a) Why is it difficult to justify further investment in the corporate website?
b) Why would fewer customers approach your company if your corporate website disappeared?
c) Why would the company management begin to get worrying feedback from their Human Resources department?
d) How do analysts normally use corporate websites?
e) Who would be phoning your press office?
f) Which costs could be saved?
g) What are many CEOs being asked to do?
2 **a)** authorise a cheque **b)** keep (something) going **c)** measure return on investment **d)** sell online **e)** serve a purpose
1 sell online **2** keep (something) going **3** authorise a cheque **4** serve a purpose **5** measure return on investment
3 **a)** measure (its) return on investment **b)** authorise a cheque **c)** selling online **d)** serve a purpose **e)** keep (their services) going
4 **a)** valuable role **b)** are likely to **c)** used to **d)** in due course **e)** get a feeling for
5 **a)** true **b)** true **c)** false **d)** true **e)** true **f)** false (perhaps this is true in general, but Mr Bowen is proposing the opposite in this article)

Unit 2

The fate of global brands

1 **a)** false (at first it seemed so, but then some awkward commercial realities started to close in) **b)** true **c)** true **d)** false (all we learn from the article is that brands have to compete with supermarkets' own products) **e)** true
2 **a)** seminal **b)** converge **c)** pour **d)** little **e)** consumer **f)** clean **g)** awkward
3 c) and f) were not mentioned in this paragraph.
4 **a)** command **b)** creating, designed (designing, created *would also work here*) **c)** throw, possessing **d)** resorted, buying **e)** owning
5 **a)** ever-proliferating brand choices **b)** packaged goods **c)** own-label products **d)** standardised products **e)** golden age

Moving your brand image upmarket

1 **a)** glory was up for grabs
b) seven-figure sum; win over an audience
c) early adopters
d) move its brand image more upmarket
e) keep up its efforts
f) enhance its hip, youth
2 **a)** Samsung was promoting its brand, its 19-inch LCD flat panel screens, its D500 mobile phone handsets and its connections to young people in Europe.
b) Samsung is trying to increase the value of its brand worldwide; it is also trying to make its brand more upmarket. Interbrand has ranked Samsung as the world's 21st most valuable brand, up from 42nd in 2001, so it has been successful in doing this.
c) Samsung is having problems because Motorola mobile phones have become more popular than its own, and it is making smaller profits on its LCD screens because there are too many on the market.
d) Europe is a difficult market for Samsung and so is the older consumer sector.
e) Samsung is turning to younger people to promote its products.
3 **a)** took part **b)** sponsored **c)** to strut **d)** to reach **e)** sector
4 They are all true.
5 **a)** The company *recently slipped back into third place behind* Motorola.
b) Samsung is suffering from falling prices for its LCD screens, *due to a glut in the market.*
c) Stimulating demand for the screens among gaming fans *could be one way to help ramp up sales.*
6 They are all false because in the article, it says ...
a) *Although* Samsung scores well in overall brand surveys and is strong in Asia, *studies indicate that ...*
b) ... in Europe Nokia and Philips are *strong local manufacturers.*
c) *the company's internal research* has shown a 25 per cent increase in positive attitudes towards Samsung in the 18 to 29-year-old age group.
7 **a)** signed **b)** makes **c)** associated **d)** gives **e)** comes

Text bank

Unit 3

Partnering among consultancies

1 **a)** 7 **b)** 2 **c)** 5 **d)** 1 **e)** 3 **f)** 8 **g)** 4 **h)** 6
2 **a)** paragraph 5 **b)** paragraph 2 **c)** paragraph 4
d) paragraph 1 **e)** paragraph 3
3 **a)** of **b)** to **c)** by **d)** from
4 **a)** capabilities **b)** a risk element **c)** echoed
d) essential
5 **i)**
a) *the rules of engagement*
b) *how will we measure progress?*
c) *seamless teamwork*
d) *personal integrity – [with complementary] strategies and approaches*
e) *personal relationships matter enormously*
f) *the commitment of all involved*
g) *the question of cultural fit and values – if [these] are not shared at the outset you will find out later to your cost*
h) *the question of joint marketing and how we protect each other's brand*
ii)
a) *an explicit commercial relationship in place*
b) *agreed milestones for the project*
e) *the interpersonal relationships are vital*
g) *you need the same ethics, the same values*
i) *explicit work-share agreements up front*
6 **a)** replaced **b)** managing **c)** been able

Blogging as a relationship tool

1 **a)** a blog **b)** blogging **c)** the blogosphere **d)** blogger
e) blogs **f)** blog
2 **a)** They all write blogs or web logs.
b) Because they would like to attract public attention, develop customer relationships, respond to criticism and (they hope) use the medium of blogging to sell more of their products.
c) They chat and they talk about the company's long-term business plans when they blog there.
d) Because they can be accessed by many more people than just the employees of a company.
e) A lot of people criticise them – and perhaps many of these people won't access that blog any more.
f) It asks its bloggers not to mention anything that the public has not already been informed about through the media. It also asks its bloggers to tell the corporate PR department if they get any enquiries from journalists.
g) Because he 'pulls no punches when it comes to his employer'. To 'pull a punch' is to not hurt someone as much as you are able to. So, in other words, if Microsoft deserves severe criticism, then Mr Scoble criticises them as severely as he can.
3 **a)** getting in on the act **b)** domain **c)** trade
d) cultivate **e)** along the way
4 **a)** enter, establish **b)** blog **c)** trade, discuss
d) targeting **e)** written
5 a, b, d and g
6 **a)** pose risks **b)** post on a blog **c)** make public
d) notify the PR department **e)** receive queries
f) cause damage **g)** spout off
1 cause damage **2** make public
3 notify the PR department **4** spout off
5 receive queries **6** post on a blog **7** pose risks
7 **a)** true **b)** false (he has been specifically hired to blog about the company, and good blogging involves telling the truth rather than just good things) **c)** false (he is quite satisfied with Microsoft's tolerance of employee blogs)
d) true

Unit 4

A company strategy for a successful product

1 **a)** 2 **b)** 1 **c)** 6 **d)** 3 **e)** 5 **f)** 4
2 **a)** distinctive **b)** obscure **c)** pagers **d)** subscribers
e) rocketed **f)** sustain
3 **a)** true (at least this was true of the market at the time the article was written)
b) true (they have been using *a canny, three-pronged strategy to keep the competition at bay*)
c) false (yes, they have been co-opting potential rivals, but we do not know from the article whether they have been developing software for RIM)
d) true
4 **a)** By allowing almost 100 distributors to have BlackBerry devices made themselves under license from RIM; and letting carriers offer BlackBerry contracts to their customers.
b) Because they earn a relatively high amount of money for each BlackBerry message their customers send and because BlackBerry messages do not take up much space (in terms of bandwidth) in their own networks.
c) RIM does not keep its technology secret. Instead it gets other companies, including potential rival companies, involved in BlackBerry projects.
5 **a)** jeopardise **b)** singles
c) being (becoming *would also work here*) **d)** possesses

A record year for a supermarket chain

1 **a)** 3 **b)** 5 **c)** 1 **d)** 4 **e)** 2
2 **a)** Integration costs **b)** operating loss
c) goodwill amortisation **d)** Disposals
e) like-for-like sales
3 **a)** to confirm (your) dominance **b)** to shrug off fears
c) to report annual profits **d)** to accelerate expansion
e) to fly in the face of (something) **f)** to rein in sales
1 to report annual profits **2** to rein in sales
3 to confirm your dominance **4** to shrug off fears
5 to fly in the face of (something)
6 to accelerate expansion
4 **a)** on, to **b)** in, for, on **c)** by, over
5 **a)** appeal **b)** businesses **c)** sales **d)** entertainment
e) finance **f)** arm **g)** phase
6 **a)** the adoption of **b)** an adverse impact **c)** cash flow
d) issue **e)** a final dividend

Unit 5

Managing flexible working practices

1 **a)** In some countries, changes in the law are forcing employers to adopt flexible working practices for certain people, yet many companies are discovering that there are many good business reasons for doing this. It is inexpensive to give employees the right IT equipment for their home offices, it is a good way of drawing on a larger pool of skills, of getting greater productivity from staff and it is a good way of retaining them – particularly older workers.
b) Women, older people and many graduates for whom a good work/life balance is important.
c) Both workers and bosses must adjust for flexible working to be effective. Managers have to learn to measure results rather than time spent doing a job – and both employers and employees must work together to build trust.

2 **a)** on the surface **b)** a fundamental change **c)** a shift (from ... to ...) **d)** herald **e)** legislation **f)** request **g)** a major catalyst to

3 **a)** true **b)** false **c)** true **d)** true

4 **a)** commissioned **b)** found **c)** attract **d)** bend **e)** prompted **f)** measure **g)** evaluate

5 **(Model answers)**
1 Do you find it difficult to attract the right skills from your local market?
2 Would you be able to attract staff if you could offer them flexible working?
3 Do you believe that staff who work from home are more likely to bend the rules?

6 **a)** ii) **b)** i) **c)** iii)

Satisfying employees and customers

1 **a)** The tracks in the depot were in poor condition and this slowed the trains down on their way to their starting platforms, and the train drivers and conductors had to wait for the cleaning and safety inspections to be carried out before they could board their trains.
b) Because the people who are most familiar with the work know where the problems are and have ideas for new products and a better service.
c) They often work for managers who don't like change, or their suggestions are processed too slowly and they become disappointed and unhappy.
d) The research looked at employees who did not deal directly with customers.
e) People who are happy like to belong to a team that they respect themselves, and that is respected by other people in the company, and they like to belong to a company that is respected by the world outside.
f) The members of the new teams have to spend time getting to know each other and how they work, often at the customers' expense.

2 **a)** became, run **b)** leaving **c)** eliminate **d)** saving, reducing

3 **a)** in great demand **b)** that extra effort **c)** where the problems lie **d)** their current strategy disrupted **e)** trapped in corporate bureaucracy

4 **a)** engaged employees **b)** corporate profitability **c)** effect, impact **d)** attitudes **e)** content **f)** admire

5 **a)** true **b)** false **c)** true **d)** false (we do not know this from the article)

6 **a)** 6 **b)** 4 and 5 **c)** 3 **d)** 2 **e)** 1

Unit 6

The priority of safety

1 **a)** true
b) true (only eight per cent of the workers at Nasa said that they saw changes for the better)
c) true (they reported that pressure to get the shuttles back into space leads the agency to make questionable safety decisions)
d) false (the Columbia Accident Investigation Board was an independent panel)
e) false (we do not know this from the article)

2 **a)** grounded **b)** disintegrated **c)** divided **e)** ensure

3 **a)** They have been working towards improving the relationship between employees and supervisors, making it easier for employees to disagree with what everyone else believes, encouraging work in teams, and making their managers act in a way that is more accountable.
b) Nasa managers say they are making time to listen to concerns of engineers and others on issues that may compromise safety.
c) According to BST assessments, the culture at Nasa has changed.
d) Perhaps not, as significantly more managers have noticed improvements than ordinary workers.

4 **a)** 4 **b)** 3 **c)** 5 **d)** 2 **e)** 1

5 **a)** In the wake of **b)** investigate **c)** expressed **d)** dismissed **e)** a lax **f)** contributing to **g)** up and running

6 **a)** doing **b)** transported **c)** called, developing **d)** getting **e)** waiting

The risk of loss of brand value and reputation

1 **a)** paragraph 6 **b)** paragraph 7 **c)** paragraph 5 **d)** paragraph 3 **e)** paragraph 2 **f)** paragraph 4 **g)** paragraph 1

2 **a)** false (while this may be true for British Airways, Royal Mail and Jaguar, as they have recently faced industrial action or threats of industrial action, other companies would probably benefit from such a reminder from time to time)
b) true **c)** true
d) false (at times when companies are losing money all issues that have nothing to do with making the company financially healthy again usually take a back seat)

3 **a)** intangible assets **b)** balance sheets
c) tainted brands **d)** branded organisations
e) industrial action
1 industrial action 2 intangible assets
3 branded organisations 4 balance sheets
5 tainted brands

4 **a)** tainted brands **b)** industrial action
c) branded organisations **d)** balance sheets
e) intangible assets

5 **a)** poor industrial relations
b) do not come about in isolation
c) reflect on
d) makes for
e) strategy

6 **a)** given, dictated **b)** goes **c)** develop, briefing
d) has

7 **a)** Potentially that, in the minds of the public, a brand will no longer be associated with a good customer relationship.
b) It is important for companies to manage the risk to their brand because, when things go wrong and a company loses the good reputation associated with their brand, this can result in problems that go on a very long time.

Unit 7

Internet shopping – ten years on

1 **a)** Retailing **b)** retail **c)** retailing or retail **d)** retail
e) retailers **f)** retailer

2 **a)** true **b)** true **c)** true **d)** false **e)** false **f)** false

3 **a)** a host **b)** taking ... to (twice in this paragraph)
c) underline **d)** decade **e)** accounted for

4 **a)** counteracting (*could also be* compensating for)
b) grew (*could also be* rose)
c) grown, suggests (*could also be* proves)

5 **a)** spending **b)** allowing
c) gain (twice in these two paragraphs)
d) neglect **e)** continue

6 **a)** communications regulator **b)** internet access
c) a broadband connection **d)** mobile commerce
e) online sales **f)** expansion area

User-friendliness

1 **a)** paragraph 5 **b)** paragraph 3 **c)** paragraph 6
d) paragraph 2 **e)** paragraph 4 **f)** paragraph 1

2 **a)** efforts are **b)** superficial **c)** an award
d) online presences **e)** beasts **f)** to get stuck into

3 **a)** false **b)** true **c)** true
d) false (at least, we cannot say this from what the article tells us)

4 **a)** see/assess/determine **b)** made, co-ordinated
c) becomes **d)** covered

5 **a)** to **b)** by, of **c)** to, to
d) out (check out *means the same as* look at)
e) by **f)** from

6 **a)** central investor area **b)** positions **c)** mix
d) subtleties **e)** stakeholders

Unit 8

Managing teams across different countries and cultures

1 **(Model answers)**
a) What sort of plan does any good virtual team have?
b) Why does using e-mail remove a lot of the hierarchy from professional communications?
c) How can people adapt most quickly to the social norms and cultural sensitivities of a new culture?
d) Who should be made responsible for setting the norms of working behaviour in a project being carried out from two different locations?
e) Why did the American's interruption to his Japanese colleague's presentation cause real problems?

2 **a)** keeping, working **b)** includes, speak **c)** studied
d) speaks, be

3 **a)** diversity **b)** challenges **c)** take into account
d) rather than by

4 **a)** of **b)** in **c)** to **d)** for **e)** for **f)** to

5 **a)** true
b) false (this is not what we learn from the article which says, 'those trying to do this [adapt to social norms and cultural sensitivities] at a distance may find it tougher to fit in, increasing the potential for misunderstandings')
c) true

6 **a)** points out **b)** appoint **c)** knows **d)** as
e) responsible for **f)** carried out

7 **a)** 3 **b)** 1 **c)** 4 **d)** 2

Team-building exercises

1 **a)** paragraph 4 **b)** paragraph 1 **c)** paragraph 2
d) paragraph 5 **e)** paragraph 6 **f)** paragraph 7
g) paragraph 3

2 **a)** The charity is called Whizz-Kidz and it helps disabled children to move around.
b) The record is called *New Shop On the Block* – a good name for an album made by a chain of department stores, and also a reference to the successful 1980s pop band New Kids On the Block.

3 **a)** given **b)** bond **c)** organised, remarked, come across
d) involved, crying

4 **a)** to understand what someone means
b) to upset someone **c)** to face the music
d) to mark a trend **e)** to get along with someone
f) to go for a drink
1 to upset someone 2 to mark a trend
3 to understand what someone means
4 to go for a drink 5 to get along with someone
6 to face the music

5 **a)** 3 **b)** 4 **c)** 5 **d)** 6 **e)** 2 **f)** 1

6 **a)** Not highly! In fact he says they 'are generally useless'.
b) He is worried that people will suffer if they have to watch, or listen to, other people's team-building exercises.

7 **(Model answers)**
a) What does Mr Sanghera think is more excruciating than being involved in a team-building exercise?
b) How many times has he listened to *New Shop On the Block*?

Text bank

c) How does John Lewis defend the release of such an album?
d) What is a mitigating factor for releasing it?
e) What does Mr Sanghera believe would make people give even more generous donations to Whizz-Kidz?

Unit 9

Options for start-up companies

1 **a)** 3 **b)** 1 **c)** 2
2 **a)** Rising inventories at semiconductor manufacturers and disappointing earnings announcements, which lead to falling share prices.
b) There are a lot of start-up technology companies in Silicon Valley – and indeed around the world – as well as more mature IT companies.
c) In a technology market that is not performing well, venture capital firms can concentrate less on preparing their companies to make initial public offerings and more on their traditional role of financing new companies in their first few years of life.
d) An initial public offering is when a new company issues shares for sale in a stock market. It is a 'prize' for entrepreneurs because it is easier for them to raise finance on a stock market than by presenting their arguments – often again and again – to different venture capitalists.
e) The danger is that people buy shares as new share issues from technology companies that almost immediately lose their value. This, in turn, weakens investors' trust in the stock market and thus weakens the market as a whole.
3 **a)** rising inventories
b) disappointing earnings announcements
c) sharp recovery
d) venture capitalists
e) long-term investment
4 **a)** true
b) true
c) false (Venture capital firms should sort out which of their companies perform the best, and are mature enough to be brought to market. If venture capitalists supported all their companies, even failing companies, they would soon go out of business!)
5 **a)** testing, consensus **b)** predicted, catch up
c) eager **d)** profitable
6 **a)** 3 **b)** 1 **c)** 2 **d)** 5
e) 4 (here 'Silicon Valley' in the article can also include other new technology companies in other parts of the world where similar financing options are available)

An alternative to the banks

1 **a)** paragraph 3 **b)** paragraph 2 **c)** paragraph 4
d) paragraph 6 **e)** paragraph 5 **f)** paragraph 1
2 **a)** bypass **b)** the high street **c)** garnered
d) according to **e)** loans **f)** creep
3 c)
4 **a)** come up with a notion **b)** tap a market
c) value stability **d)** assess as creditworthy
e) parcel out money **f)** charge a fee
g) earn commission
1 tap a market **2** earn commission
3 assess as creditworthy **4** parcel out money
5 value stability **6** charge a fee
7 come up with a notion
5 **a)** true
b) true
c) false ('borrowers who fail to pay will be pursued through the usual channels' that is, in the same way as other companies try to get their money back from bad payers)
d) true
e) false ('for the lender, their investment is not protected by any compensation scheme')
f) false ('for the lender, their investment is not protected by any compensation scheme unless they have been defrauded.')
g) true
6 **a)** set up **b)** working, finding **c)** see **d)** catch on
7 **(Model answers)**
a) How has Zopa carried out/done its marketing so far?
b) What does Zopa want to achieve?
c) Why is this such a big challenge?

Unit 10

Using technology to handle customers

1 **a)** paragraph 3 **b)** paragraph 4 **c)** paragraph 6
d) paragraph 2 **e)** paragraph 5 **f)** paragraph 1
2 **a)** 3 **b)** 5 **c)** 4 **d)** 6 **e)** 1 **f)** 2
3 *With the right telephony techniques ...*
b) e) f)
With good customer support software ...
a) c) d)
4 **(Model answers)**
a) How does interactive voice response work?
b) What will a good customer service application do?
c) When do customer histories appear in front of the agent?
d) What information will these histories show?
5 **a)** reduce **b)** encouraging **c)** seek **d)** posting
e) build **f)** resolved **g)** fed
6 **a)** ultimately **b)** integrated (with) **c)** pool
d) credit control **e)** a warranty **f)** is past due payment
g) cash-conscious businesses

Customer satisfaction surveys

1 Can't get no *satisfaction* (from the song by the Rolling Stones)
a) paragraph 5 **b)** paragraph 3 **c)** paragraph 2
d) paragraph 4 **e)** paragraph 1
2 **a)** noticed, become **b)** pop up, visiting **c)** quizzed
3 **a)** opportunity **b)** plaudits **c)** brickbats **d)** seemingly
e) attention **f)** a refreshing change
4 **a)** false (according to Prof Barwise, 'Placing someone else's needs above your own just does not make sense unless it helps perpetuate your genes.')
b) true ('we may deduce that employees are rarely predisposed to give any customers good service unless they fancy them.')

c) false (he says that everyone lies to their boss, but he doesn't say anything about them never telling the truth)
d) true ('but bosses always underestimate the extent of the deceit')
e) true
f) true
g) false ('if you are responsible for dealing with customers every day, and your customers are intensely dissatisfied, are you going to risk getting the blame by telling the management?')

5 **a)** Because they are a way of finding out about customer satisfaction directly from the customers rather than through the employees.
b) Not especially effective as they don't always help to identify problems and – even when a problem has been identified – they don't always help to solve them.

6 **(Model answers)**
a) What is the author's main criticism of these surveys?
b) How do good companies with good products and services measure customer satisfaction?
c) How do many companies destroy the value created by their spending on advertising and branding?
d) What does the author think the intelligent response would be?

Unit 11

Managing crises effectively

1 **a)** paragraph 4 **b)** paragraph 3 **c)** paragraph 6 **d)** paragraph 5 **e)** paragraph 2 **f)** paragraph 1

2 **a)** inevitable **b)** robust, fallible **c)** essential **d)** appreciate **e)** customer preferences **f)** established, put in place

3 **a)** true (Arthur Andersen has gone out of business and Marconi has been taken over – see the following lesson 'Desperate days, drastic measures' to find out more about how Marconi managed its crisis)
b) true
c) false ('closer to home' means 'more relevant' or 'less global' here)
d) true

4 **a)** They quickly withdrew Concorde from service, announced an investigation into the accident and reassured the travelling public that it was still safe to fly Air France.
b) It went down the next day, but not by much and not for very long.

5 **(Model answers)**
a) Why did Intel suffer a huge and unforeseen crisis?
b) What did the company do about it?
c) How much did it cost them?
d) Why did Intel's customers respond positively?

6 **a)** 2 **b)** 4 **c)** 1 **d)** 3

7 **a)** incident **b)** disease **c)** key **d)** seismic **e)** subtle **f)** undermine **g)** swiftly

Carrying out a rescue plan

1 **a)** 3 **b)** 1 **c)** 2

2 **i)** c **ii)** g **iii)** f **iv)** a **v)** e **vi)** d **vii)** b

3 **a)** dried **b)** brought **c)** fix, implicated **d)** given, seek

4 **a)** defaulted **b)** debts **c)** trimmed **d)** supply chain **e)** made redundant **f)** relisted **g)** retained **h)** confidence

5 **a)** true
b) false ('answerable' here means 'responsible to')
c) true
d) not quite true (but they certainly persuaded them not to hold them up in any way)
e) true
f) false (they continued to invest heavily in R & D, but the article doesn't say whether they made a loss or not)
g) true (they managed to raise operating margins)

6 **a)** revive **b)** a set period **c)** faced **d)** intended to hit **e)** eventually **f)** procedures **g)** counselling **h)** dropped **i)** keeping product costs steady

Unit 12

Leadership qualities

1 **a)** 6 **b)** 2 **c)** 5 **d)** 3 **e)** 1 **f)** 4

2 **a)** legendary **b)** getting in the way **c)** inspire **d)** determine

3 **a)** operate, premise **b)** succession planning **c)** Nature, nurture **d)** management consultancy **e)** long term

4 **a)** true **b)** true **c)** true
d) true (this is 'seconding staff to particular roles')
e) true (this is 'individual coaching for executives')

5 **a)** make, acknowledge, required
b) look, tend **c)** able, turn

6 **a)** 3 **b)** 1 **c)** 4 **d)** 2

The advantages of diplomats

1 **a)** 3 **b)** 5 **c)** 6 **d)** 7 **e)** 1 **f)** 2 **g)** 4

2 **a)** 'Content' corporate leaders manage with systems and with their authority. 'Context' leaders are more concerned with the ways people in companies can effectively work together.
b) Large companies that are in trouble appear to be best suited to 'context' corporate leaders.

3 **a)** t'ain't **b)** engage **c)** inspire **d)** tenure

4 **a)** heed **b)** an alpha male **c)** shake **d)** chat genially **e)** write **f)** turn

5 **a)** true
b) false (at least we do not know this from the article)
c) true
d) true (as 'It turns out [that] he was talking to the right people')

6 his (Sir Howard Stringer's) *rise*
the elevation of Dick Parsons
the ascent of Chuck Prince
to get the top job
Mr Parsons *was promoted*

7 **a)** drew a distinction **b)** emphasise **c)** considering **e)** been brave **f)** rejuvenating

8 **a)** be cyclical **b)** most effective **c)** with good grace **d)** awry

Unit 13

A year after a merger

1 **a)** 4 **b)** 6 **c)** 1 **d)** 5 **e)** 2 **f)** 3
2 **a)** paragraph 3 **b)** paragraph 5 **c)** paragraph 1 **d)** paragraph 4 **e)** paragraph 2
3 **a)** achieving, forecast **b)** said, forecast **c)** account
4 **a)** the flag carrier **b)** a pioneering step **c)** fragmented **d)** planned acquisition
5 **a)** true **b)** true
6 **a)** 3 **b)** 4 **c)** 2 **d)** 1

How to manage takeovers and mergers

1 *In a successful merger or acquisition ...*
c, e, g, l
Most mergers and acquisitions involve ...
d, h, j
Mergers across different countries often involve ...
a, f, i
Implementing successful mergers and acquisitions can be achieved by ...
b, k, m
2 **a)** true **b)** true
c) false (according to this article long-term benefits of mergers to shareholders are rare, though there are probably some short-term benefits not mentioned here)
d) true
e) false (according to the article, acquirers who have made unsuccessful mergers would have done better if they had expanded their companies from within)
3 **a)** ostensibly **b)** extra complexity **c)** fail **d)** synergy **e)** assist **f)** expertise
4 It may cost less than hiring consultants, it gives companies greater control over the process and, with practice and experience, it will make future acquisitions far more likely to succeed.
5 **a)** an in-house methodology **b)** a set of guidelines **c)** documented processes **d)** collective knowledge **e)** pre-acquisition processes **f)** key individuals **g)** specialist expertise **h)** company parameters
1 collective knowledge **2** company parameters **3** key individuals **4** specialist expertise **5** an in-house methodology **6** a set of guidelines **7** pre-acquisition processes **8** documented processes
6 **a)** collective knowledge
b) set of guidelines, documented processes
c) in-house methodology, pre-acquisition processes
d) company parameters
e) key individuals, specialised expertise
7 **a)** argue **b)** getting deals wrong **c)** returns to the corporate agenda **d)** high time **e)** to determine

Unit 14

Solving impossible problems

1 **a)** 5 **b)** 3 **c)** 2 **d)** 4 **e)** 6 **f)** 1
2 **a)** find, make, tackle, put **b)** working, taking, facing
3 **a)** impeccable credentials **b)** huge margin **c)** extraordinary speed **d)** computational resources **e)** chief executives **f)** business performance
1 extraordinary speed **2** computational resources **3** chief executives **4** business performance **5** impeccable credentials **6** huge margin
4 **a)** false ('upstate' indicates that the organisation is in New York state, but not actually in New York City)
b) false (the CBO is an in-house think tank, drawing on expertise from across the IBM group, but not outside the company)
c) false (in the article this was just given as an example of what the CBO could do)
d) true
5 This is potentially a good money-making idea for IBM because they believe companies will pay a lot of money for this kind of service, on top of what they normally pay for information technology.
6 **a)** This is an advantage of the 'firefighting' problem.
b) This is an advantage of the 'flow of passengers through airports' problem.
c) This is an advantage of the 'diagnosis and treatment of illness' problem.
7 **a)** cannot afford to have **b)** on end **c)** the more likely **d)** a significant chance of failure **e)** to take (something) on

Keeping up with technology

1 **a)** He is chairman of News Corporation, the global media company that owns the *New York Post* in the US and *The Times* and *The Sun* in the UK.
b) Mr Murdoch is mapping out an internet strategy for his company, and is discussing ways for News Corp to embrace the internet.
c) Because at that time people were spending more money on advertising on the internet and the circulation of newspapers was going down.
2 **a)** proprietors **b)** editors **c)** complacent **d)** effects **e)** excitement **f)** admitted **g)** limp along **h)** grasp
3 **a)** true
b) false (they have been avoiding (shunning) this since the internet bubble burst)
c) true
d) false (there has been a recent growth in advertising spending on the internet)
e) true
4 **a)** losing **b)** include **c)** access **d)** rely, tell **e)** making, relegated
5 **a)** a bland repurposing **b)** print content **c)** internet portals **d)** news coverage **e)** advertising dollars
1 print content **2** news coverage **3** advertising dollars **4** internet portals **5** a bland repurposing
6 **a)** true **b)** false
c) probably true (at least he said it was important to find 'ways to incorporate blogs into news coverage')
d) true
e) false (the article says that he would like the newspaper industry to 'garner [its] fair share of the advertising dollars that will come from successfully converging these media')

Resource bank

Teacher's notes

Introduction

These Resource bank activities are designed to extend and develop the Skills sections in the main Course Book. Each Resource bank unit begins with a language exercise that takes up and takes further the language points from the Course Book unit, and then applies this language in one or more role play activities.

What to give the learners

You have permission to photocopy the Resource bank pages in this book. In some units, you will give each student a copy of the whole page. In others, there are role cards which need to be cut out and given to participants with particular roles. These activities are indicated in the unit-specific notes below.

The **language exercises** at the beginning of each Resource bank unit can be used to revise language from the main Course Book unit, especially if you did the Skills section in another lesson. In any case, point out the connection with the Course Book Skills material. These language exercises are designed to prepare Ss for the role play(s) that follow and in many cases can be done in a few minutes as a way of focussing Ss on the activity that will follow.

A typical two-person **role play** might last 5 or 10 mins, followed by 5 mins praise and correction. An animated group discussion might last longer, and longer than you planned: in this case, drop one of your other planned activities and do it another time, rather than try to cram it in before the end of the lesson. If you then have 5 or 10 minutes left over, you can always go over some language points from the lesson again, or, better still, get students to say what they were. One way of doing this is to ask them what they've written in their notebooks during the lesson.

Revising and revisiting

Feel free to do an activity more than once. After one run-through, praise strong points, then work on three or four things that need correcting or improving. Then you can get learners to change roles and do the activity again, or the parts of the activity where these points come up. Obviously, there will come a time when interest wanes, but the usual tendency in language teaching is not to revisit things enough, rather than the reverse.

Fluency and accuracy

Concentrate on different things in different activities. In some role plays and discussions, you may want to focus on *fluency*, with learners interacting as spontaneously as possible. In others, you will want to concentrate on *accuracy*, with learners working on getting specific forms correct. Rather than expect Ss to get everything correct, you could pick out, say, three or four forms that you want them to get right, and focus on these.

Clear instructions

Be sure to give complete instructions *before* getting students to start. In role plays, be very clear about who has which role, and give learners time to absorb the information they need. Sometimes there are role cards that you hand out. The activities where this happens are indicated below.

Parallel and public performances (PPP)

In pair work or small group situations, get all pairs to do the activity at the same time. Go round the class and listen. When they have finished, praise strong points, and deal with three or four problems that you have heard, especially problems that more than one group has been having. Then get individual pairs to give public performances so that the whole class can listen. The performers should pay particular attention to these two or three points.

1 to 1

The pair activities can be done 1 to 1, with the teacher taking one of the roles. The activity can be done a second time reversing the roles and getting the student to integrate your suggestions for improvement.

Unit 1 Communication

Problem–solving on the phone

- With the whole class, look again at the expressions on page 11 of the Course Book and get Ss to read them with realistic intonation. Then do the same with the expressions here, completing the unfinished ones with possible continuations.

1 d j	**2** a i	**3** e h	**4** c g	**5** b f

Resource bank

- Point out that 'widget' is used to talk about an imaginary product that a company might produce: it doesn't matter what it is. Divide the class into pairs and hand out the role cards for Phone call 1. Get Ss to sit back to back to simulate the phone calls, or even better, get them to use real phone extensions.
- When the situation is clear, the role play can begin in parallel pairs. (There is quite a big element of information exchange here, as A has to communicate information about the order to B before B can deal with the problem.)
- Circulate and monitor. Note language points for praise and correction, especially in the area of problem-solving.
- Praise good language points from the role play and work on three or four points that need improvement, getting individual Ss to say the correct forms.
- Hand out the role cards for Phone call 2.
- Follow the same procedure for monitoring and correction as above.
- Get one of the pairs to do a public performance of their role play for the whole class.

Unit 2 International marketing

Brainstorming

- Refresh Ss' memories about the advice for brainstorming on page 19 of the Course Book. Then ask them to correct the expressions here in pairs. Circulate and assist.
- With the whole class, ask Ss for the answers.

1. We're trying to come up with some completely fresh thinking on this subject.
2. It doesn't matter what your positioning in the company is. All ideas are (no 'the') welcome.
3. We're going to stop at 5 on the dot, so we have an hour ahead of us to think of something.
4. Don't criticise other people's contributions. At this stage, everything is acceptable.
5. Just say everything that comes into your head. We should consider every idea, however crazy it seems at first!
6. You don't have to stick to the point. We get some good ideas when people digress.
7. Let other people (no 'to') finish when they are talking. Don't butt in.
8. We mustn't get bogged down in details at this stage.

(B)

- Divide the class into groups of three or four, and appoint a leader for each group. Allocate a situation to each group. Point out that money is no problem, at least for the moment!
- When it's clear what Ss have to do, the brainstorming sessions can begin.
- Circulate and monitor, but do not interrupt the flow of the brainstorming. Note language points for praise and correction, especially brainstorming-type language.
- Praise good language points from the discussion and work on three or four points that need improvement, getting individual Ss to say the correct forms.
- Ask representatives (not necessarily the leaders) of the different groups for a brief summary of their brainstorming discussions and conclusions.

Unit 3 Building relationships

Networking

- Remind Ss about the language of networking on page 27 of the Course Book.
- Divide the class into pairs. Cut up, shuffle and hand out the 'turns' to each pair. Obviously, be careful not to mix the different sets of turns, as this could lead to some surreal conversations!
- Get the pairs to piece together the conversation in parallel.
- You can hand out a complete conversation as printed in this book as a key and get Ss to read it sitting back to back to simulate a phone conversation, paying attention to friendly intonation.
- Ask for a performance of the conversation from one of the pairs for the whole class.

(B)

- In Exercises B and C, students A and B both have access to the same information.
- Point out that the conversation in B takes place in the week *before* the one in A.
- Divide the class into pairs and get them to rehearse the conversation.
- Circulate, monitor and assist with natural expression and intonation of the kind you hear between old friends.
- Praise good language points from the role play and work on three or four points that need improvement, getting individual Ss to say the correct forms.
- Ask for a performance of the conversation from one of the pairs for the whole class.

(C)

- Point out that the conversation in C takes place a few days *after* the one in A.
- Divide the class into pairs and get them to rehearse the conversation.
- Circulate, monitor and assist with natural expression and intonation of the kind you hear between people who have just met.
- Praise good language points from the role play and work on three or four points that need improvement, getting individual Ss to say the correct forms.

- Ask for a performance of the conversation from one of the pairs for the whole class.
- Ask the other pairs what happened when they continued the conversation.

Unit 4 Success

Negotiating

- Get Ss to look again at the expressions on page 35 of the Course Book, then do this exercise as a quick-fire whole-class activity.

1 d	**2** b, c, f, g	**3** a, e, h

(B)

- Divide the class into groups of four or six, with two or three Ss on each side.
- Cut up and hand out the relevant role cards and give Ss a few minutes to study them.
- Explain the situation to the whole class, and that the points system is meant to represent the priorities of each side. In the final agreement, points will be calculated on a pro rata basis, so, for example, if the local authority makes 45 teachers' assistants redundant, they will get 37.5 points.
- Explain that each side will give reasons for its demands. For example, teaching union representatives might point out that their main priority is avoiding redundancies among teachers because they are the backbone of the system and more important than anything else. They might say that under present circumstances, building the new technical school can wait a few years, etc.
- When everyone is clear, the role play can begin. Circulate and monitor. Note language points for praise and correction, especially negotiation language.
- When the groups have reached a conclusion, bring the class to order and praise good language points from the role play and work on three or four points that need improvement, getting individual Ss to say the correct forms.
- Then ask a representative from each group for an account of what happened, and the final score. Compare and contrast the discussions and scores from each group.

Unit 5 Job satisfaction

Handling difficult situations

- Get Ss to look at the expressions on page 43 of the Course Book, then do this exercise in pairs.
- Circulate and assist.
- Ask the whole class for the answers.

1 I'm terribly sorry. How clumsy of me!
2 Excuse me, but I really must be off. It was nice talking to you.
3 It's very nice of you to offer, but I'm very busy at the moment.
4 Sorry I'm late, but the traffic was a nightmare.
5 That's really bad news. I'm really sorry to hear that.
6 I don't know how to tell you this, but I've had an accident with your car.
7 I must apologise. I thought the meeting was *next* Tuesday.
8 The same thing happened to me. I know how you must be feeling.
9 You mentioned that you might be able to help me out.
10 Could you possibly help me to finish this report?

(B)

- Divide the class into pairs and hand out the role cards.
- Point out that situations 1–5 are between colleagues, and situations 6–10 between potential supplier and customer. They are just meant to be separate, isolated exchanges, not form a continuous conversation.
- Point out that Ss can give the real reason for saying 'no' in an appropriately polite form, or if more suitable, a pretext.
- When the situation is clear, the parallel exchanges can begin.
- Circulate and monitor. Note language points for praise and correction, concentrating on appropriate and tactful expressions. For example, in situation 1, B could say: 'I'm rather busy at the moment. I've got an important deadline coming up. Sorry I can't help', etc.
- Praise good language points from the expressions and work on three or four points that need improvement, getting individual Ss to say the correct forms.
- With the whole class, ask different pairs for different exchanges.

(C)

- Practise intonation of the expressions with the whole class.
- Do as a quick-fire whole-class activity. Ask different pairs to enact different exchanges, adding other comments according to the context, for example, for situation 10: 'Yes, I'd like that. I haven't been sailing for a long time. It'll be great', etc.

Unit 6 Risk

Reaching agreement

- Remind Ss about the expressions on page 51 of the Course Book, then ask them to match expressions 1–7 with their equivalent versions.

1 d	**2** a	**3** g	**4** e	**5** b	**6** c	**7** f

- Point out that in the situation that follows, negotiators should be using expressions a–g from A, rather than expressions 1–7!
- Divide the class into groups of four: two buyers and two suppliers in each group.
- Explain the basic situation. The idea here is that Ss concentrate on clarification in a negotiation, rather than the other stages. The activity is an information exchange to clear up misunderstandings about what has been decided. Get the Chief Buyer in each group to start by saying:
  – 'Let's just run over what's been agreed.'
  Point out expressions for correcting, such as
  – I don't think that's what we decided.
  – There's some sort of mistake there, surely.
  etc.
- When the situation is clear, the parallel clarification sessions can begin.
- Circulate and monitor. Note language points for praise and correction, especially in relation to the language of checking and clarification. Also, be strict with Ss saying numbers correctly. Work on the language of clarification and summary, as well as the stress and intonation of exchanges such as:
  – 'So we agree that we'll buy 20,000 dresses at 35 euros each?'
  – 'No, it was 25,000 dresses at 37 euros each.'
- Bring the class to order. Praise good language points from the role play and work on three or four points that need improvement, getting individual Ss to say the correct forms.

Unit 7 e-commerce

Presentations

- Point out the link with the presentations language on page 59 of the Course Book.
- Get Ss silently to read through the example presentation here individually or in pairs, identifying the steps.

> OK, it's two o'clock. Let's make a start (10). Good afternoon everyone (7) and thank you all for coming (1). My name's Steve Suarez and I'm head of the Anglo-Latin American Chamber of Commerce (6). This afternoon, I'm going to talk to you about doing business in Latin America. I'm going to begin by giving an overview of the different markets in Latin America, and then look in more detail at two key markets that I know a lot of you are interested in: Brazil and Mexico. I'll talk for about 45 minutes, and then we'll open up the session for a general discussion (14). But if you have any questions while I'm speaking, please feel free to ask them at any point (2). Can I just ask how many of you have been on business to Latin America? Can we have a show of hands? (13) Thank you.
>
> When I was in Rio last year, I was being shown round the city by an importer of European machine tools. We were having a beer together when he said, 'You know Steve, the problem with exporters who try to break into the Brazilian market is that they approach Brazil as if it was just like the Spanish-speaking countries of South America. But I can tell you, it's a very different kind of market, that's for sure!' (3) ...

- Go through the answers with the whole class.

- Make enough copies so that every student has a series of steps. Hand them out. Ss can talk about subjects in their presentations that they have already used in earlier presentations. The idea here is to concentrate on the opening few seconds of the presentation, as this is key.
- Get Ss to write out the text of their presentation corresponding to the steps you have given them. Circulate, monitor and assist.
- Give Ss time to memorise as far as possible what they have written. Circulate and help with natural delivery.
- With the whole class, get individual Ss to come to the front and give the beginnings of their presentations, corresponding to the steps you have given them. Keep the pace moving.
- If you have a very large class, get some Ss to give the beginnings of their presentations now, and other Ss in later session(s).

Unit 8 Team building

Resolving conflict

- Draw Ss' attention to the link between these expressions and those on page 73 of the Course Book. Ask them to identify the errors in the expressions here in pairs or individually. (All the headings are correct.)

Expressing your feelings
I'm really <u>worried</u> about ...
Making suggestions
<u>We can always look</u> into other possibilities ...
Expressing satisfaction
Yes, that <u>sounds</u> like an ideal solution.
Expressing dissatisfaction
That's <u>just not</u> feasible.
Agreeing action
Right. Now we've fixed our goals, let's plan a course of action to put them into <u>effect</u>.
Showing sympathy
I'm sorry to <u>hear</u> that.
Stating common goals
<u>Ideally</u>, we should all be working together on this.
Identifying the real problem
What are you really <u>concerned</u> about here?
Resolving the conflict
We must <u>reach</u> some sort of compromise on this.
Reviewing the situation
We should get together next month and check on <u>progress</u> towards our objectives.

- Divide the class into groups of three. Student A is the Sales Manager. B is a senior rep and C is a junior rep. All three have copies of the different proposals and the amounts that each would save. A has no role card apart from this information. Explain that A's role is to chair the meeting, explain the proposals, and get reactions from the members of the sales force, who are representing their colleagues, not just putting their own point of view. Emphasise that C also has a conciliatory role between the sales force head and B, the senior sales person.
- Hand out the relevant role cards to Students B and C.
- Give Ss time to absorb the information.
- When the situation is clear, the role play can begin. Circulate and monitor. Note language points for praise and correction, especially in relation to language for resolving conflict.
- Bring the class to order. Praise good language points from the role play and work on three or four points that need improvement, getting individual Ss to say the correct forms.
- Ask different groups to explain briefly what happened in their meetings and which combination of cost savings they chose.

Unit 9 Raising finance

Negotiating: tactics

- Point out the connection with the expressions on page 81 of the Course Book.
- Ask Ss to do the exercise individually or in pairs.
- Check the answers with the whole class, discussing any difficulties.

1 Let's check ~~up~~ the points we've covered so far. *(summarising)*
2 How do you see ~~at~~ the future development of the plant? *(open question)*
3 Have you considered setting up ~~to~~ operations in other European Union countries? *(closed question)*
4 I regret that this is the case, but under European Union ~~the~~ competition laws, there's no way we can offer more government money. *(softening phrase)*
5 I'd like to suggest something. If your government can guarantee the currency here will be relatively stable against the currencies of other countries over ~~when~~ the next five years, there's a much bigger chance of us investing here. *(signalling phrase)*
6 I'm sorry, but if you do not offer us a ~~more~~ bigger incentive, we'll have to look elsewhere. *(softening phrase)*
7 How about ~~for~~ this? If you can guarantee to employ 5,000 people, we can sell you some government-owned land at a very reasonable price. *(signalling phrase)*

B

- Explain the situation and divide the class into groups of four: two senior Kara managers and two UK government officials.
- Give Ss copies of the information for their side of the negotiation. Point out that the idea here is not to have a complete negotiation, but to apply the language seen above in A and in the Skills section of the Course Book, following the stages separated by continuous lines.
- When the situation is clear, the role play can begin.
- Circulate and monitor, especially the language relating to this unit. Note language points for praise and correction.
- With the whole class, praise good language points from the role play and work on three or four points that need improvement, getting individual Ss to say the correct forms.
- If there is time, reverse the roles and do the activity again, getting Ss to integrate corrections and improvements from the first run-through.

Unit 10 Customer service

Active listening

- Tell Ss they are going to look specifically at active listening in interviews, in this exercise by the interviewee.
- Ask them to discuss the points in pairs or threes.
- Circulate and monitor. Explain any difficulties.

1. The ideal amount of eye contact varies from culture to culture. In an interview situation this could vary from 0 to almost 100%, depending on the culture.
2. This and other mannerisms are best avoided everywhere. But in some cultures, this particular mannerism is viewed especially badly.
3. This might show you are paying attention, but it's probably better to adopt a more neutral position. Ask Ss to show how they would sit in an interview.
4. Some people might do this to show they are paying attention, but it probably would be seen as disrespectful in most places.
5. Not good. Creates a barrier between you and the interviewer and looks disrespectful.
6. More acceptable in some places than others, but probably best avoided.
7. In some cultures, this gesture is used (consciously or unconsciously) to show that you don't understand. Probably best avoided.
8. Probably the right thing to do in many places, but may be interpreted as being over-passive in some cultures.
9. In the UK, 'sir' is rarely heard outside the army and the schoolroom. More commonly used in the US, for example to ask strangers for directions in the street. May be heard in both places in very conservative institutions. Might be good to say 'Mr Brown', 'Mrs Smith', etc. occasionally.
10. Done in some cultures, but not others.
11. Acceptable in many cultures, but be careful not to ask about something that has already been explained.
12. Probably safer to do this than pretend you have understood and then find you answered a question that was not asked.

(B)

- Divide the class into groups of three. A is Head of Recruitment at Novia and is interviewing B for the job of Head of Research at their Canadian labs. C is an observer, who will note the stages of the interview, and the sort of language used in the questions and answers, especially in relation to techniques for active listening.
- All three members of each group should get copies of Karl Eriksson's CV, and be given time to study it. Explain any difficulties.
- When the situation is clear, the role play can begin in parallel threes.
- Circulate and monitor, but do not pre-empt the role of the observer, who should be noting the stages in the interview and the language being used.
- When the interviews are over, ask the observer from each three to give an account of what happened and the language used.
- Praise good language points from the role play and work on three or four points that need improvement, getting individual Ss to say the correct forms.

Unit 11 Crisis management

Asking and answering difficult questions

- Relate this to the language for asking and answering difficult questions on page 97 of the Course Book.
- Explain the situation here and get Ss to do the exercise individually or in pairs.
- With the whole class, ask Ss for the answers and explain any difficulties.

1. Could you tell me how many tons of oil have leaked from the tanker?
2. Would you mind answering the question? What is your policy on compensation for those affected?
3. Do you deny that serious environmental damage has been caused?
4. Do you mind if I ask whether the oil tanker had (or has) a good safety record?
5. I am interested in knowing if you consider Natoil to be a safety-conscious company?
6. Isn't it true that you don't care for the environment, only profits?
7. May I ask why you did not react more quickly?
8. Are you saying that you deny responsibility?
9. Could you clarify what efforts are being made to clean the affected beaches?
10. What can you tell us about the long-term effects on seabirds and other animals?

(B)

- Tell Ss that the questions in A anticipated this role play. Read 'The facts so far' with the whole class.
- Divide the class into groups of four or five. In each group, two Ss represent the government side, and there is a journalist from each newspaper. Hand out the relevant role cards.
- Point out that at this press conference, the officials are very defensive, trying to minimise their involvement in the disaster. The journalists are very persistent and do not believe the officials.
- When Ss have absorbed all the necessary information, the role play can begin.
- Circulate and monitor. Note language points for praise and correction, especially in relation to asking and answering difficult questions.

- Praise good language points from the role play and work on three or four points that need improvement, getting individual Ss to say the correct forms.
- If there is time and interest, organise another press conference, where the politicians are more open and forthcoming.

Unit 12 Management styles

Socialising: putting people at ease

- Relate this exercise to the one on page 105 of the Course Book. Point out the way that questions in informal speech can be shortened like those in 1–4. Work on friendly delivery.
- Get your Ss to do the exercise individually or in pairs.
- With the whole class, ask for the answers.

1 c	**2** d	**3** a	**4** f	**5** b	**6** e

- Then ask Ss to have a continuous conversation in parallel pairs, incorporating the expressions 1–6 and a–f as naturally as possible. Circulate and monitor.
- Ask one of the pairs do a public performance for the whole class.

Ⓑ

- The idea here is that Ss must incorporate their one-liner seamlessly into a small-talk conversation without Student A realising what is on Student B's card.
- Cut out copies of the cue cards. Hand out copies of the first five or six randomly to Ss in a way that prevents Ss from seeing each other's cards: one one-liner for each student. Do the small talk conversations in parallel pairs. To keep things simple, do not monitor for language in this activity.
- Tell Ss that they can start by discussing what they are each going to have for lunch (from an imaginary menu).
- Student A then starts the conversation in a general way, e.g. by saying
  – What have you been up to since we last met?
- Ss must then try to 'steer' the conversation so that they can place their one-liners inconspicuously!
- At the end of the conversation, each student tries to guess the other's expression.
- If Student A guesses correctly, A 'wins'. (A variation on this is to have A, B and C, where C is an observer, guessing what is on the cards of both A and B.)
- Ask Ss about their tactics for placing their one-liners, how easy / difficult it was, etc.
- If there is time and interest, do the activity again, handing out new one-liners, perhaps getting one pair to perform for the whole class.

Unit 13 Takeovers and mergers

Summarising in presentations

Ⓐ

- Make the link with the Skills section on page 113 of the Course Book.
- Ask Ss to do the exercise individually or in pairs.
- Circulate and monitor.
- With the whole class, ask for the answers, explain any difficulties.

1 A zoo is a combination of three things: a visitor attraction, an education centre, and an animal conservation centre. *(making points in threes)* ✓
2 Firstly we'll look at zoos as visitor attractions, then we'll examine them from the educational point of view, and last but by no ~~way~~ means least, we'll turn to the conservation issues. *(ordering)*
3 What are the key issues ~~in~~ relating to animal conservation in zoos? *(rhetorical question)*
4 As I pointed out ~~more~~ earlier, planning a zoo requires great expertise. *(referring back)*
5 Of course, if a dangerous animal escapes from your zoo, this is an absolute disaster. *(emotive language)* ✓
6 These days visitors have higher expectations. They're saying we want more, more, more! *(repetition)* ✓
7 For ~~the~~ example, zoos have a big role to play in the conservation of certain types of monkeys. *(exemplifying)*
8 Have I covered ~~over~~ everything you wanted me to cover? *(asking for feedback)*

Ⓑ

- The idea here is for Ss to put into practice the language for ordering, referring back, etc. The points on theme parks, football stadiums, etc. have been provided as subject matter in which they can use the key language.
- Hand out a subject card to each student. Emphasise to Ss that the points are suggestions, and that they should feel free to mention others.
- Allow time for Ss to prepare their presentation, concentrating on the language for the particular functions in A.
- If short of time, tell Ss that they won't have to make the complete presentation, just be ready to illustrate the key phrases in context.
- Ask individual Ss to come to the front of the class and give their presentations, where necessary 'fast-forwarding' to the next point where they use a key expression, explaining what they would be saying between the key expressions.
- Note language points for praise and correction, especially in relation to presentations language.
- Praise good language points from the presentations and work on three or four points that need improvement, getting individual Ss to say the correct forms.

Unit 14 The future of business

Telephoning: getting the right information

- Remind Ss about the language for telephoning on page 121 of the Course Book.
- Divide the class into pairs. Cut up, shuffle and hand out the 'turns' to each pair. Obviously, be careful not to mix the different sets of turns, as this could lead to some surreal conversations!
- Get some students to work in threes on Conversation 1 and other Ss to work in pairs on Conversation 2.
- Circulate, monitor and assist.
- Hand out copies of the complete versions and get Ss into threes to read aloud the first conversation together, sitting back to back to simulate a phone conversation: Maria, the switchboard operator and John Reed.
- Get Ss in pairs to read aloud the second conversation in pairs: Maria and Tim Reed, paying attention to friendly intonation.
- Ask for a performance of each conversation from one of the pairs for the whole class.

B

- Explain that there will be a series of phone conversations following on from the first one in A.
- Divide the class into pairs. Student A is Maria, Student B, Tim.
- Hand out copies of the role cards progressively for each situation, so as not to pre-empt the final dénouement.
- Get Ss in parallel pairs to role play the first situation. Circulate and monitor.
- Get one pair of Ss to do their version of the role play for the whole class.
- Do the same for the second situation.
- For the third situation (three weeks later), hand out the role cards to just one pair, so that they do a performance for the whole class. Tell Ss that in this situation, they can interpret 'end suitably' as they wish, without going over the top, of course!

UNIT 1 Communication

Problem-solving on the phone

A **Look again at the expressions for problem solving on page 11 of the Course Book. For each category 1–5, there are two new expressions in a–j. Match each expression to its category.**

1 Stating the problem
2 Offering to help
3 Apologising / showing understanding
4 Making suggestions
5 Requesting action

a) I'll see what I can do.
b) Could you deal with this?
c) Have you thought of checking the database?
d) I'm phoning about a mix-up that there's been with ...
e) You must be very upset.
f) I'd be grateful if you could find out ...
g) This is just an idea, but ...
h) I know how frustrating this must be.
I) I'll get on to this right away.
j) I'm calling to see what's happening with ...

B **Work in pairs on this situation. Use the expressions on page 11 of the Course Book, plus the expressions a–j above.**

Phone call 1

A You work for Rod Engineering. You have received a consignment of widgets and related parts and supplies from Reliable Widget Supplies. (Widgets are essential components in the machines that Rod makes.) However, the consignment you received does not correspond to the order you made by phone last week.

You ordered:
- PBX widgets: 10,000 units
- widget sheets: 4,000 square metres
- widget oil: 500 litres
- Grade D widget powder: 10 tonnes

You received:
- BVX widgets: 10,000 units
- widget sheets: 1,000 square metres
- widget oil: 5,000 litres
- Grade E widget powder: 10 tonnes

B You work for Reliable Widget Supplies (RWS).
- Note down the problems with one of your customers.
- Say you can't check A's order on screen because your computer network is down.
- Ask A to give details of the order for
  - widgets
  - widget sheets
  - widget oil
  - widget powder.
- Say you will phone back later when you've found out what went wrong.

Phone call 2

A
- B phones you back.
- Note down B's explanations.
- Ask how they are going to rectify the situation.
- Say if you are happy with the solutions offered.

B
- You phone A back.
- Explain what went wrong and offer apologies and solutions.
  - PBX 10,000 widgets. The person taking the order on the phone misheard, and noted 'BV' instead of 'PB'. The correct widgets will be sent today.
  - Widget sheets. RWS was low on widget sheets last week and was only able to send 1,000. Now you have more in stock and will send another 1,000 today and 2,000 next week.
  - Widget oil. You don't know what happened. With the next delivery, you will ask the delivery driver to bring back the 4,500 extra litres.
  - Widget powder. Grade E has replaced Grade D, and is even better. It costs the same as Grade D. Tell A that they will be very pleased with the results!

UNIT 2 International marketing

Brainstorming

A **Look again at the good and bad advice about brainstorming on page 19 of the Course Book. Then correct these expressions at a brainstorming session related to it.**

1 We're trying to come off with some completely fresh thinkings on this subject.
2 It doesn't mind what your positioning in the company is. All ideas are welcome.
3 We're going to stop at 5 on the point, so we have an hour up front of us to think of something.
4 Don't critic other people's contributes. At this stadium, everything is acceptable.
5 Just say everything that comes across your head. We should considerate every idea, whatever crazy it seems at first!
6 You don't have to glue to the point. We get some good ideas when people digression.
7 Let other people to finish when they are talk. Don't butt inside.
8 We mustn't get bogging down in detailings at this stage.

B **Hold brainstorming meetings about these situations. (Money is not a problem at this stage!)**

1 Behind its main building, your company owns a piece of unoccupied land. The company is doing well and its Chief Executive wants to spend money on facilities for staff. Brainstorm the different ideas for facilities that could later be put to employees in a vote. These ideas have already been suggested:
   - ornamental garden
   - go-kart track
   - gym ...

2 It's your company's 50th anniversary. You and your colleagues have been asked to brainstorm suitable ways of marking and celebrating this important event.
3 You work in the R&D department of a chemical company. You have developed an invisible, odourless glue that can be applied to paper, textiles, plastics and even metal. The glue is sticky enough to hold something in place, but it comes unstuck if someone pulls on one of the things that it is being used to hold together. Brainstorm the possible applications for this glue.
4 You work for a European airline. There is now a delay of 30 mins or more in the departure of 45 per cent of the flights, and there have been instances of air rage in the departure lounges, with angry passengers abusing staff. Brainstorm all the ideas you can think of for keeping passengers calm while they are in the departure lounges.
5 Your city owns a huge disused power station on a prestigious riverside site. The building is an impressive listed monument from the 1930s, and it cannot be demolished. You and your fellow city councillors brainstorm the different uses to which it could be put.

UNIT 3 Building relationships

Networking

A **Look again at the useful language for networking on page 27 of the Course Book and rearrange the 'turns' that your teacher will give you into a logical phone conversation.**

JM: Jane Montgomery.

LP: Oh, hello. My name's Linda Persson. I'm a friend of Silvana Belmonte. She said I might be able to track you down through your New York office. I hope you don't mind me phoning. Is this a convenient time, or shall I call back later?

JM: No, this is fine. How is Silvana?

LP: Very well. She said to give you her regards.

JM: The last time I saw her was at our office in Rio two or three years ago. What's she up to these days?

LP: She's still working in advertising down there. In fact that's why I'm calling. I work for Smithson, you know, the European food products company.

JM: Ah, Smithson, right.

LP: We're looking for an advertising agency to help us get into the American market. Silvana said you had a lot of contacts in advertising here in New York.

JM: Yes, I know one or two people. Maybe I could help you out there. Do you work in marketing or general management?

LP: Marketing. I'd be very grateful for any ideas you could give us. The US market is unknown.

JM: Why don't you come round to my office later this week, and we could go out to lunch. It's near the Metropolitan on East 86th Street: Montgomery and Associates, 450 East 86th.

LP: How about Wednesday? Shall we say about one?

JM: That would be good. Just ask for me at reception. See you then.

LP: Looking forward to it. Bye for now.

JM: Bye.

B **This conversation takes place the week *before* the one above in A. Student A is Linda Persson. Student B is Silvana Belmonte. They are old friends: they did an MBA together at Harvard 10 years ago. Linda is on holiday in Rio, visiting Silvana who lives and works there.**

- You reminisce about your time together at Harvard.
- Silvana talks about her job in advertising in Rio.
- Linda talks about her work at Smithson, their plans to get into the US market, and their need for a US-based advertising agency.
- Silvana mentions Jane Montgomery, who might be able to help: she knows a lot of people in advertising in New York.
- Linda asks Silvana if she has Jane's number.
- Silvana says she'll find it if she looks for 'Montgomery and Associates' on the Internet.
- Linda thanks Silvana.

C **This conversation takes place a few days *after* the one above in A. Student A is Linda Persson. Student B is Ross Klein, of the advertising agency Daponte Klein Jameson. They were put in touch by Jane Montgomery and they are meeting in the DKJ offices in New Jersey.**

- Ross meets Linda at reception and takes her to his office, asking if she found the address OK.
- Linda says it was no problem.
- Ross says that DKJ used to be in Manhattan, but they recently moved to New Jersey (easier to commute and to park): Linda shows interest.
- Ross asks if she would like some coffee, tea or juice and Linda responds.
- They talk about their mutual contact, Jane Montgomery, and Linda explains how she met her.
- Ross says he understands that Linda works for Smithson, and that they are looking for an advertising agency in the US.
- Linda confirms this, and they continue the conversation.

UNIT 4 Success

Negotiating

A **Look at the expressions for 1) signalling, 2) checking understanding and 3) summarising on page 35 of the Course Book. Then put each of the expressions a–h under the correct heading.**

a) Let's just summarise the key points again.
b) If I understand you correctly, you're not willing to make a concession on this.
c) What sort of lead-time do you have in mind?
d) Do you mind if I make a suggestion here? Let's adjourn for lunch.
e) Right. That seems to be it. Just to recap ...
f) So, you're offering a 10 per cent discount if we can pay 30 per cent up front, is that right?
g) To put that in non-technical language, you're bankrupt, is that correct?
h) Great! We have a deal! We'll go through the main conditions again now, and then our lawyers can draw up a contract based on them.

B **A local government authority in a big city has budget problems. Schools are paid for through local taxes, and the authority must cut spending on schools in order to stay within this year's budget. City officials meet members of the teaching union to discuss the cuts.**

Local authority officials

- In order to cut enough from the budget, you must gain at least 180 points by obtaining the agreement of the teaching unions to a combination of these items:
- Making teachers redundant
  100 teachers or more: 100 points
  50 teachers: 50 points
  no change: 0 points.
- Making teachers' assistants redundant
  60 assistants: 50 points
  30 assistants: 25 points
  no change: 0 points.
- Asking teachers to take early retirement
  50 teachers or more: 30 points
  25 teachers: 15 points
  no change: 0 points
- Cutting maintenance of school buildings
  10% cut or more: 50 points
  5% cut: 25 points
  no change: 0 points
- Cutting expenditure on school books
  10% cut or more: 10 points
  5% cut: 5 points
  no change: 0 points
- Cancelling the construction of a new technical school: 10 points
- If the unions agree to your maximum demands, you will score 250 points.

Teaching unions

- In order to protect the interests of your members, you feel you must gain at least 180 points by reaching agreement on a combination of these items:
- Making teachers redundant
  100 teachers or more: 0 points
  50 teachers: 75 points
  no change: 150 points.
- Making teachers' assistants redundant
  60 assistants or more: 0 points
  30 assistants: 15 points
  no change: 30 points.
- Asking teachers to take early retirement
  50 teachers or more: 0 points
  25 teachers: 20 points
  no change: 40 points.
- Cutting maintenance of school buildings
  10% cut or more: 0 points
  5% cut: 10 points
  no change: 20 points.
- Cutting expenditure on school books
  10% cut or more: 0 points
  5% cut: 2.5 points
  no change: 5 points.
- Cancelling the construction of a new technical school: 5 points.
- If the local authority agrees to your maximum demands, you will score 250 points.

Resource bank

UNIT 5 Job satisfaction

Handling difficult situations

A **Look again at the expressions for handling difficult situations on page 43 of the Course Book. There is one wrong word in each of the utterances 1–10. Cross it out and put the correct word.**

1 I'm terribly sorry. How clumsy with me!
2 Excuse me, but I really must be out. It was nice talking to you.
3 It's very nice from you to offer, but I'm very busy at the moment.
4 Sorry I'm later, but the traffic was a nightmare.
5 That's really bad news. I'm really sorry to listen that.
6 I don't know how for tell you this, but I've had an accident with your car.
7 I must apology. I thought the meeting was *next* Tuesday.
8 The same thing happened to me. I know how you should be feeling.
9 You mentions that you might be able to help me out.
10 Might you possibly help me to finish this report?

B **Work in pairs. Student A makes requests or invitations, B politely says 'no', and A replies suitably.**

Student A
In situations 1–5, you and Student B are work colleagues with the same seniority. Politely ask Student B to do these things, and reply politely to the reason they give.

1 Help finish a report
2 Answer your phone while you're out
3 Give another colleague, C, a sensitive message that might make C annoyed
4 Go for a drink after a meeting
5 Have a game of tennis at the weekend

In situations 6–10, you have invited a potential supplier, Student B, to your country.

6 See the sights of the city
7 Go to a karaoke bar
8 Go to a nightclub
9 Come and have dinner at my house
10 Go sailing at the weekend

Student B
In situations 1–5, you and Student A are work colleagues with the same seniority. Say 'no' politely, using a different expression each time. You might give the real reason shown below, or not, depending on the situation.

1 Too busy – other important deadlines
2 Can't be bothered
3 Not your job, and you feel used
4 Long day – too tired
5 Not very good at tennis

In situations 6–10, you are a supplier who has been invited by a potential customer, Student A, to their country.

6 Have been there before – ugly city
7 Can't sing
8 Don't drink alcohol and can't dance
9 Potentially embarrassing – not done in your country
10 Prefer to be by yourself

C **Now change roles, and practise saying 'yes' in as many different ways as possible to the requests and invitations. Here are some suggestions. Try to think of other ways of saying 'yes'.**

- Yes, no problem.
- Yes, that would nice.
- Yes, I'd like that.
- Yes, thanks. That would be great.
- Yes, good idea.
- Yes, I can do that.

UNIT 6 Risk

Reaching agreement

A **Look at the useful expressions for reaching agreement on page 51 of the Course Book. Match each expression 1–7 to another version of the same expression a–g.**

1 Does anyone have really serious objections if we ... ?
2 I totally and absolutely disagree with you.
3 I agree with you a hundred and ten percent on that one.
4 I've said this before and I'll say it again because no one takes any notice ...
5 It's blindingly obvious we should ...
6 This is bad news, but we're certainly going to be forced to ...
7 I'm going to summarise because I don't think you've understood and there are bound to be problems if I don't go over the main points.

a Well hold on. I'm not sure I agree with you on that one.
b I think it's pretty clear we should ...
c Well, unfortunately, I think we'll probably have to ...
d Does anybody have any strong feelings about ... ?
e I keep repeating this, but as I've said several times already ...
f Can I just clarify that by looking again at the main points ...
g I think I'd agree with you there.

B **Buyers for a department store chain are negotiating with clothing suppliers. They have been negotiating all day. The Chief Buyer for the department stores thinks they have reached agreement and summarises what he / she thinks has been agreed. The suppliers disagree and indicate this politely.**

Buyers

You think you have agreed the following:
20,000 women's dresses @ 35 euros each
15,000 men's jackets @ 30 euros
12,500 pairs of women's slacks @ 27 euros
10,000 pairs of men's trousers @ 25 euros
Delivery: 1 month from now
Payment: 90 days after delivery
Currency of payment: euros

Suppliers

You think you have agreed the following:
25,000 women's dresses @ 37 euros each
15,000 men's jackets @ 35 euros
10,000 pairs of women's slacks @ 25 euros
8,000 pairs of men's trousers @ 27 euros
Delivery: 3 months from now
Payment: 30 days after delivery
Currency of payment: US dollars

UNIT 7 e-commerce

Presentations

A **Look at the beginning of this presentation. Which of the steps a–k does the speaker go through, and in what order? (He does not go through all of the steps mentioned.)**

1 thanks the audience for coming
2 tells the audience if / when they can ask questions
3 tells a story
4 states a problem
5 offers an amazing fact
6 introduces himself
7 greets the audience
8 greets latecomers
9 tells latecomers where there are seats available
10 brings the audience to order
11 asks if everyone can see the data projection screen
12 asks if everyone can hear at the back
13 asks a question
14 announces the structure of his talk

OK, it's two o'clock. Let's make a start. Good afternoon everyone and thank you all for coming. My name's Steve Suarez and I'm head of the Anglo-Latin American Chamber of Commerce. This afternoon, I'm going to talk to you about doing business in Latin America. I'm going to begin by giving an overview of the different markets in Latin America, and then look in more detail at two key markets that I know a lot of you are interested in: Brazil and Mexico. I'll talk for about 45 minutes, and then we'll open up the session for a general discussion. But if you have any questions while I'm speaking, please feel free to ask them at any point. Can I just ask how many of you have been on business to Latin America? Can we have a show of hands? Thank you.

When I was in Rio last year, I was being shown round the city by an importer of European machine tools. We were having a beer together when he said, 'You know Steve, the problem with exporters who try to break into the Brazilian market is that they approach Brazil as if it was just like the Spanish-speaking countries of South America. But I can tell you, it's a very different kind of market, that's for sure!' ...

B **Prepare the beginning of a presentation on a subject of your choice, going through the steps that your teacher will give you.**

Scenario 1

1 Greet the audience.
2 Thank the audience for coming.
3 Introduce yourself.
4 Start to tell a story.
5 Greet latecomers.

Scenario 2

1 Ask if everyone can hear at the back.
2 Introduce yourself.
3 Offer an amazing fact.
4 Announce the structure of your talk.
5 Go into the first point of your talk.

Scenario 3

1 Bring the audience to order.
2 Ask if everyone can see the screen.
3 Introduce yourself.
4 State a problem.
5 Tell latecomers where there are seats available.

Resource bank

UNIT 8 Team building

Resolving conflict

A Look again at the expressions for resolving conflict on page 73 of the Course Book. Correct the mistakes in these expressions used in talking about problems. (All the headings are correct.)

Expressing your feelings
I'm really worry about ...
Making suggestions
Always we can look into other possibilities ...
Expressing satisfaction
Yes, that sound like an ideal solution.
Expressing dissatisfaction
That's not just feasible.

Agreeing action
Right. Now we've fixed our goals, let's plan a course of action to put them into effectiveness.
Showing sympathy
I'm sorry to heard that.
Stating common goals
Idealistically, we should all be working together on this.
Identifying the real problem
What are you really concerning about here?
Resolving the conflict
We must gain some sort of compromise on this.
Reviewing the situation
We should get together next month and check on progression towards our objectives.

B After a year of very bad sales at Repro Photocopiers, the Sales Manager (responsible for three senior reps and nine junior reps) has been told to cut expenses by $300,000. Repro believes in its managers consulting staff about changes. The Sales Manager meets members of the sales force to discuss ways of doing this.

Proposal	Savings $
• Reduce the number of reps by 10 per cent and increase sales target of each rep	80,000 per senior rep, 50,000 per junior rep
• Replace all sales reps' cars with smaller models	130,000
• Reduce the maximum amount to be spent on each lunch with clients from $100 to $50	30,000
• Annual sales conference to be held locally in the US rather than in Cancun, Mexico, the usual venue	35,000
• Move the sales team to a smaller office within the company HQ	30,000
• Abolish the perk of a yearly clothing allowance	25,000
• Economise on stationery	5,000

Student B **Senior sales force member**

You are a senior member of the sales force, representing the three senior reps. You could imagine firing junior reps, but not senior ones. You cannot accept the loss of status that would go with a smaller car and a reduced expense account. You can just about accept the idea of giving way on some of the other issues, but you are not in a conciliatory mood.

Student C **Junior sales force member**

You are a junior member of the sales force, representing all your junior colleagues. You try to conciliate between the senior rep and the head of the sales force. You would prefer one or two senior reps to be fired rather than junior ones, because their results last year were particularly bad, but you can't say so openly, of course. You are less status-conscious than your senior colleagues and willing to consider the other budget reduction proposals.

UNIT 9 Raising finance

Negotiating: tactics

A **Look again at the negotiations language on page 81 of the Course Book. There is one word too many in each of the expressions 1–7. Cross out the extra word in each expression.**

1 Let's check up the points we've covered so far. *(summarising)*
2 How do you see at the future development of the plant? *(open question)*
3 Have you considered setting up to operations in other European Union countries? *(closed question)*
4 I regret that this is the case, but under European Union the competition laws, there's no way we can offer more government money. *(softening phrase)*
5 I'd like to suggest something. If your government can guarantee the currency here will be relatively stable against the currencies of other countries over when the next five years, there's a much bigger chance of us investing here. *(signalling phrase)*
6 I'm sorry, but if you do not offer us a more bigger incentive, we'll have to look elsewhere. *(softening phrase)*
7 How about for this? If you can guarantee to employ 5,000 people, we can sell you some government-owned land at a very reasonable price. *(signalling phrase)*

B **The above expressions come from a negotiation between Kara, an Asian car company that wants to build a plant in the UK, and British government officials. Role play part of these negotiations, following the instructions for each side. (You don't have to use the expressions in A above.)**

Kara company representatives	**British government officials**
• Summarise the situation so far: • British government will provide £100 million in state aid and sell government land cheaply for building the plant. • Kara will guarantee 5,000 jobs. • Key issues remaining: price for land, and UK currency stability.	• Agree that summary is correct. • Price for the land not an obstacle; can be discussed later. • Say that British government is aiming for currency stability, but can give no guarantees.
• Agree to come back to land price later. • You need guarantees on British currency stability so costs of components from outside the UK will be stable.	• Again say you can offer guarantees. • Ask about Kara's future plans in the UK if this investment is successful.
• Say that you envisage long-term commitment.	• Ask if Kara have considered other countries for their plant.
• Avoid answering question directly, but say all options are open. • Suggest that you discuss the price of the land.	• Agree to the suggestion.

Resource bank

UNIT 10 Customer service

Active listening

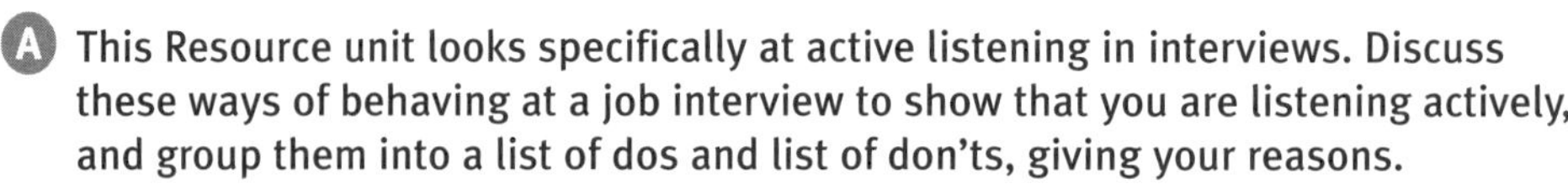

A **This Resource unit looks specifically at active listening in interviews. Discuss these ways of behaving at a job interview to show that you are listening actively, and group them into a list of dos and list of don'ts, giving your reasons.**

1 Face the interviewer, but keep direct eye contact only about half of the time. Do not stare continuously at the interviewer.

2 Run your fingers through your hair.

3 Hold your chin between your thumb and your forefinger.

4 Hold your hands together vertically, with only the fingertips touching.

5 Cross your arms in front of you.

6 Cross your legs.

7 Scratch your forehead.

8 Speak only when spoken too.

9 Use a polite form of address to the interviewer when answering questions, e.g. 'Sir', 'Mrs Smith', etc.

10 When the interviewer asks about your qualifications, show the certificates relating to them.

11 Ask the interviewer a question about the job if there's something you want to know.

12 Ask the interviewer to repeat a question if you have not understood.

B **Student A is interviewing candidates to head the North American research centre of Novia, a large pharmaceuticals company in Montreal, Canada. Student B is a candidate for the job. Student C is an observer. Role play the interview, showing that you are listening actively to the other person.**

Karl Eriksson's CV

- 1999–present **Deputy head of research, Novia Pharmaceuticals Research Labs, Reading, England** Assisted head of research in all types of drug trials. Supervised staff (250 researchers) in the absence of the head of research
- 1990–1999 **Researcher, Novia Pharmaceuticals Research Labs, Hamburg, Germany** Worked under research team leader on anti-cancer drugs. Specialised in computer simulations of drug effectiveness.
- 1986–90 **PhD in Pharmacology, Stanford University, California**
- 1983–86 **Degree in Pharmacology, Stockholm University**
- 1982–83 **Gap year** Backpacked round Asia
- 1975–82 **Secondary school, Kalmar, Sweden** Science specialisation
- Good interpersonal skills
- Computer skills: advanced programming skills in drug testing software
- Languages: Swedish (mother tongue), fluent German and English, intermediate Italian (have been taking evening classes in the UK)
- Interests: Ice hockey, sailing, travel, languages

Student A Head of recruitment, Novia Pharmaceuticals

You consider yourself a sympathetic interviewer. Try to use the language for active listening on page 89 of the Course Book, as well as the extra expressions you found.

You have a copy of Karl Eriksson's CV. Base the interview on it. In particular, you want to know

- why he wants to leave England for Canada
- if he speaks French (the working language of the research labs is English, but he will need French outside)
- how he looks back at his time in Hamburg and the US
- why he didn't go straight to university from secondary school
- how he feels about having lived outside Sweden for so long
- what his interpersonal skills are like. (Ask him how he would deal with particular situations like disputes between colleagues.)
- how he keeps his knowledge of computer applications in pharmaceuticals up-to-date

Student B Karl Eriksson

- You're looking for new challenges in a new job. You think of yourself as a permanent expat (=someone who works abroad), and like the idea of moving on regularly. (So do your family: wife and two teenage children.)
- Professionally, you're happy with your time in Reading, but you're fed up with the weather (and you want more opportunities to play ice hockey, which is not popular in England).
- Hamburg was also a good experience. Apart from specialising in cancer drugs, you learnt that you're good at managing people.
- You keep up with computing in pharmaceuticals by reading a lot and going to professional conferences about it.
- You have pleasant memories of your studies. You like the world of commercial pharmaceuticals. You could never have become a university teacher.
- Your gap year was an enriching experience, and you hope your children will do the same thing.
- You feel you have a gift for languages (but be modest about this!) and could learn French quite quickly.

Student C Observer

- Be ready to provide a (tactful) report on what happened during the interview.
- Note the stages in the interview and the language being used.
- Also note the body language and the way it relates to the language being used, either to reinforce it or contradict it.

UNIT 11 Crisis management

Asking and answering difficult questions

A **Complete these questions from journalists to officials at a press conference about an oil spill from an oil tanker that has sunk off the coast. Each slash represents one missing word. Put the words in brackets into their correct form.**

1 Could / tell me / many tons / oil / (leak) / the tanker?
2 Would / mind (answer) the question? What / your policy / compensation / those affected?
3 Do / deny / serious environmental damage has (be) (cause)?
4 Do / mind if / ask whether / oil tanker (have) /good safety record?
5 I / interested / knowing if / consider Natoil / be / safety-conscious company?
6 Isn't / true that / don't care for / environment, only profits?
7 May / ask why / did / react more quickly?
8 Are / (say) / you deny responsibility?
9 Could / clarify / efforts are (be) made to clean the affected beaches?
10 What can / tell us about / long-term effects / seabirds / other animals?

B **Role play the press conference where the above questions were asked. Students in Group A are government officials and senior managers at Natoil, the state oil company. Students in Group B are journalists from national, local and professional newspapers.**

The facts so far. The accident happened last night when a tanker sank in stormy weather. The coastline has been polluted. 10,000 seabirds have been killed and many more are likely to die because of the oil. Cultivation of shellfish may also be affected.

Minister for the Environment. You maintain the line that damage will be limited. The wind direction is about to change, and this should blow the oil away from the coast. You think that the estimate of 10,000 seabirds killed is exaggerated. You do not think there is any danger to shellfish, as they are 200 km away from the site of the spill.

These are the facts as you see them, and you are sticking to them. If the journalists ask any questions not covered by the information above, you use a 'blocking' answer, or ask the Chief Executive of Natoil to answer it.

Chief Executive, Natoil. The shipwrecked tanker did not belong to Natoil: it was subcontracted. You do not see the accident as Natoil's responsibility, but that of the shipping company whose tanker it was. In any case, you think the long-term damage will be minimal.

These are the facts as you see them, and you are sticking to them. If the journalists ask any questions not covered by the information above, you use a 'blocking' answer, or ask the Minister for the Environment to answer it.

Journalist from 'Petroleum Inquirer'. You ask questions about the general situation, but also particularly about the rumour that the captain of the tanker was drunk at the time of the accident. You want to know what action is being taken to ascertain the complete facts surrounding the accident, and what action the government will take against Natoil and the shipping company.

Journalist from 'Environment Concern'. You ask questions about the general situation, but also particularly about the effect of pollution on the coastline.

Journalist from 'Shellfish Trade Weekly'. You ask questions about the general situation, but also particularly about compensation for fishermen if their fishing grounds are destroyed by oil.

UNIT 12 Management styles

Socialising: putting people at ease

A **Two business contacts who know each other quite well are talking. Match the questions 1–6 to their answers a–f. Then have a natural conversation containing them.**

1 Good flight?	a) It's been a hell of a year. Let's hope things calm down a bit.
2 Family alright?	b) I've been trying to work on my technique, but you know how difficult it is to find the time.
3 Been busy recently?	c) Fine, but my luggage didn't turn up. I think it's probably still in Brussels.
4 Hotel OK?	d) My son has been feeling a bit off: you know, a bug that's been going around. But he's OK now.
5 How's the golf?	e) It's been a very wet autumn, and now they're forecasting snow.
6 What's the weather been like with you?	f) Very comfortable, but the traffic noise is a bit of a problem.

B **This is a role play where two business contacts are making small talk over lunch. They know each other quite well. One of the business people must include a particular expression in what he / she says. The other must guess which one it is.**

Jobs
The labour market is getting really tight here. We're having trouble finding specialists in our field.

Hobbies
I try and go sailing every weekend. But you know how difficult it is to get away!

Families
My son's into the latest rock music. I just can't keep up with the trends these days!

Weather
It's more and more unpredictable. First we had the flooding. Then it felt like summer in the middle of February!

Holidays
We're going walking in the Pyrenees for a week. Less crowded than the Alps from what I hear.

Food and restaurants
You must try the latest Japanese place while you're here. It's difficult to get a table, but I've booked for this evening.

The market
Business is booming. But we're worried that the recession in the US will eventually affect us here.

IT topics
Our company intranet is finally working just like we want it to.

The building you are in
I love modern architecture. So much light and space! It gives you this feeling of freedom!

Cars
Have you tried the latest Jaguars? They're really amazing. I'm thinking of getting one.

How you travelled here
Everything went very smoothly. No hold-ups. No lost luggage. Magic!

UNIT 13 Takeovers and mergers

Summarising in presentations

A **A specialist in zoo management is giving a presentation about her subject. In most of these extracts from her talk there is one extra word that does not fit. Cross out this word. Some of the extracts, however, are correct. If an extract is correct, put a tick (✓) against it. (The labels in brackets are all correct.)**

1 A zoo is a combination of three things: a visitor attraction, an education centre, and an animal conservation centre. *(making points in threes)*

2 Firstly we'll look at zoos as visitor attractions, then we'll examine them from the educational point of view, and last but by no way means least, we'll turn to the conservation issues. *(ordering)*

3 What are the key issues in relating to animal conservation in zoos? *(rhetorical question)*

4 As I pointed out more earlier, planning a zoo requires great expertise. *(referring back)*

5 Of course, if a dangerous animal escapes from your zoo, this is an absolute disaster. *(emotive language)*

6 These days visitors have higher expectations. They're saying we want more, more, more! *(repetition)*

7 For the example, zoos have a big role to play in the conservation of certain types of monkeys. *(exemplifying)*

8 Have I covered over everything you wanted me to cover? *(asking for feedback)*

B **You are an expert talking about running a particular type of visitor attraction. Use your own expressions for the functions in brackets in A above in giving your presentation. Some key issues are given to help you, but you can mention others, of course.**

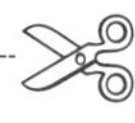

Theme park
- Interesting attractions for an increasingly sophisticated public
- Transport and access to the park
- Crowd and queue management for popular attractions
- Value for money: parades, etc.
- Safety
- Cleanliness
- Restaurants

Football stadium
- Architecture and atmosphere
- Sitting versus standing. Safety of terraces: should terraces for standing be allowed?
- Facilities for spectators
- Facilities for players
- Facilities for broadcasters, photographers, etc.
- Policing
- Ticketing
- Transport and access

National park
- Traffic and crowd control
- Damage by people to paths, fences, etc.
- Litter
- Relations with local people, including farmers
- Possible charging for entry
- Building of tourist facilities versus need to keep the place 'untouched'
- Manage restaurants and shops directly, or franchise them? Control?
- Allow other activities, e.g. mining?

Open-air rock concert
- Choice of venue
- Choice of bands
- Ticketing
- Keeping out gatecrashers (=people who haven't paid)
- Facilities for musicians
- Facilities for fans
- Crowd control
- Transport and access

UNIT 14 The future of business

Telephoning: getting the right information

A Look again at the useful language for telephoning on page 121 of the Course Book and rearrange the 'turns' that your teacher will give you into a logical phone conversation.

Conversation 1

Switchboard: Iberia Wine Importers, good morning.

Maria: Hello. Can I speak to Tim Reed in Accounts?

Switchboard: Do you know the extension?

Maria: No, I'm afraid I don't.

Switchboard: Sorry to keep you waiting. ... I'm putting you through.

John Reed: Reed.

Maria: Is that Tim Reed?

John Reed: No, this is John Reed. You seem to have got the wrong extension. I'll try and transfer you back to the switchboard.

Switchboard: Switchboard.

Maria: I phoned just now but I got put through to the wrong extension.

Switchboard: Which extension did you want?

Maria: Tim Reed in Accounts.

Switchboard: Sorry, I don't follow you. There's no one in Accounts by that name.

Maria: But I've been dealing with him for years!

Switchboard: Let me just check. Reed ... Reed ... Reed. Ah, here he is. Timothy Reed. Putting you through.

Conversation 2

Maria: Hello, Tim. Got through to you at last! This is Maria Soares at Vinhos Portugueses in Porto.

Tim: Hi Maria. Has the switchboard been playing you up? There's a new receptionist every week. It's a nightmare. Anyway, what can I do for you?

Maria: I'm phoning about an invoice we sent some time ago. As far as we can see, it still hasn't been paid.

Tim: Have you got the invoice number and the date?

Maria: 193 987A. It was dated 1st March, and it was for 120,534 euros.

Tim: 193 987A. 1st March. Sorry, I didn't get the amount.

Maria: 120,534 euros. It was for 5,000 cases of Vinho Verde we shipped in late February.

Tim: Right, I've got that. Vinho Verde. Nice wine, but I can't see any trace of it on our system.

Maria: Are you saying you've lost the invoice?

Tim: Maybe we never received it here in Accounts. The mail distribution in this place is hopeless. I'll check it out and get back to you as soon as I can.

Maria: Thanks Tim. Be hearing from you soon, I hope.

Tim: You can count on me, Maria. Bye for now.

Maria: Bye.

B Maria and Tim have a series of conversations over the following weeks. Role play these conversations, using the key information for each one.

Maria — **One week later**

- You have heard nothing from Tim.
- You call him again and get through first time. Make small talk.
- Say politely that you've heard nothing from him, despite sending two e-mails.
- Listen sympathetically to his explanations and say that you're looking forward to receiving payment.
- End the conversation appropriately.

Tim — **One week later**

- Maria phones you again. She gets through first time.
- Apologise for not having contacted her. (Find an excuse.)
- The invoice has just turned up: someone found it behind a cupboard in the post room.
- Promise that it will be paid soon by bank transfer.
- End the conversation appropriately.

Maria — **Two weeks later**

- You still haven't received payment. Phone Tim again.
- No small talk this time: get straight to the point. Your company is in serious financial difficulty because of non-payment of this invoice.
- Say that you are really concerned about the situation. Ask Tim what he means when he says the invoice will be paid 'soon'.
- End politely but coldly.

Tim — **Two weeks later**

- Maria phones you again.
- Apologise for the fact that the invoice still hasn't been paid.
- You understand the financial difficulty caused. Say that the invoice will be paid soon.
- End politely.

Maria — **Three weeks later**

- Phone again.
- You are desperate for payment. Your boss has threatened to make colleagues redundant if payment is not received.
- When you hear that Iberia Wines is in receivership, ask why Tim didn't tell you before. You feel really let down.
- End suitably.

Tim — **Three weeks later**

- Maria phones you again.
- Explain that Iberia Wine Importers is bankrupt and unable to pay its bills.
- Apologise and say that you had no idea this was going to happen. You only found out yesterday.
- Sympathise with Maria.
- End suitably.

Resource bank

Pearson Education Limited
Edinburgh Gate
Harlow
Essex CM20 2JE
England

First published 2006
Fourth impression 2009

CD-Rom Pack:
ISBN: 978-1-4058-4346-1

Book for CD-Rom Pack:
ISBN: 978-1-4058-1320-4

DVD Pack:
ISBN: 978-1-4058-1345-7

Book for DVD Pack:
ISBN: 978-1-4058-1321-1

Set in 9/12pt Metaplus

Printed in China
SWTC/04

www.market-leader.net

Acknowledgements

We are grateful to the following for permission to reproduce copyright material:

David Bowen for the articles "Now about this web thing" published in *The Financial Times* 12th May 2005 and "Webhikers guide to galaxies" published in *The Financial Times* 6th April 2005; Richard Gillis for the article "One strike and you're down" published in *The Financial Times* 5th October 2004; Nancy Hubbard for the article "Caveat emptor: a rule for the new deal" published at www.FT.com 23rd August 2004; Sarah Murray for the article "Virtual teams: Global harmony is their dream" published in *The Financial Times* 12th May 2005; Keith Rodgers for the article "Balance between cost control and service" published at www.FT.com 9th March 2005; Financial Times Limited for the following articles published in *The Financial Times* "Super-fast Blue Gene looks for answers" by Alan Cane published 6th May 2005, "Why it pays to put the workers in the picture" by Alicia Clegg published 6th April 2005, "Lending exchange that bypasses high street banks attracts interest" by Paul J Davis published 22nd August 2005, "Air France-KLM ahead on savings" by Kevin Done published 11th April 2005, "Papers must embrace the internet, Murdoch tells editors" by Aline van Duyn published 14th April 2005 "Silicon Valley's lesson in patience" by John Gapper published 20th July 2004, "Desperate days, drastic measures" by John Gapper published 1st November 2004, "When companies need diplomats" by John Gapper published 10th March 2005, "NASA's exercise in managing risk" by Victoria Griffith published 14th April 2005, "Tesco breaches £2bn profit mark for first time" by Lucy Killgren published 12th April 2005, "More about results than time" by Philip Manchester published 23rd February 2005, "The rise of the corporate blogger" by Scott Morrison published 15th July 2005, "Samsung plays to the young generation" by Maija Pesola published 29th March 2005, "A field marshall's baton in every soldier's knapsack?" by Gill Plimmer published 6th April 2005 "Online shopping expected to grow by 35% this year" by Elizabeth Rigby published 6th April 2005, "Team building for charity brings tears to my eyes" by Sathnam Sanghera published 11th February 2005, "Message machine creates a buzz" by Bernard Simon published 8th April 2005, "How to engage your employees" by Michael Skapinker published 31st May 2005, "Teams seek strength in affiliations" by Stefan Stern published 28th April 2005, "Can't get no....." by Richard Tomkins published 5th September 2005, "Goodbye to the golden age of global brands" by Richard Tomkins published 6th June 2003 and "FT Summer school: expect the unexpected" by Morgan Witzel published 19th August 2004.

In some instances we have been unable to trace the owners of copyright material, and would appreciate any information that would enable us to do so.

Layouts by John Dickinson www.johnddesign.co.uk